Arthur J. Albano

W9-CCV-605

TRUTH AND IDEOLOGY

Truth
and Ideology

by Hans Barth

TRANSLATED BY Frederic Lilge
FOREWORD BY Reinhard Bendix

UNIVERSITY OF CALIFORNIA PRESS

Berkeley   Los Angeles   London

Original German title: *Wahrheit und Ideologie*
Published by Eugen Rentsch Verlag, Erlenbach-Zurich and Stuttgart;
second, enlarged edition, on which this translation is based, 1961 (original edition, 1945)

University of California Press
Berkeley and Los Angeles, California

University of California Press, Ltd.
London, England

Copyright ©1976 by
The Regents of the University of California

ISBN 0-520-02820-1
Library of Congress Catalog Card Number: 74-81430
Printed in the United States of America

Contents

Foreword

HANS BARTH was born in Winterthur, Switzerland in 1904 and died in Zürich in 1965. He completed his law degree at the University of Zürich in 1928, but he had begun publishing articles in the *Neue Zürcher Zeitung* in 1924. Following his academic work, he joined the editorial staff of that paper in 1929, at the age of 25, and assumed responsibility for the paper's "scientific feuilleton." Barth's articles in this section of the paper were of a novel kind. They usually extended a column or two and contained commentaries on recent publications primarily in German philosophical literature. Sometimes those commentaries would extend over several issues; occasionally they would respond to a commemorative occasion rather than a recent publication. They would deal with complex philosophical questions and extensive works by singling out a salient issue for appreciative or critical comment. Barth continued this "journalistic" activity from 1929 onward. In 1946, he accepted a position as professor of philosophy and political science at the University of Zürich, and in 1949 he resigned from his editorial position at the *Neue Zürcher Zeitung*. His book, *Wahrheit und Ideologie*, was originally published in 1945, a summation and philosophical underpinning of the journalistic commentary which he had written during the preceding sixteen years.

The dictionary states that ideology means both visionary theorizing and a systematic body of concepts about human life and culture.

Stated baldly, the book by Hans Barth tells us that since the eighteenth century every set of ideas to which the second definition applies has been discredited as "visionary" or "false." In one way or another, men have come to think of ideas as weapons which serve the fulfillment of our desires or interests, rather than the discovery of truth. Bacon said that what a man wishes were true, he the more readily believes, and we commonly speak of the wish being father to the thought. But Barth tells us that this position cannot (and has not) been held consistently. For any assertion that all ideas are mere contrivances to enhance our interests, implicitly claims to state a truth, even though the statement itself denies that it is within man's capacity to achieve truth. This famous paradox goes back to the ancient Greeks, but this book traces the modern development in a detailed examination of Bacon, Helvetius, Destutt de Tracy, Marx, Schopenhauer, and Nietzsche. Barth is concerned to show that each author reveals the impossibility of radical doubt. Ultimately, each not only develops his views of "ideas as weapons," but reveals his belief that these views are true. And that obviously provokes the skeptical reader to ask what interests might be served by the assertion that "all ideas serve our interests."

Professor Barth's work is an important contribution to the history of ideas; that is why it is of value to make the book available to English readers. This study carefully delineates the ideas of each writer considered; only in this way can one appreciate, and do justice to, the full complexity of different intellectual perspectives. Indeed, Barth's work is a prime example of scholarship in this field. Only if we give full weight to the views of those who went before us, have we any reason to hope that future generations will take our own ideas seriously as well. But to enter fully into the ideas of a thinker is a difficult task. This fine translation makes Barth's work readily accessible, but it may help the reader with a difficult text if I outline here the main intellectual tendency documented in this study.

Bacon's typology of idols—his term for certain types of common human prejudices—appears in the second chapter of the book, but comes first chronologically. Bacon lived between 1561 and 1626. His typology is part of an eloquent advocacy of science as contrasted with scholastic philosophy. Barth takes it for granted that the reader will be familiar with Bacon as a highly placed courtier in Elizabethan England, who incurred the Queen's displeasure. He rose to prominence under James I, only to fall from royal grace once again near the end of his life. Bacon devoted the many years spent out of royal favor to what we would call propaganda on behalf of science. His typology of idols was an effort to come to grips with the many sources of error which men are heir to and must guard against. He believed that once recognized as such, errors could be eradicated by an act of will, because God has endowed men with reason, and truth is man's reward for the proper exercise of his God-given faculties.

Bacon's ideas were taken up by the philosophers of the Enlightenment. Men like Helvetius (1715–1771) and Holbach (1723–1789) lived in an intellectual world in which Bacon's assumptions about man's God-given qualities were no longer taken for granted. Barth shows that in their interpretation, Bacon's idols of the mind were turned into prejudices actively fostered by state and church. These eighteenth-century philosophers were concerned with man's emancipation from the constraints imposed by an absolutist state and especially by a church that controlled the system of education. Since these constraints were justified by prejudiced opinions, philosophy has the emancipatory task of unmasking these opinions by showing that they served the interests of state and church.

In the work of Destutt de Tracy (1754–1836) this doctrine was elaborated into a scientific theory of the human mind that was to be made the basis for educational reform, free of the vested interests of the church. Note that in the transition passage from Bacon in the early seventeenth to the French enlightenment in the eighteenth and nineteenth centuries the ground had shifted. Where Bacon had analyzed "idols" confident that they would be removed by an effort of reason and good will, Helvetius, Holbach, and de Tracy were persuaded that reason and good will were not enough because vested interests stood in the way of the needed reform. Only a thoroughgoing reform of the educational system based on a scientific analysis of ideas would be adequate to the task.

With Marx (1818–1883) and Nietzsche (1844–1900) skepticism deepens and the measures needed to remove the obstacles to truth become more radical. For Marx, human thought is bound up with the class struggles that are the moving force of world history. For Nietzsche, human thought is bound up with the struggle for survival which is rooted in our biological makeup. In these views, men have not searched for truth at all. Rather, men use knowledge as a weapon to further their material interests, whether these aim at economic or physical superiority. Accordingly, human fallibility is grounded in the conditions of human existence and can be overcome only when those conditions are transcended. For Marx that transcendence will be achieved by revolution which will end human pre-history and initiate an age in which class struggles will cease, and with them the need for the ideological distortion of the human condition. For Nietzsche, that transcendence will be achieved by men larger than life *(Übermenschen)* though the political implications of this view are left uncertain.

In this way, Barth's book traces a transformation of Western philosophy from the Renaissance to the mid-twentieth century. (The footnotes to the work show the extensions of these ideas in Central European thought until the late 1930's.) Men have become more skeptical of the human condition, they have discovered ever new sources of human fallibility. Bacon had offered an inventory of the ways in which human thought goes astray. His approach concerned the human condition, and under God the prospect of human reason was bright. The French philosophers offered a diagnosis of their time, maintaining that vested interests prompted man's thought to go astray. Their approach concerned the human condition in French society and they proposed educational reforms that would provide safeguards against the prejudices promoted by vested interests. Marx enlarged upon this view in the sense that prejudice was not just due to this or that vested interest, but to the way in which every man's existence and ideas are bound up with the class to which he belongs. And as we approach the modern period, Nietzsche and Freud advanced views which made man's very quest for knowledge suspect because that quest tends to disguise the craving for power over others and the urge to seek sense gratification, in which these thinkers see the root motivation of our species. In the past three centuries we have traveled along a route that has ended in profound pessimism regarding the human condition. For many, revolution or therapy seems to remain the only hope.

Barth's study of this major intellectual transformation specifically disclaims the intention of characterizing "currents of thought." His analysis attempts to let ideas speak for themselves by close attention to the individual achievement of each thinker. So the main part of the text dispenses with any attempt at criticism. The author's

foreword expresses the view that the most radical reductionism becomes self-contradictory so that "in little-noted passages" Marx
and Nietzsche seek to vindicate the truth of their respective theories,
even as these theories attribute all other ideas to economic interests
or biological drives. Barth believes an explicit critique becomes
superfluous where close analysis reveals such self-contradictions.
But although this self-restraint is sustained throughout the book,
the conclusion does carry the analysis a step further. For on his last
pages the author makes clear that "to charge consciousness with being ideological requires a prior distinction between 'true' and 'false'
consciousness. . . . The disastrous effect of ideological thinking in its
radical form is not only to cast doubt on the quality and structure of
the mind that constitute man's distinguishing characteristic, but also
to undermine the foundation of his social life. Human association is
dependent on agreement, and the essence of agreement (be it concerned with common behavior, rational action, or scientific investigation) is the idea of truth." Written in the spring of 1945,
following the devastations of the Nazi regime and World War II,
these sentences reflect the author's passionate and personal conviction with which he concludes a very dispassionate, scholarly book.
How should we interpret this personal dimension, which is in fact
the vantage point from which this book was written? As it happens,
the answer is found in Barth's preparatory work as a journalist
which sheds much light on his commitment to the ideal of truth.

It is remarkable that the young Barth articulated this position at
the age of twenty-five. In a lead essay on European philosophy,
published in 1929 (*Neue Zürcher Zeitung* or *NZZ*, No. 2012), he
stated his belief that man can think validly only as a whole human
being, bound to a particular place and inextricably involved in the
relationships of a human community. European philosophy consists
of a series of national philosophies. Each of these may be typical of
a national community, but is not for that reason the exclusive
property of a particular group. Contrasts and conflicts result from
this condition, but they are not the last word. At this early point in
his career, Barth indicated that his work would aim toward the ar-
ticulation of a unitary perspective of European philosophy as a
whole, despite these manifest differences.

In the articles immediately following this introduction, Barth sur-
veyed aspects of Russian, Spanish, and German philosophy and
concluded with an essay on political philosophy (*NZZ*, No. 915,

May 11, 1930), taking as his motto Jacob Burckhardt's statement that European civilization involved not only love of power and money, but love of the spirit. This emphasis on the value of intellect was worth underscoring in deliberate contrast to the fashionable denigration of the mind. For it was commonplace in the 1930's, as it has been more recently, to praise man's vital urges instead. Nationalism was (and remains) one of these supposedly nonintellectual values and it is interesting to see how Barth handled the issue. He acknowledged that thought is not merely the result of an individual's will, but expresses as well the tendencies or cross-currents of the whole community. National thought may lose itself in the past greatness of one's country and thus reveal its weakness; Barth cites the nationalism of Maurice Barrès as an example. But national thought may also have recourse to the foundations of the nation and can in this way lead to a comprehensive stock-taking and self-scrutiny. That should not mean deliberate primitivism, Barth adds, like enthusiasm for African sculptures or for archeology. That way, flirtation with "a primitive, brutal life force, the glorification of an endless procreative primal matter, an intoxication with mythology" develop without let or hindrance. Against these aberrations of his day (and, in barely altered ways, of ours) Barth demanded a political philosophy in a positive sense. Opportunism is not enough. Creative decisions are possible only if they are founded on an understanding of contexts, which retains its validity beyond the current emergency. Action without guidelines makes as little sense as human life without order, without participation in the cultural and political context of our country and our time.

Thus, Barth's conclusion in 1930 was the same as at the end of *Wahrheit und Ideologie,* namely, that human association and the quest for truth are intimately related to one another. In 1963, the Swiss literary scholar Karl Schmid published a small but deeply probing volume entitled *Unbehagen im Kleinstaat* (Discontent in the Small State). Schmid analyzed five Swiss writers who shared a sense of alienation in part because their country stood among the great cultures and nations and was destined to be a spectator rather than a historical participant. This was *not* Barth's problem. He was a fully engaged witness to the decline of German culture into barbarism and he had seen it as his task as early as 1929–1930 to define an intellectual position from which to uphold the value of the individual and the community. He had been convinced from the beginning that neither of these values could be maintained without a belief in truth. In a critique of the holistic philosophy of Othmar Spann he had upheld the value of individualism, saying that no whole can exist without its parts, however justified we are in criticizing exaggerated forms of individualism (*NZZ*, No. 1384, July 24, 1932). Yet in criticizing the reductionist tendency which attributed ideas to various nonideational factors including the group and the community, Barth also maintained that this critique was only valid within limits. As he put it in another article (*NZZ*, No. 2301, December 8, 1932): "It seems to me that a maximum of internal ties [to social norms and to the community] becomes necessary as a kind of compensation, wherever a maximum of political and intellectual freedom is attained." It was from this vantage point as a Swiss critic of the rapidly deteriorating German cultural scene that Barth perceived the link between a human community and the belief in truth. It is a perception worth pondering in our own day.

REINHARD BENDIX

Preface

THE CREATOR of the concept of ideology gave it a purely scientific and philosophical meaning. Yet, common usage appropriated and characteristically transformed it. In the daily press and in parliament, in the speeches of political agitators, and in the lecture halls of humanists and social scientists, the concept of ideology has developed a variety of possible meanings upon which the users as a rule do not reflect. People speak of the ideologies of parties, classes or estates, and of ideological wars. The complex of ideas and beliefs on which a political constitution is founded is called ideology, and so are philosophic systems or prevailing interpretations of man and the world. In each case the concept exhibits some of its original characteristics. The person using it always tries to devalue his opponent's intellectual or political position by proving that it is only a perspective conditioned by interest and point of view. At the same time he attempts, before the court of reason, to legitimize his own views and attitudes as universally valid. This first phase in ideological denunciation is quickly left behind, however, for with the same arguments the side under attack can charge the accuser's position of being likewise ideology-infected and nothing but an unjustified rationalization of a subjective prejudice. When opponents thus mutually reproach each other with holding ideologically tainted positions, the need arises for an objective judgment to resolve the conflict. But clearly no such judgment can be forthcoming. For if the accusation be true that the human mind produces only ideologies, there is no court of appeal with criteria for arriving at an objective judgment.

XV

We are thus faced with two questions: how is the human mind constituted to produce only ideologies, and under what social and economic conditions does this occur? To answer them in this investigation required expanding its scope to consider those anthropological, historical, and philosophical suppositions which, directly or indirectly, are related to the whole problematics of the doctrine of ideology and the rise of ideological consciousness. It was also necessary to include some tendencies in eighteenth- and nineteenth-century intellectual history. This was not done in order to characterize "currents" of thought, but rather, by reference to specific philosophical works, to focus on various forms of intellectual influences and ground-breaking preparation—for intellectual currents always become manifest in individual achievements.

We have attempted in the course of the historical interpretation to let the necessary critique grow out of the "objects" themselves. This intention can succeed only if it is granted that even inadequate attempts at the solution of philosophic and scientific problems may somewhere contain within themselves the "right thing" and thereby act as an explosive force within the framework of the proposed solution. This procedure was justified by the discovery that neither Marx nor Nietzsche was able to carry out the ideological reduction of intellectual products to economic factors and vital urges without exposing at the same time in little-noted passages the rectifying countertheses.

HANS BARTH

Spring 1945

About the Second Edition

As books, too, take form in a certain frame of mind and under certain historical circumstances, we decided to let this book stand as first written. There has been added to the second edition an inquiry into Rousseau's idea of human self-alienation. This is justified because alienation and its elimination are central to the philosophy of Marx, which, like that of Hegel, nowhere denies its eighteenth-century ancestry, The references to the immense literature have been supplemented, without any claim to completeness.

HANS BARTH

May 1961

Translator's Note

THIS translation diverges from the German text in several ways. To speed the flow of the exposition, I eliminated a certain amount of repetition and redundancy. The sequence of sentences was altered when it appeared that the author's thought could thereby be given greater force in English. Some passages of doubtful relevance which distracted attention from the main problem under discussion were either briefly summarized or omitted. Paragraphs of excessive length were subdivided. Throughout I have tried to unravel a somewhat knotty Germanic style and to render the author's ideas in the form of plain and direct statements. These changes obviously make this a free rather than a literal translation. The reductions made in the original text also entailed the omission of a number of footnotes, but as these contained references to works already cited, the large bibliography has not been curtailed.

F. L.

I

The Ideology of Destutt de Tracy
and Its Conflict with
Napoleon Bonaparte

THE TERM *idéologie* originated in the period of the French Revolution. It was created by Antoine Destutt de Tracy to designate a philosophical discipline that was to provide the foundation for all the sciences. But following the transformation of France from a democratic republic into a despotic autocracy, a derogatory and contemptuous meaning was attached to the concepts of ideology and ideologue which goes back to Napoleon Bonaparte. Ideology was alleged to be the product of a theoretical attitude out of step with reality, especially with political and social reality. The hatred with which Bonaparte pursued ideology would scarcely be intelligible had it merely been divorced from the world. It appears, however, that ideology as theory had a distinct bearing on political practice. Down to the present the concept has retained the connotation of an invective and accusation. Spengler, who also liked the pose of the strong man, still distinguished, much as the Corsican, between the doer and the spectator. "In times of uncertainty such as the Attic enlightenment or the French and German revolutions," he wrote, "it is an all too frequent presumption of the ideologue as writer or public speaker to want to be active in the actual destiny of nations instead of building systems. He misconceives his place. With his principles and programs he belongs in the history of literature

1

and nowhere else. Real history does not pass judgment on the theorist by refuting him but by leaving him alone with his ideas."[1]

For Destutt de Tracy ideology meant "the science of ideas."[2] He regarded Condillac as the real founder of this science though in de Tracy's view he only continued and extended what had originally been Locke's contribution to the history of philosophy—to observe and describe the human mind in the same way as a natural object, a mineral, or plant. Ideology for Destutt is a part of zoology. Though Condillac granted animals a soul and thereby the capacity to feel, judge, and remember, his Christian belief led him to uphold the infinite difference between animal and human souls.[3] Destutt accepted no such difference. He reserved the investigation of man's mental capacities to the method of ideology, which, disregarding religious considerations of any kind, proceeded in the manner of untrammeled scientific inquiry. Hence it gave true access to the knowledge of man. Neither the metaphysical origin of nature nor man's religious and moral vocation were objects of scientific research.[4] The solution of such questions Destutt referred to metaphysics, which belonged to the "arts of the imagination" whose "purpose was to gratify, not to instruct us." In a manner reminiscent of Kant, he assigned to ideology the tasks of defining the sources of human knowledge, its limitations, and the degree of its certainty. But since knowledge and its dissemination rely on ideas, the "science of ideas" was fundamental. It investigated the origin and law governing the formation of ideas. Only the reduction of ideas to their underlying sensations guaranteed the certainty indispensable for constructing a knowledge of nature and man. Only success in avoiding false ideas could assure scientific progress. Thus Bacon's *Instauratio Magna* was just as important to the ideology of de Tracy

1. Oswald Spengler, *Der Untergang des Abendlandes* (Munich, 1922), 2:22.

2. Antoine Louis Claude Destutt, Comte de Tracy, *Eléments d'Idéologie* (Brussels, 1826), 1:3. The first edition appeared in 1801.

3. Etienne Bonnot de Condillac, *Traité des Animaux*. Oeuvres complètes (Paris, 1798), 3:592.

4. See the excellent work by François J. Pivacet, *Les Idéologues* (Paris, 1891), p. 21. Very summary information on the ideologues is given by Gottfried Salomon, "Historischer Materialismus und Ideologienlehre," *Jahrbuch für Soziologie* (Karlsruhe, Gottfried Salomon, 1926), vol. 2.

as it was to the philosophy of the French Enlightenment. In his theory of idols Bacon attempted to prevent the conception of false ideas by exposing all possible sources of error. Condillac resumed these endeavors,[5] and the ideologues continued them, citing Condillac as their authority.

From the beginning, however, ideology had a practical and not just a theoretical significance because in the view of its proponents it alone provided an adequate foundation for the political, moral, and educational sciences. Educational, economic, and political theory depended no less than the knowledge of nature and man on ideology for the investigation of the origin and formation of the linguistic expression of ideas. Except in name, Plato's doctrine of ideas has nothing in common with Destutt de Tracy's "science of ideas." Indeed, it forms part of the centuries-long process in which the Platonic idea was subject to reinterpretation and gradually disintegrated. For Destutt de Tracy the idea was no longer, as for Plato, the objective criterion by which truth and justice could be known. Since the term idea had come to designate sensual experience, the existence of a substance independent of human consciousness and possessing the character of an archetype and model was ruled out. "We need merely note that only individuals have real existence, and that our ideas are by no means substances existing outside us but are pure creations of our minds, ways of classifying our perceptions of individuals."[6] Descartes still distinguished three types of ideas: those that were innate, those formed by man himself, and those acquired from the external world.[7] Of these, de Tracy retained only those which man formed on the basis of sensations received from the outside world. In this radical repudiation of innate ideas de Tracy and Condillac agreed.

5. Condillac, *Essai sur l'Origine des Connaissances Humaines.* Oeuvres, 1:507.

6. Destutt de Tracy, *Eléments,* 1:301, 19–20.

7. René Descartes, *Meditationes de Prima Philosophia.* Oeuvres de Descartes, ed. C. Adam and P. Tannéry, 12 vols. (Paris, 1897–1910), 9:29. Also "Brief an Mersenne," 3:383. Descartes meant by idea "tout ce qui peut estre en nostre pensée." He identified three kinds: "à sçavoir quaedam sunt adventitiae, comme l'idée qu'on a vulgairement du soleil; aliae factae vel factitiae, au rang desquelles on peut mettre celle que les astronomes ont du soleil par un raisonnement et aliae innatae ut idea dei, mentis, corporis, trianguli et generaliter omnes quae aliquas essentias veras, immutabiles et aeternas repraesentant."

Condillac started with the assertion that the word idea expressed something that had never been adequately explained.[8] He saw his philosophical task in the removal of this deficiency and "in going back to the very origin of our ideas." A sensation was for him feeling and idea in one. "It is feeling in relation to the soul, which it modifies; it is idea in relation to a thing of the external world." Only in memory was the idea distinguished from feeling. Condillac insisted on "well ascertained facts"[9] as the sole basis of the sciences. His *Traité des Systèmes* was filled with an insurmountable mistrust of such concepts as substance, spirit, soul, and of all abstract principles, which he rejected as philosophical jargon. Locke still assumed two sources of ideas, sensation and reflection. Condillac admitted only one, sensation, "perhaps because reflection is principally sensation, or perhaps because it is less the source of ideas than the canal through which the ideas flow from the senses."[10]

From Condillac, who he confessed had awakened him philosophically, de Tracy took over the view that all ideas consisted of sensations. But he did not follow his teacher without some restrictions and criticism. Whereas Condillac had sought to present even mental activities such as judging, remembering, perceiving, and willing as forms of sensations, de Tracy, though maintaining the sensualistic principle, reintroduced reflection as a "particular sensibility" and thus reversed the radical reduction of the human mind to the senses. His first concern was to relate all ideas to their origin in sensuality, leaving their total reduction as the exclusive task of ideology. By means of this reduction, a grammar and language modeled after mathematics were to be created in which each idea was assigned its corresponding linguistic sign. This reduction was also to prevent the formation of false abstract principles that would vitiate not only mutual human understanding but the construction of the state and society. With respect to these eminently practical consequences of ideology, de Tracy was in agreement with Condillac, who never tired of pointing out, principally in his *Cours d'Etudes pour l'Instruction du Prince de Parme,* that right thinking was the basis of right political action. "Everybody knows that the

---

8. Condillac, *Traité des Sensations.* Oeuvres, 3:39.
9. Condillac, *Traité des Systèmes.* Oeuvres, 2:8, 13.
10. Condillac, *Traité des Sensations.* Oeuvres, 3:13.

projects of those in power are defective only because they rest on principles that are adopted in part whereas they should be accepted as a whole."[11] Again like Condillac, de Tracy wanted to derive all ideas from the basic capacity of human nature to have sensations. This derivation did not mean, however, that all special capacities such as judging or remembering should be reduced to a single ultimate sensation. Within sensation, which for de Tracy was equivalent to thought, different special capacities were supposedly contained which gradually unfolded through use. Sensibility was that capacity by which impressions of widely differing kinds were transmitted to us. But sensibility also included the very consciousness of our having sense impressions, and so became reflection. "To feel is for us everything. It is the same as to exist. For our existence consists in the fact that we feel it, and our perceptions are nothing but ways of being or existing. No matter what one feels, one never feels anything but what one is."[12] Whereas Condillac regarded all human capacities, including thought, as modified sensations and retained the concept of a psychic substance,[13] de Tracy taught that "sensibility in its true sense" is divided into five abilities that must be strictly differentiated from each other. He reversed Condillac's attempt to conceive all psychic contents and mental operations as transformations of simple sense impressions, and referred to five "particular kinds of sensibilities," namely, feeling, remembering, judging, willing, and self-motion.[14] All of them participated in thought. "To think is to feel a sensation, thinking is always feeling."[15] These five capacities could not be derived from each other, but together constituted man's basic capacity, sensation. Therefore de Tracy called them "modes of sensation." Yet the fact of sensibil-

---

11. Condillac, *Traité des Systèmes,* 2:44, 384.

12. Destutt de Tracy, *De la Logique,* p. 151. Concerning the connection between body and soul, simple experience and reflection, see Vera Stepanowa, *Destutt de Tracy; Eine historisch-psychologische Untersuchung* (Zurich, 1908). pp. 16, 22.

13. Condillac, "C'est l'âme seule qui sent à l'occasion des organes." *Traité des Sensations,* 3:1. Mario dal Pra is emphatic and convincing about the basically spiritualistic character of Condillac's sensualism in his excellent monograph, *Condillac.* Storia universale della Filosofia (Milan, 1942), vol. 49, especially pp. 235 ff. See also Ernst Cassirer, *Die Philosophie der Aufklärung* (Tübingen, 1932), pp. 21 ff., 133 ff.; and Emile Bréhier, *Histoire de la Philosophie* (Paris, 1934), 2:1, 382 ff.

14. Picavet, *Les Idéologues,* p. 306.

15. Destutt de Tracy, *Eléments,* 1:18, 291–2.

ity also implied an ego that feels. "I exist only because I feel." "My existence and my sensibility are one and the same thing." In his *Traité de la Volonté et de ses Effets,* de Tracy explained that "to feel anything is to feel oneself as a feeling self, to know oneself as feeling."[16] But this still was not enough; for even reflection—the distinguishing characteristic of the mind—was assimilated to sensation as one of its original qualities. To feel, he said, was "to possess the possibility of distinguishing between one's self and what one feels, that is between one's self and oneself."

He proceeded similarly in his analysis of the concept of society. Here, too, de Tracy wanted to apply his principle of the universal reduction of ideas to their constitutive sensations. But again irreducible facts forced him constantly to broaden the concept sensation and thus to estrange it from its original meaning. For what sense was there in speaking of sensation when it also meant thought? The analysis of society, which was the basis for analyses of such economic phenomena as the division of labor, wealth, value, industry, money, distribution of goods, and population growth, was at least illuminating in the sense of confirming a basic relatedness: as every sensation pointed to a felt object, so one economic subject referred to another. The social condition was man's natural condition. But this only meant that related to the ego, as originally and necessarily implied in sensation, was another to whom it was attracted by the need for survival and by sympathy. Society consisted in nothing but an indissoluble chain of mutual business transactions. This exchange, in which both parties sought and found their advantage, produced the cooperation of forces, economic growth, enlightenment, and the division of labor.

De Tracy expected ideology to possess the same measure of certainty and reliability as the physical and mathematical sciences. The reduction of all ideas held out the promise of a science of man that would provide the foundation for the whole of political and economic life.[17] Only such indubitable knowledge would enable the legislator and ruler of the state to establish and maintain a just and rational order. It was a natural consequence of these insights that the ideologues, and de Tracy above all others, devoted themselves to

16. Destutt de Tracy, *Traité de la Volonté et de ses Effets,* p. 14.
17. Picavet, *Les Idéologues,* p. 306.

the education of the French people once the revolutionary turmoil had subsided. "Enlightenment always produces some good effects," Condillac had written,[18] and the ideologues acted in the same belief. By reason of their scientific knowledge they sought to influence the formation of the postrevolutionary state and particularly its system of instruction and education.[19] They claimed that their theory, whose different aspects have been described, would guarantee nothing less than a just social order and the happiness of mankind. Was not the progressive knowledge of man, Condorcet asked, proof "that nature links truth, happiness and virtue indissolubly together?"[20] Reason as the instrument of the knowledge of truth, combined with the innate moral goodness of human nature, vouched for the eventual emergence of a social state in which individual interests would harmonize with the common interests of all. "Must not the perfection of the laws and public institutions that follows on the progress of the sciences result in drawing together and eventually merging the public interest of the individual and the public interests of all?"[21]

De Tracy's work *Eléments d'Idéologie* was meant to render a service to the system of public education. But education made sense only if one believed in the educability of human nature, and this belief pervaded "the science of ideas." The knowledge of human nature to which ideology aspired was normative; it hoped to discover principles that would be universally valid for the many-sided education of social man. The reduction of all ideas to their sensual origin necessarily led, it was claimed, to a knowledge of those ideas lying at the base of human coexistence and issuing from the indubitable fact of its interdependence. The radical reduction of ideas was not an end in itself, but rather the means for constructing a comprehensive system of education. Analysis would expose the principles of such a system, and theory would thus fulfill its ultimate

---

18. Condillac, *Traité des Systèmes,* 2:384.

19. A detailed description of the ideologues' influence on French school legislation during the Revolution is given by Charles H. van Duzer in *The Contribution of the Ideologues to French Revolutionary Thought* (Baltimore: Johns Hopkins Press, 1935).

20. Marie Jean Antoine Nicolas Caritat, Marquis de Condorcet, *Esquisse d'un Tableau historique des Progrès de l'Esprit humain* (Paris, 1822), p. 293.

21. Condorcet, *Esquisse,* p. 292.

purpose of serving as a guide to practice. The maxim of liberating reason from "the yoke of prejudices" to which the French Enlightenment owed its persuasive power was also de Tracy's own conviction.

Although the ideologues rejected and condemned metaphysics as an intellectual pastime founded on religious prejudices, their own anthropology and social philosophy likewise rested on a metaphysical conception of nature. Nature was for them a well-ordered system in which everything happened according to knowable laws. They made it their task to discover these laws since these were to form the basis of the state and society. Freedom was a necessary condition of the knowledge of nature, as it was also the aim of their political, economic, and educational endeavors. Only in freedom could man grow and live according to his nature, and through the free exchange of the goods he produced achieve a maximum of material welfare. De Tracy's social philosophy and economic theory rested on a faith in the harmonious balance of social forces, so far as everyone acted according to his own well-understood interests. These views brought the ideologues into inevitable conflict with Bonaparte, who sacrificed political liberty to his autocratic and imperialistic drives. Though not all ideologues were men of political action, their philosophical labors nevertheless acquired a political character when they attempted to make their ideas effective through public education and enlightenment. Only intellectual means were at their disposal. They believed in the power of reason; and because they did, they also believed the world could be arranged to the advantage of the human race by a general application of the ideas to which the study of nature and man had led them. Bonaparte's ruthless behavior toward the ideologues showed only too well that he was anything but indifferent toward these "sinister metaphysicians" who, he disdainfully remarked, crept about him like vermin. His persecution of them made it evident that their faith in reason was a power to be reckoned with. Enlightenment has always had a political potential, and in this case it proved effective because it provided a measure of the original intent of the Revolution and its consequent destruction by Bonapartist despotism.

There simply are no philosophic or scientific ideas without some effect, directly or indirectly, on the political thought and events of a period. As the "science of ideas" became the foundation of popular education, the ideologues turned into politicians, compelled to affirm and demand conditions favorable to instituting their pedagogical reforms. And this led to the conflict with General Bonaparte.

The political motive that turned the future emperor into an opponent of the ideologues, after he sought and received their appreciation and company at the start of his career, is clearly reflected in his changing relations to the *Institut National,* of which he became a member in 1797. In his letter of gratitude the general declared that "the true conquests, and the only ones that cause one no regret, are those of ignorance." How proud he was of his membership is also shown by the way he signed his proclamations to the army during the Egyptian campaign: commanding general, member of the Institute. He could with good faith claim the title of a "hero of liberal ideas."[22] No wonder, then, that the members of the Institute considered him as one of their own and entertained the delusive hope that this young general, geometrician, and philosopher was the man who would turn the republic of their dreams into reality.[23] This faith alone may help explain why they approved the *coup d'état* of the 18th of Brumaire by which he made himself consul. They expected that order and freedom, peace and calm would be restored by his strong hand.[24] What had been won by the Revolution, the ideologues did not want to surrender. Their trust in the general's political principles, by the way, was not without foundation. On the day his consulate was established, Bonaparte reassuringly and with high promise declared: "We want a republic founded on true freedom, on civil liberty, and national representation, and we shall have it. . . . That I swear!"[25]

The peace between the ideologues and Bonaparte was deceptive and turned into irreconcilable conflict as the autocratic, despotic proclivities of the first consul became apparent. On 23 January 1803 he struck a blow against one section of the National Institute that was bound to provoke him, the section of the moral and political

22. Louis Antoine de Bourienne, *Mémoires sur Napoléon,* cited by van Duzer, *Contribution of the Ideologues,* p. 146.

23. François Victor Alphonse Aulard, *Histoire politique de la Révolution française,* 6th ed. (Paris, 1926), p. 694.

24. Jean Philibert Damiron, *Essai sur l'Histoire de la Philosophie en France au 19ème Siècle.* 5th ed. (Brussels, 1835), p. 55.

25. See van Duzer, *Contribution of the Ideologues,* pp. 143 ff., 147.

sciences; it was abolished and its members reassigned to the remaining sections. The newly established second section for French language and literature was specially commissioned to prepare a dictionary of the French language and to translate Greek, Latin, and Oriental authors into French. Bonaparte wanted to prevent all independent scientific research in matters political and economic in order to stifle any opposition it might inspire. This decree condemned the ideologues to political ineffectiveness.

The ideologues were moderate republicans for whom intellectual and civic freedoms were the noblest achievements of the Revolution. The more Bonaparte's politics aimed at their restriction and at the expansion of his personal power, the more eloquent the expression of the ideologue's grief became.[26] Bonaparte's policy toward religion and the Church further intensified the opposition between the emerging autocrat and the French intellectual élite as represented by the Institute and particularly by the former section on the moral and political sciences. For the most part, though not exclusively, the members of the Institute were libertarians.[27] Freedom of conscience, freedom of scientific research, and religious tolerance they regarded as uninfringeable republican rights. They were unwilling to give them up because to them were attributed the undeniable gains they had made in their relentless and passionate struggle against the Catholic Church.

During the eighteenth century criticism of religion preceded criticism of the state. But the first necessarily expanded into the second because the state sided with the religious authority, and made its powers available to the Church for the persecution of anticlerical and atheistic literature.[28] The ideologues upheld the principle of tolerance that had spread throughout France well before 1789. The Christian was replaced by the natural man on whom the moral law, as well as state and society, were to be founded. In the eyes of the *philosophes,* nothing endangered social peace as much as divisive religious conflict. Hence, toleration alone seemed to guarantee the

26. Marin Ferraz, *Histoire de la Philosophie pendant la Révolution (1789–1804).* (Paris, 1889), p. xvii.
27. See Aulard, *Histoire politique,* p. 732; and van Duzer, *Contribution of the Ideologues,* pp. 71–73.
28. Daniel Mornet, *Les Origines intellectuelles de la Révolution française.* 2nd ed. (Paris, 1934), pp. 471–2, 138, 143–4.

peaceful coexistence of different faiths and to assure the elementary moral claim to freedom of conscience.

Bonaparte, however, came gradually to appreciate the value of a positive religion firmly rooted in the social order. It dawned on him that religion could be an excellent instrument of political power, an idea neither new nor harmless. His change of mood was signaled far and wide when in 1802 Chateaubriand dedicated the first edition of *Le Génie du Christianism* to him. With his novel, *Atala,* glorifying the Catholic religion and the Christian message, this author had scored a success a year earlier comparable to that enjoyed by the works of Montesquieu, Voltaire, and Rousseau.[29] Religious feeling, which the cult of the "supreme being" sought to satisfy during the Revolution, now reverted to traditional forms of fulfillment. In 1825, in a foreword to *The Genius of Christianity,* Chateaubriand masterfully characterized the general spiritual situation at the turn of the century with these words:

> The victims of our troubles (and what victims they were!) took refuge at the altar much as the shipwrecked cling to the rock on which they seek salvation. Imbued with the memory of our kings, the genius of Christianity permeated the whole of the old monarchy. The rightful heir was, so to say, concealed in the depths of the sanctuary from which I lifted the veil and elevated the crown of Saint Louis over his holy altar.

Not without vanity, he made this telling comment about Napoleon:

> Bonaparte, who wanted to erect his power on the most secure social foundation, and who had just come to terms with the Roman curia, did not at all object to the publication of a work that enhanced the popularity of his plans. He had to fight the men around him and the avowed enemies of all religious faiths. He was therefore glad to have the support of public opinion evoked by *The Genius of Christianity.* Later he regretted his mistake, and at the time of his downfall confessed that the work which had most harmed his power was *The Genius of Christianity.*

29. Louis Madelin, *La Contre-révolution sous la Révolution (1789–1815)* (Paris, 1935), p. 175. See especially chaps. 7 and 8 on "La Reaction catholique" and "Le Concordat et la Contre-revolution."

Bonaparte intended to found his power and the new political order of France on the traditional basis of European society, the Christian religion. Religion was to be the *mystère* of the social order. He did not put his trust in any natural order legitimized by universal reason common to all men, but rather in religion because it sanctioned divinely ordained inequalities within a hierarchical social structure. It also permitted him to speak out sharply against the revolutionary sociopolitical currents and the rationalistic critique of the state derived from natural law. "Society cannot endure without inequality of property, and inequality of property cannot be maintained without the help of religion." Man should be promised a different distribution of goods in the next world.[30] In his dispute with the astronomer Lalande, an atheist, the emperor was emphatic in this regard: "I shall have to remind myself that my first duty is to prevent the morale of my people from being poisoned, for atheism is the destroyer of the morality of nations if not of individuals." He forbade Lalande to publish further, and the aged scientist complied with this "fraternal request."[31]

It became dangerous to bring the canons of Christian faith and the Catholic Church before the court of reason. It became dangerous, too, to demand a state founded on human reason and freedom, as well as to criticize the existing state by these criteria. Chateaubriand risked nothing in subjecting Diderot and d'Alembert to ridicule because, as he put it, they "had lined up the documents of human wisdom by alphabetical order in their *Encyclopedia*—that Babel of the sciences and reason."[32] The declared enemies of all religious faiths whom he mocked and attacked were, of course, the ideologues.

In the end, the autocratic politics of the usurper collided head on with the aspirations of that intellectual élite to which it had once been his burning ambition to belong. He not only denounced the ideologues as enemies of religion and of the Christian state, but made them scapegoats for the catastrophic mistakes of his im-

30. Aulard, *Histoire politique*. Napoleon to Pelet de la Lozère and to Roederer, p. 734.

31. François Victor Alphonse Aulard, "Napoléon et l'Athée Lalande," *Etudes et Leçons sur la Révolution française*, 2nd ed. (Paris, 1908), 4:313–4.

32. François Auguste René, Vicomte de Chateaubriand, *Le Génie du Christianisme*, book 1, chap. 1.

perialism and all the troubles that had befallen the country since the revolutionary wars. "It is to ideology, that sinister metaphysics," Napoleon proclaimed in the State Council on 20 December 1812, "that we must attribute all the misfortune of our beloved France. Instead of adapting the laws to knowledge of the human heart and the lessons of history, ideology seeks to base the legislation of nations on those first principles into which it so subtly inquires."[33]

The ideologues had proposed an inquiry into human understanding that ignored religious ideas even though they, too, might have some share in shaping man's self-image. Despite de Tracy's hostility to metaphysics and his claim to provide a purely scientific knowledge of man, he nevertheless retained the general intellectual assumptions of the Enlightenment. It was these above all else that provoked the sharpest opposition from the proponents of the Restoration. Their political struggle against the Revolution was accompanied by a critique of the intellectual temper that had made it possible in the first place. The indictment of the "Babel of reason" was framed by men of clerical, Christian persuasion and supported by social groups interested in maintaining or restoring prerevolutionary conditions. The Revolution might be condemned by Stahl as a "world-historical catastrophe,"[34] or by Bonald as "the crime of Europe,"[35] but what really concerned these men was the intellectual climate preceding it. Thus, the Restoration philosophers considered the thinkers of the eighteenth century to be really responsible for the great historical break. At first their critique of religion and despotism seemed not to have any political consequences. But the parties under attack sensed what was in the wind. Bonald wrote:

> In the case of a literate people, the greatest wrong one can do to society is to allow the publication of false doctrines of religion, morality, or politics. Governments have an excessive fear of the influence newspapers may have on the public peace whereas they underestimate the slow but profound corruption worked by serious writings. A bout of ephemeral fever alarms them more than a

33. Cited by Hippolyte Taine, *Les Origines de la France contemporaine. Le Régime moderne.* 5th ed. (Paris, 1898), 2:219–20.

34. F.J. Stahl, *Geschichte der Rechtsphilosophie,* 3rd ed. (1856), p. 300.

35. Louis Gabriel Ambroise, Vicomte de Bonald, *Pensées sur divers Sujets.* Oeuvres (Paris, 1858), 3:369.

gangrene. The remedy against a dangerous newspaper article can be found in another paper the next day. The refutation of a bad book sometimes does not occur for a century and may even require a revolution. The spectacle of contemporary writers of equal force locked in battle, group against group, is rare. Bossuet and Fénelon were born in one century, Voltaire and Rousseau in another.[36]

Catholic doctrine was the main criterion for deciding which moral and political theories were correct. The radical difference between the spirit that prepared the Revolution and that which sought to negate it is graphically expressed in the opposition between Rousseau and Bonald. For Rousseau, the individual compared with society as good with evil; for Bonald the reverse was true. *Emile* opened with the famous words: "God makes all things good and they turn to evil in the hands of man. . . . All social institutions in which we find ourselves submerged stifle man's nature and put nothing in its place." Bonald replied: "We are evil by nature, good through society." From these contradictory anthropological assumptions issued antithetical conclusions: the necessity of changing the social order, on the one side, and its absolute immutability on the other. The theologians of the Restoration, too, assumed that there was a natural order in human society, but they grounded it in God's will and law. Revelation provided them with the basis of every concrete philosophy of society as well as with the necessary condition for the knowledge of man. All spokesmen of the counter-revolutionary movement attacked the absolutism of reason as a hubris of the human spirit: Burke in England; Rivarol, Bonald, and de Maistre in France; Adam Muller, Ludwig von Haller, Franz von Baader, and Friedrich Julius Stahl in Germany; and Donoso Cortes in Spain. To these men scientific inquiry unrestricted by religious faith, as practiced by the ideologues and their predecessors, was blasphemy.

Philosophy outside France took only sporadic notice of the concept of ideology.[37] Hegel mentioned it in connection with his dis-

---

36. Bonald, *Pensées*, 3:360–1.

37. The later response to ideology as "science of ideas" outside Germany was also scanty. The sense of a purely scientific discipline in which Destutt de Tracy used the term remained alive. His metaphysical presuppositions, however, were rejected,

cussions of John Locke and defined it as "the reduction of thought to sensation."[38] Schopenhauer, who held the ideologue Cabanis in high esteem, equated the ideological method with Kantian transcendentalism.[39] Franz von Baader, finally, referred to the ideologues contemptuously as "those sophistical rationalists who inquire into the origin of ideas and pretend to have discovered the art of manufacturing them and their linguistic symbols. This discovery seemed to them quite plausible because their entire philosophy derived from the axiom that rational man was called upon to make everything over, including himself." To Baader the ideologues were the embodiment of "the spirit of irreligion" that rose up against the very source of spirit, God, and "thereby they fell victim to the Tantalus-like ambition of creating their own reason."[40] He also stigmatized them for "the vile leveling" of human and animal nature.

A curious interpretation of ideology is found in Heinrich Heine. In his review of German intellectual life written in Paris for the French and entitled *On the History of Religion and Philosophy in Germany,* Heine described how the philosopher Fichte was accused of atheism and forced to resign his professorship at the University of Jena in 1799. He then quoted from a letter Fichte wrote on May 22 of that year to Reinhold, his predecessor at Jena. "It is absolutely certain that unless the French achieve complete supremacy and bring about a change in Germany or at least in a substantial part of it, nobody who is known for ever having had a free idea in his life

---

or else ideology was allied with opposite metaphysical conceptions. In Italy, Pasquale Gallupi gave this definition, "L'ideologia è la scienza dell'origine e della generazione delle idee," in his work *Elementi di Filosofia* (1820), 2:2. Gallupi was, however, an opponent of Condillac's and Destutt de Tracy's sensualism. See Giovanni Gentile, *Storia della Filosofia italiana dal Genovesi al Gallupi,* 2nd ed. (Florence, 1937), 2:43. See also Melchiorre Gioja, *Ideologia* (1822), and d'Aquisto, *Trattato d'Ideologia* (1858). In Spain, the Catholic thinker Jaime Balmes used the concept of ideology in a nonpolemical sense: "La intelligencia da origen a la ideologia y la psychologia," *Filosofia fundamental* (1846), vol. 4, chap. 21, sec. 285.

38. Georg Wilhelm Friedrich Hegel, *Werke,* 15:387, 474.

39. Arthur Schopenhauer, *Die Welt als Wille und Vorstellung,* vol. 2, chap. 22.

40. Franz von Baader, ed. Franz Hoffman, *Sämtliche Werke* (Leipzig, 1854), 5:81-2. Baader took issue with the French ideologues in a review of Bonald's "Recherches philosophiques sur les premiers object des connaissances morales" (1825).

will be left in peace."[41] On this passage Heine commented: "Far worse things would have happened to the friends of liberty who remained in Germany if a few years later Napoleon had not defeated the Germans. Napoleon can hardly have suspected that he would become the savior of ideology. Without him, however, our philosophers would have been strung up on the gallows and put to the wheel."[42] Heine's assertion makes sense only if ideology is equated with philosophy in general and if one bears in mind that the French ideologues were defenders of political liberty. Napoleon, who ousted them from their important positions in France, saved the ideologues in Germany, so Heine seemed to argue, by invading the country and giving a powerful impetus to political and intellectual freedom.

41. J.H. Fichte, ed., *Fichtes Leben und literarischer Briefwechsel*, 2nd. ed. (1862), 2:257–8.
42. Heinrich Heine, *Sämtliche Werke* (Hamburg, 1861), 5:243.

II

Bacon's Theory of Idols and Its Political, Anticlerical Interpretation by Helvetius and Holbach

Bacon's Theory of Idols

PHILOSOPHERS have always been aware that their knowledge of the world was impeded by a variety of obstacles, some of them located in man's cognitive capacity itself. A critical examination of the latter became imperative when man recognized that his control of nature and society depended on the reliable use of his own understanding. If nature and its laws were to serve as guide for his educational, moral, and political purposes, he had to ask himself why philosophers disagreed in their definition of natural law. The philosophy of the eighteenth century, being interested especially in the practical aspects of enlightened understanding, devoted its constant attention to this grave difficulty. In its struggle against everything that obstructed the introduction of a rational order in human relations, it had to confront two problems: what were the causes that prevented man from ordering his life according to reason and nature; and what was the source of the obstructions that impeded the advancement of knowledge? Faith in man's ability to discover the immanent laws of nature, which were equivalent to the laws of reason, was beyond doubt. It became the substitute for the content of Christian religion. The transformation of religion into a universal moral faith led the representatives of militant rationalism to advance their demands with the passion of secular missionaries. Nevertheless, this faith did not prevent them from

17

recognizing that the actual use of man's reason was severely impeded and at times rendered completely ineffectual. They were equally certain that the natural, rational order was as yet nowhere realized. History and ethnology showed that any attempt at such a realization met with resistances that were both difficult to discover and to overcome. But unless the aim of establishing a rational order was to be abandoned at the start, the nature of the obstructions had to be known.

These were the problems that confronted the "science of ideas" as founded by Condillac and developed by de Tracy. Ideology accordingly fought on two fronts; it aimed to create a scientific foundation of knowledge, and to shed light on all types of intellectual behavior which, for whatever reasons, tried to prevent full disclosure of the truth. For this dual engagement seventeenth-century English philosophy supplied the decisive weapons. Just as Condillac and de Tracy honored Locke's *Essay on Human Understanding* as the work that prepared and in part anticipated the critique of ideas, so Helvetius and Holbach resorted to Bacon's *Great Instauration* as the arsenal to equip themselves for their battle against all forces that resisted the effort of making knowledge fully effective. Condillac summarized the philosophical program of all these thinkers in a phrase which, by its later literal incorporation in the *Encyclopedia,* revealed the almost canonical respect Bacon enjoyed for an entire period: "No one knew better than Bacon the causes of our errors. For he realized that the ideas produced by the mind were faulty and had therefore to be remade if the search for the truth was to advance."[1] Already the first part of the *Instauration,* devoted to the organization of the sciences, contained a remarkable list of errors and sources of errors that impeded the activity of the inquiring mind. Of crucial importance, however, was the second part, the *Novum Organon.* It set forth the famous theory of idols of which the eighteenth century was to avail itself. What Bacon called idol was termed prejudice by the French Enlightenment,[2] whose fight for

---

1. Etienne Bonnot de Condillac, *Essai sur l'Origine des Connaissances humaines.* Oeuvres complètes (Paris, 1798), 1:507. Literally the same remark in the article on Bacon in the *Encyclopédie,* vol. 3. In his "Preliminary Discourse," d'Alembert paid enthusiastic tribute to Bacon and his importance for the organization, method, and execution of the *Encyclopédie.*

2. Condillac translated the Baconian *idolum* with *préjugé.*

reason was a fight against the idols or prejudices of mankind. Ideology described the right technical procedure to be followed in the formation of ideas, whereas the theory of idols was charged with exposing the fallacies of pseudoscientific thinking and the misuse of man's intellectual powers. By accepting the first book of the *Novum Organon,* ideology entered into a momentous alliance with Bacon's theory of idols, the consequences of which were to become fully apparent only with Feuerbach and Marx.[3]

Bacon's theory of idols has its place in the "destructive part" of the *Novum Organon.* Like that of philosophy generally, its function was to discover whether the foundations of human power and greatness could be made more secure as well as broadened.[4] "The kingdom of man" could only be erected on his knowledge of nature. Man acquired power over nature by obeying it, and he could obey it only after he had learned to understand it. Bacon complained that progress in this direction had long been lagging and turned his attention to what obstructed it. He could not claim, he said, that the human mind reflected the world as it really was unless man gained access to nature and its laws. "What is worthy to exist is also worthy of science; science is the reflection of being." Nothing Bacon had to say about the relation between thought and being allows any conjecture about the mind's possible unfitness to understand nature. On the contrary, man achieved such understanding precisely by "the mind's own innate power" through the method of induction. "This type of explanation is the true and natural method of the mind once

3. Karl Mannheim thinks that "to some degree Bacon's theory of idols anticipates the modern concept of ideology," *Ideologie und Utopie,* 2nd ed. (Bonn, 1930), p. 14. This interpretation is rightly contradicted by Siegfried Landshut, *Kritik der Soziologie* (Munich, 1929), p. 89, fn. 4. He points out that Bacon was concerned not with the relation of being and consciousness, but with the injurious effect of false conventional notions on the growth of the understanding of nature. It is important not to overlook the fact that Bacon's theory differed both from the theory of prejudice of the French Enlightenment and from Marx's concept of ideology. It is true that Bacon as well as the *philosophes* identified a socially conditioned way of interpretation and evaluation. But the common intent of their philosophies was to destroy the idols and prejudices in order to secure the autonomy of the mind, thereby protecting it from sociological relativism.

4. Francis Bacon, *The Works of Francis Bacon,* comp. and ed. James Spedding, R.L. Ellis, and D.D. Heath, new ed. (Longon, 1879). The major quotations on the pages immediately following are from *Novum Organon,* 1:41–139.

all impediments have been cleared away." The cognitive power of man being beyond doubt, the poverty of his knowledge of nature must have other reasons. Bacon found them in the deductive method and in syllogistic logic, and also in the "idols" that preoccupy the mind. He therefore directed his first efforts at a critique of traditional philosophy and the human intellect itself. Medieval and Greek philosophy—Democritus excepted—he accused of being guided by concepts and words instead of by nature, also of passing too hastily from the particular to the general, undermining thereby the reliability of knowledge. To deductive and syllogistic logic he opposed induction, in which the testimony of the senses was corrected and supplemented by experiments that compelled nature to answer specific questions put to it.

The critique of the understanding, as conducted by the theory of idols, was necessary because the human mind was deformed, reflecting reality much as a warped mirror "whose shape and curvature change the rays of objects." To correct this deformation Bacon created a "science for purging the mind so that it might become skillful in the truth," a "mind purged and scraped." The purgation was administered by the theory of idols.

> The idols and false notions that have already taken hold and are firmly lodged in the human understanding not only make it difficult for the truth to gain access; even if such access is granted, the idols return and obstruct the restoration of the sciences as long as men are not on their guard and take precautions against them. The idols were of dual origin. They either entered the mind from the outside, or they were innate. The first could be eliminated, even though laboriously, but the second could in no way be destroyed. All that could be done was to bring them out into the open so that this treacherous power of the mind could be recognized and vanquished.

Even these few statements show sufficiently that Bacon's theory was not free of contradictions. It distinguished imperfectly between two aspects, the epistemological and logical, and the psychological. If what he called idols was something inborn with the power to influence the results of knowledge, then it is difficult to see how the purging of the mind could succeed in eliminating this source of errors. If, however, the idols were merely whims of the mind, the aim of Bacon's theory would be realizable. Were the innate idols to lead the mind to apprehend and explain things "by analogy to man"—instead of "by analogy to the universe," as should be the case—the very principle of Bacon's interpretation of nature would be in question. Yet it was for him axiomatic that science transmitted a true picture of things, a conviction implied by his theology as well as by his epistemology. He held that in contrast to idols, ideas were not "arbitrary abstractions" but "the true inscriptions of the Creator upon his creations," and therefore accessible to human understanding. Because of their direct relationship to the Creator, the things themselves were true. It made sense to assert the "aberrations of human nature," and to differentiate the pure from the impure intellect if one granted the possibility of an intrinsically true mind. This need not necessarily exclude the formation of idols; but one had to assume that even though they interfered with the process of understanding, they were unable to prevent it absolutely. Nevertheless, Bacon's frequent comparisons of the intellect to a "distorting" or "enchanted" mirror suggest that the intellect was constitutionally unsuited for the comprehension of nature. Still, bearing in mind what he propounded in the *Great Instauration* and in *The Proficiency and Advancement of Learning,* one may conclude that the idols formed part of our cognitive ability not by any logical necessity, but merely by psychological accident. Only in the latter case was it justifiable to expect that the mind may be so guided "as to acquire the ability to apply itself to the nature of things by all appropriate methods."

Bacon warned that the activity of the understanding was liable to be dominated and prepossessed by the will. "The human mind is not a pure light, but is influenced by will and feeling. Consequently, sciences come into being in compliance with desire. Feeling penetrates and infects thinking in innumerable and often unnoticeable ways." Thus, Bacon held the will responsible for preventing the mind from understanding and explaining nature. True, the intellect itself was inclined to assume a greater regularity and sameness in things than was warranted. Yet this weakness for premature conclusions could be counteracted just as the influence of will and feeling could be eliminated or at least kept in bounds. Since idols were the productions of the will, Bacon's theory about them amounted in fact to a "pathology of representation and judgment."[5] His critique was primarily directed at the psychological assumptions with which the intellect worked, making us conscious of the affective and social elements that impeded understanding. Bacon saw in such an effort the promise of a decisive correction because once the source of error was identified, it could be rendered harmless. For though he believed the human mind was inclined to explain the world in human terms, *"ex analogia hominis,"* he did not consider it unfit for an adequate understanding of the nature of things. On the contrary, he remained convinced that because of our insight into possible anthropomorphic falsification, the knowledge of nature could be made secure, provided the counsel of caution against the "storms of passion" was duly heeded.[6] Bacon's conception of truth presupposed a correspondence between being and consciousness. The possibility of a basic inadequacy of the intellect did not enter his mind. His theology protected him from that, for it assumed that man and nature were of the same divine origin and therefore in harmony with each other.

It would be difficult to overestimate the historic as well as the systematic significance of Bacon's theory of idols. In the eighteenth century it inspired the theory of prejudices developed in England and particularly in France, and for a long time thereafter helped protect scientific work from obscurantism. At the same time the battle fronts shifted. Whereas Bacon's chief interest was to protect the study of nature from the influence of idols and from the interference of theology and superstition, later on, other fields such as political science and history, sociology and economics became the main objects of concern. They, far more than the natural sciences, appeared to be affected by class and national interests, and it was against these that the dignity of objectivity had to be established.[7]

5. This apt characterization belongs to Ernst Cassirer, *Das Erkenntnisproblem in der Philosophie und Wissenschaft der neueren Zeit,* 3rd ed. (Berlin, 1922), 2:7. His criticism of Bacon's role in the establishment of empiricism is generally relevant in this connection.

6. Bacon, *Of the Proficience and Advancement of Learning Divine and Human.* Works, 3:315-6. "In general and in sum, certain it is that veritas and bonitas differ but as the seal and the print: for truth prints goodness; and they be the clouds of Error which descend in the storms of passions and perturbations."

7. The line of critical sociological inquiry established by Bacon and the Enlightenment continued through the nineteenth into the early twentieth century. In

Bacon distinguished four types of idols. Their general nature, origin, and effect have already been presented; a brief description of each type will therefore suffice. They were the Idols of the Tribe, the Idols of the Cave, the Idols of the Marketplace, and the Idols of the Theatre. The first were common to the human species. The second were peculiar to the individual and resulted from his natural idiosyncrasies, education, social intercourse, and the kind of authority he cultivated and revered. The third derived from the social life of man. "Men associate with each other by means of speech; but words are imposed according to the apprehension of the crowd. And therefore the ill and unfit choice of words wonderfully obstructs the understanding . . . Words do violence to it and spoil everything."[8] The fourth and last derived from the doctrines, fables, and fallacies of philosophy.

It was a matter of great consequence that the religious struggles of the sixteenth century exerted so strong an influence on Bacon's theory of idols, and that he regarded the effect of superstition on scientific understanding as equally obnoxious as that of the "idols of

---

The Study of Sociology (1873), Herbert Spencer described in great detail all those psychological and social factors which impede the scientific investigation of society. By his analysis of how these affect theoretical attitudes, he hoped to free sociology from the reproach that it merely reflected the political and economic interests of groups and nations. Scientific objectivity is to be guaranteed by the exposure and elimination of the typical prejudices of education, patriotism, social classes, churches, and nations. Two treatises by the Swedish sociologist Gustaf F. Steffen serve the same purpose: *Die Irrwege sozialer Erkenntnis* (Jena, 1913) and *Der Weg zu sozialer Erkenntnis* (Jena, 1911). For him, too, the problem of the truth of social knowledge is of central importance. He describes "the errors of social thinking" that are caused by social superstition, prejudices, lies, and mysteries. Steffen rightly calls attention to the fact that the search for truth in social science encounters difficulties not only in the subjectivity and prejudices of the investigator, but also in the object, social life, which is "an object of inquiry equipped with the will and power to deceive the observer and to conceal itself from him." Mention should also be made of the book by L.B. Hellenbach, *Die Vorurtheile der Menschheit* (1883), which, with reference to Bacon, attempts to promote a philosophical world view, and the happiness of mankind, by the destruction of prejudices. Unfortunately, this popularly written book itself adopts contemporary views as criteria by which prejudices are to be measured, thus paying considerable tribute to the prejudices of its own time. Since Hellenbach considers every philosophy to be subject to this pitfall, the "critique of our cognitive capability" remains the only possible object. The book by Max Nordau, *Die conventionellen Lügen der Kulturmenschheit* (1883), which at one time went through many editions, is of similar caliber.

8. Bacon, *Novum Organon,* 1:43, 59.

the soul." He thus set a precedent for the later use of his theory by the French *philosophes* in their criticism of the Christian churches and dogmas. In his attempt at the restoration of the sciences, Bacon was most careful to separate philosophy from theology because, to him, the religious claim to truth rested on revelation whereas philosophic truth consisted in the faithful representation of nature.[9] Theology rightly objected to having its doctrines deduced from philosophic principles and to thereby being deprived of any appeal to divine authority. Philosophy, in turn, had to reject the attempt of theologians to explain nature by invoking divine mysteries. Bacon's rejection of scholasticism rested chiefly on its failure to separate theology from philosophy. "From the unhealthy mixture of the divine and the human," he feared, there arose not only a "phantastic philosophy" but an "heretical religion." The relation between the two disciplines could be made clear by assigning to each its proper field of inquiry and method.

The corruption of philosophy by superstition would cease if the cause, effect, and concept of superstition were clarified. "It must not be overlooked," he wrote, "that natural philosophy had at all times to contend with such troublesome and dangerous enemies as superstition and blind religious zealotry." Particularly illuminating is a passage from *The Proficiency and Advancement of Learning,* in which Bacon ascribed to superstition the very same influence he later attributed to the idols in the *Novum Organon.* "The mind of men," he wrote, "is rather like an enchanted mirror, full of superstition and imposture, if it be not delivered and reduced."[10] Thus, to the four idols he added superstition, whose likeness to religion made it all the uglier, just as the ape's ugliness was increased by his likeness to man.[11] Because superstition projected an "unworthy" image of the divinity, it was for Bacon worse than atheism, which professed to have no such image at all. In order to determine what superstition was, one had first to know God as revealed in Holy

9. Kuno Fischer, *Franz Bacon von Verulam* (Heidelberg, 1856), is well informed on Bacon's position on religion, his differentiation of theology and philosophy, and the influence of his views on the philosophy of the eighteenth century. See especially pp. 269 ff.

10. Bacon, *Of the Proficience and Advancement of Learning,* 3:395.

11. Bacon, *The Essays of Counsels, Civil and Moral: Of Superstition,* 6:416.

Scripture. However, in view of the multifarious theological controversies, Bacon stressed the importance of ascertaining, through a comprehensive work, the true content of divine revelation.[12]

Superstition was reprehensible not only in that it heaped mockery and disgrace on the divinity, but because it destroyed the natural system of law and morality by subjecting the mind to an uncontrollable force. Superstition transferred the leadership and power of the state to the popular mass. This meant that rational discussion on which society must rely was sacrificed or accommodated to practical considerations and hence to arbitrary rule.[13] To the extent that superstition appropriated the power of the state, it destroyed freedom of conscience and instituted uniformity of opinion in society. Lacking a base in either the doctrines of revelation or the rational understanding of nature, superstition destroyed the supernatural and the natural order, surrendering both to human whim.

To appreciate the future consequences of Bacon's strictures of pseudoreligious behavior, we need to bear in mind that the effects of superstition and of the idols on the state and on science were identical. He thus anticipated the later view of the eighteenth century in which idols and superstition merged into a single complex of antirational urges that were essentially interest-oriented and originated in arbitrary or "unconscious" deformations of the intellect. The connection between Bacon and the French Enlightenment is apparent in his reflections on the motives of superstition, among which

12. Bacon, *De Dignitate et Augmentis Scientiarum,* book 9, 1:829 ff. Also, *A Confession of Faith,* 7:219.

13. Bacon, *Of Superstition,* 6:415–6. "It were better to have no opinion of God at all, than such an opinion as is unworthy of Him. For the one is unbelief, the other is contumely: and certainly superstition is the reproach of Deity. . . . And as the contumely is greater towards God, so the danger is greater towards men. Atheism leaves a man to sense, to philosophy, to natural piety, to reputation; all which may be guides to an outward moral virtue, though religion were not; but superstition dismounts all these, and erecteth an absolute monarchy in the minds of men. Therefore atheism did never perturb states; for it makes men wary of themselves, as looking no further: and we see the times inclined to atheism (as the time of Augustus Caesar) were civil times. But superstition hath been the confusion of many states and bringeth in a new primum mobile, that ravisheth all the spheres of government. The master of superstition is the people; and in all superstition wise men follow fools; and arguments are fitted to practice, in a reversed order."

he regarded the social interests of the clergy as of decisive importance.[14] Once it was discovered that certain religious customs, institutions, and ideas no longer reflected "true" religion—in his case
Christian revelation—but served the interests of a certain social es-
tate, the criticism of the idols and superstition was transformed into
social criticism. When it was further observed that the interests of
the leading group in a state coincided in some way with the interests
of the clergy, and that the social hierarchy and the political con-
sititution were sanctioned by religion, the critique of religion expanded into a critique of the state. For its part, a state founded on
religion was bound to regard any criticism of church and religion as
aimed against itself and therefore made available its instruments of
power for their defense. This expansion of the original theory of
idols into a broad criticism of society and the state occurred during
the French Enlightenment.

The separation of theology and philosophy had for Bacon certain
consequences concerning the relationship of church and state.
Though he regarded the unity of religious faith as useful and
desirable for the state, he rejected all compulsion in matters of conscience, and this for two reasons. History showed that religious
compulsion all too easily inflamed the passions and interests of
special parties;[15] and theological differences engendered controversies that lacked significance or else were of such subtlety and
obscurity as to be meaningless.[16] In either case the state ran the risk
of settling theological differences that were far removed from the
purity of God's word.

14. Ibid., p. 416. "The causes of superstition are pleasing and sensual rites and
ceremonies; excess of outward and pharisaical holiness; over-great reverences of
traditions, which cannot but load the church; the stratagems of prelates for their
own ambition and lucre, the favouring too much of good intentions, which openeth
the gate to conceits and novelties; the taking an aim at divine matters by human,
which cannot but breed mixture of imaginations; and lastly, barbarous times, especially joined with calamities and disasters."

15. Bacon, *Of Unity in Religion*, 6:384. "It was a notable observation of a wise
father, and no less ingenuously confessed; that those which held and persuaded
pressure on conscience, were commonly interested therein themselves for their own
ends."

16. Ibid., p. 382. "Men ought to take heed of rending God's church by two
kinds of controversies. The one is when the matter of the point controverted is too

Bacon only expected his theory of idols to act as a safeguard for the understanding and explanation of nature. But this restricted use could not be maintained because it was difficult to see why all branches of knowledge should not be protected from the influence of idols. It was therefore natural that his limited theory should be expanded by the *philosophes* of the eighteenth century into a general theory of prejudice and applied, more severely than before, to religion and, radically, to state and society. Bacon still drew a sharp distinction between innovations that affected the intellectual and in-stitutional bases of civil society and those that merely changed the logical foundations of knowledge. A new popular movement, even if it attempted to improve the conditions of life, was always dangerous because of the disturbances it caused in the habitual course of social affairs. Any progress in the sciences, however, any new point of view or experiment, was to be welcomed. "Civil society," he stated, "rests on authority and consensus, on fame and opinion, not on proofs."[17] Since public order and social institutions were not reducible to rational constructions, the critique of idols did not apply. Public opinion and uniformity of views were rooted in irrational, accidental conditions and prejudices. What guaranteed the stability of social conditions was a tried and tested tradition.

At this point the critique of the Enlightenment departed from Bacon's position. It asserted the existence of a natural, lawful order of state and society that could be disclosed; if it did not exist in actuality, the reason simply was that prejudices concealed it from common view. The theory of idols, broadened into a theory of prejudice, now acquired a pronounced political character: it claimed to replace a social order founded on divine authority and sovereignty with a secular order justified by reason. The irrational basis of the state and religion, already admitted by Bacon, was now perceived as one more idol to be brought before the court of reason. If it did not pass the test, it would be exposed as the machination of class interest and group will.

---

small and light, not worth the heat and strife about it, kindled only by contradiction. . . . The other is when the matter of the point controverted is great, but is driven to an over-great subtilty and obscurity; so that it becometh a thing rather ingenious than substantial."

17. Bacon, *Novum Organon,* 1:90.

The Unmasking of Prejudices by
Helvetius and Holbach

In the eyes of the men of the Enlightenment prejudice
had a dual effect. In the individual it appeared in the form of career
and status preconceptions, leading him to a biased selection of the
facts, to biased interpretation and evaluation that barred him from a
true knowledge of state and society. At the same time, these institutions themselves took an interest in the way they appeared to
the observer. Thus subject and object conspired to obscure the true
order of human coexistence. The work of Helvetius and Holbach
monotonously and aggressively voiced this complaint. The preface
to Holbach's *Système de la Nature* expressed a common concern of
the period when it presented the struggle for truth as having both intellectual and political importance.

> Man is unhappy solely because he fails to understand nature. His
> mind is so infected by prejudices that one is tempted to think of
> him as forever condemned to error. . . . Reason guided by ex-
> perience must at last attack at their source the prejudices by
> which mankind has so long been victimized. The time has come
> for reason, so unjustly debased, to quit the pusillanimous attitude
> that has made it the accomplice of lies and madness. . . . The
> truth is one; man has need of it. The crushing chains forged
> everywhere in nations by tyrants and priests we owe to error.

The battle of reason against the prejudices threatening to flood
and drown understanding was the prime subject of the writings of
Helvetius and Holbach. Diderot, for one, praised Helvetius's book
De l'Esprit as "a fierce knockout blow delivered against prejudices
of every kind."[18]

Why did man shrink from self-knowledge and renounce, for
motives as yet unknown, the objectification of reason? Why was

---

18. Denis Diderot, *Réflexions sur le Livre "De l'Esprit,"* Oeuvres complètes
(Paris, 1875), 2:274. Diderot here offers an excellent criticism which has stood the
test of time.

society afraid to expose the principles and articles of its constitution to public consciousness? This peculiar situation appeared to imply a conspiracy by which society and the individual had agreed to declare plain prejudices as the truth. This was the situation from which Helvetius and Holbach started.

In the judgment of the nineteenth and twentieth centuries, Helvetius was not a thinker of any philosophic importance. By dismissing his books *De l'Esprit* and *De l'Homme* as feeble derivatives of the sensualism of Condillac, as did Ernst Cassirer,[19] for example, serious appreciation of his work was blocked from the very outset. This representative of the spirit of the Enlightenment did not even escape the reproach that his writings amounted to no more than an "absurd exaggeration and distortion of the French movement."[20] His reputation also suffered from the religious and clerical condemnation of the entire philosophy of the Enlightenment, a verdict based less on knowledge than on political and theological partisanship. Finally, exponents of the Restoration and Romanticism censured Helvetius for what had formerly brought him renown—his contribution to the intellectual ferment preceding the French Revolution and his participation in efforts at comprehensive educational reform. One might have supposed, nevertheless, that the generous tribute paid Helvetius by two German philosophers, Karl Marx and Friedrich Nietzsche, would have induced others to examine whether this wholesale repudiation was justified. Such an examination would have yielded a more balanced estimate of his work. On the one hand, his sensualistic epistemology would have been pronounced unsound for the simple reason that specific intellectual capacities were derivable from sensation only because they were already contained in it. His philosophical materialism, too, would have been faulted for its internal contradictions, which could not be resolved by the suggestion that matter was endowed with the

19. Ernst Cassirer calls *De l'Esprit* a "weak work of little originality" that carried further Condillac's attempt to present psychic experience as a metamorphosis of simple sensation. See *Die Philosophie der Aufklärung* (Tübingen, 1932), p. 33. See also Emile Bréhier, *Histoire de la Philosophie* (Paris, 1934) 2:1, 438, for the place of Helvetius in the history of French thought.

20. The judgment of Hermann Hettner, *Geschichte der französischen Literatur im achtzehnten Jahrhundert,* 5th ed. (Braunschweig, 1894), p. 397.

capacity of feeling.[21] On the other hand, it would have been apparent that, with all his rationalist predilections he recognized the importance of the affective components of the soul and gave a brilliant defense of the passions as the "creative germ of the mind."[22] In short, the obvious faults of Helvetius need not have obscured the merits of his work.

It would be strange indeed if two such relentlessly critical minds as Marx and Nietzsche were appreciative of Helvetius without some good reason.[23] True, they were interested in preserving certain of his insights which were obscured by the tendencious, denunciatory use of such labels as materialism, rationalism, and utilitarianism. Thus, Marx was attracted to the sociological aspect of Helvetius's analysis of man, Nietzsche to his psychology of the "love of power." Both were aware also that Helvetius's psychology and sociology incorporated certain keen insights from such writers as Montaigne, Pascal, Fontenelle, and La Rochefoucauld. Marx was especially struck by the idea that man's practical and theoretical behavior as related

---

21. Claude Adrien Helvetius, *De l'Esprit* (1758), p. 32. The *Oeuvres complètes* (London, 1777) contain a work entitled "Les Progrès de la Raison dans la Recherche du Vrai." There we read, "What is called nature cannot contain anything except intelligence and matter," 2:340. Georg Plechanov argues with some good reasons against the authenticity of this work in his contribution to the history of materialism, *Holbach, Helvetius, Marx* (Stuttgart, 1896), p. 80, fn. 2. But his opinion, and Marx's too, that Helvetius expounded a pure materialism is unconvincing.

22. Helvetius, "Les Progrès de la Raison," p. 297. The passions "must . . . be considered the seminal element of the mind and the powerful spring propelling men to great deeds."

23. Karl Marx and Friedrich Engels, *Die heilige Familie* in *Historisch-kritische Gesamtausgabe,* I,3, p. 306. "The French lent English materialism *esprit* and eloquence, flesh and blood. They gave it temperament and charm, which it lacked. They civilized it. Helvetius stamps materialism with a typically French character and relates it to social life. Sensual qualities and love of self, pleasure, and intelligent personal interest constitute the basis of morality. His system is characterized by the natural equality of all human intelligence, direct correspondence between the progress of reason and industry, the natural goodness of man, and the omnipotence of education."—For Nietzsche, Helvetius represents "the last great event in morals." He taught that people seek power in order to acquire the enjoyments of the powerful (which is only half true). XIX:179. He has remained, Nietzsche said, "among all good moralists and all good men the best insulted in Germany to this very day," even though his work "pointed the right way," IX:301. Schopenhauer, too, had a positive relation to Helvetius, whom he counted as a "privileged mind" among the French and English moral critics, *Parerga*, II;21.

to matters of public life was a product of the social milieu. Nietzsche was drawn to Helvetius as to a precursor of the doctrine of the will to power. These two perspectives must be kept together, however, if we are to do justice to the significance his work holds for the problems of this investigation.

In contrast to Condillac, who attempted to derive all ideas from basically simple sensations, Helvetius wanted to know which ideas owed their origin to man's social life.[24] He therefore avoided Condillac's procedure of starting with the artifice of an isolated, simple human being registering a succession of external impressions. Nor was he interested in returning to the historical beginnings of human societies. He used historic figures and events for illustration, but his interest centered on man as he appeared in the present. His work attempted a sociological interpretation of the ideas by which men oriented their behavior and which they believed to be objective reflections of the social order. He inquired into what share society had in the birth and content of ideas. The word "idea" he used in an almost unlimited sense. It comprised the conceptions we form of the relations between men and things, and between men and men; also the affect-laden perceptions that precipitate positive and negative judgments concerning things we know or expect to be either beneficial or harmful to ourselves. In Helvetius's view, an idea was able equally to express subjective prejudice and adequate knowledge. It would therefore be a misunderstanding to conclude that for him the social conditioning of ideas reduced them to reflections of social interests emptied of all social knowledge. His intention was the very contrary, namely, the independence and objectivity of sociological knowledge.

Helvetius thus was principally in the same epistemological position as Bacon. His analysis of human understanding, including ideas, prejudices, and cognitive ability, often involves, it is true, long-winded descriptions of the dependence of ideas on social facts. However, the possibility of demonstrating such a dependency presupposed the existence of an objective criterion. Besides, Helvetius did not draw the radical conclusion that all ideas, without excep-

24. Alois Dempf refers to *De l'Esprit* as the "brilliant work" in ideological research. "Kulturphilosophie," *Handbuch der Philosophie,* ed. Alfred Baeumler and Manfred Schröter (Munich, 1934).

tion, reflect the living conditions of different groups and societies. That was reserved for Marx and his followers. Helvetius was protected from this radicalization by his conception of reason and natural law. We nowadays reproach such a position with being unhistorical. But we might well consider whether this objection does not overlook the fact that rational constructions of the social order contain a certain universal element or substance all men have in common. This is not to question that social institutions are rooted in and affected by a great variety of unique historical conditions and traditions, including feelings and passions, religious and moral convictions, economic interests and ethnic origin, the sense of a common political destiny. All these differences do not, however, contest three fundamental facts. First, all forms of social life are actualized by concrete human beings as the representatives of a common social will. Second, it is the same human essence that objectifies itself in the variety of historic cultures. And third, all social formations require moral and rational assumptions. These three insights represent the great heritage and deep concerns of the eighteenth century. Hegel preserved that heritage and gave expression to those concerns when he wrote: "Man is rational by nature; this makes possible the idea of equal rights for all and invalidates the rigid distinction between men who have rights and those who are rightless."[25] "It is a part of intellectual culture to conceive of the ego as a *general* person and a universal in whom *all* are identical. *Hence man has value because he is man,* not because he is a Jew, Catholic, Protestant, German, Italian, etc."[26]

True to the spirit of the eighteenth century, Helvetius did not merely call attention to the variety of social associations and their corresponding ideas, but wanted above all to reveal the underlying unity and universality of the human mind. Behind the infinite variety of cultural achievements lay, he assumed, an "essential equality of mind," for all men were equipped with what he called "rightmindedness" that manifested itself in their capacity for objective understanding and remained identical through different cultures. It would appear, therefore, that the true intent of the rational

25. Hegel, *Enzyklopädie der philosophischen Wissenschaften im Grundriss*, VII/2:65, §393 Zusatz.
26. Hegel, *Grundlinien der Philosophie des Rechts*, VIII:264, §209.

construction of social forms was the discovery of those general principles that made them possible in the first place. No human association could exist or endure without trust and the idea of truth. Though this was just an assertion, it could become confirmed as a general insight of social philosophy; and in that case, the rationalism of the eighteenth century might come to be viewed in a new light. Critics have, of course, rightly objected to the abstract schematism of its moral and social theories because it ignored national and cultural differences. It is true, also, that rationalism and natural-law theory led to the fiction that all social organizations could be founded or reconstituted according to abstract criteria, in violation of individual historic culture growth. Yet we should remember that Helvetius would not have been tempted to put together a codex of rational propositions, had he lacked a universal image of man.

The central theme of his thought is the dependence of ideas on man's social organizations. "Our ideas," he wrote, "are the necessary consequences of the societies in which we live."[27] More specifically, he aimed to demonstrate how the members of different strata and of groups differentiated by profession, rank, and achievement perceive events and actions, how they evaluate them and incorporate them into their respective world views. The same social situation fostered a common point of view. Men's emotional reactions differed according to their social position and condition. Individual psychological behavior was determined by the modes of thought and valuations characteristic of the group. In short, anticipating the environmental determinism of the nineteenth century and its errors, Helvetius presented man as a product of the intellectual and social environment in which he was born. Because he held to a passive concept of the mind, he underestimated individual spontaneity and creativity, which cannot be restricted to the appropriation of already existing cultural contents. The passive concept of the mind also led him to overestimate the power of education, as in the oft-quoted phrase, *L'éducation peut tout.*[28] This belief in the omnipotence of education had political consequences. Since education is everywhere closely related to the prevailing form of government, its principles cannot be reformed without also

27. Helvetius, *De l'Esprit,* p. 114.   28. Helvetius, *De l'Homme,* II:332.

changing the constitution of the state. "If under a liberal regime men are generally open, loyal, and industrious, but under a despotic one, deceitful, base, lacking in genius and courage, this difference in character is due to the different types of education they have received under the two types of government."[29]

Though Helvetius believed that human thought and action were motivated by personal interest, he also observed that interest was always qualified by social condition, actual need, and disposition. Men had no interest in seeing things as they really were, and this was why their views on morality, politics, and metaphysics differed. In his work *De l'Esprit,* Helvetius tried to show that self-love makes man what he is. But since he cannot have what he wants unless he also possesses the means for achieving his purposes, self-love must be allied with the love of power. Nietzsche later welcomed the introduction of this basic concept, in which he saw a precursor of his own "will to power." But at the time, the concept helped to round out the picture thus far developed by the sociology of prejudice. In the last analysis, Helvetius thought, ideas and prejudices masked and disguised a will to power. Therefore, enlightenment meant essentially unmasking and revealing, gaining insight into the misuse of ideas such as justice and virtue for the purpose of disguising special power interests. "Everyone wants to command because everyone wants to increase his happiness and have all his fellow citizens take notice of it. Now the surest means to make them do so are power and force. Hence, love of power founded in the love of happiness is the common aim of all our desires. Wealth, honor, fame, envy, respect, justice, virtue, intolerance—all these are but different names and disguises of our love of power."[30]

Thus, the psychology of power undergirded the sociology of power. Like individual behavior, the structure and lawfulness of social formations became intelligible in terms of power drives. This was not in itself a momentous insight. Its significance became apparent, however, when it was explained that organized social power nurtured and disseminated certain kinds of prejudices, namely, those that promised to provide ideological support for the maintenance of its position. More specific consequences followed. Religion and political theory were open to the suspicion that they were only

29. Ibid., II:333.   30. Ibid., I:239; similarly, pp. 248, 269–70.

"pretexts," that is, instruments for maintaining the established order. "The prejudices of the great," Helvetius said, "are the laws of the little."[31] Inevitably, the prejudices and pretenses disseminated by political and religious authorities would collide with the philosophy of rationalism. For though they had no truth content, they nevertheless served to legitimate the existing authorities. This the philosophers could not tolerate because they aimed to found the social order on rational laws inherent in nature itself. Their criticism, however, created a new political problem not limited to their own period, but of lasting importance. This was the problem of political and religious tolerance. It formed the center of Helvetius's social criticism and also of his anthropology because tolerance obviously conflicted with the love of power. We follow his analysis of this conflict further.

Nature and history, he wrote, tell the same story: "Power is everything on earth."[32] Since man loves virtue only for the wealth and respect they may yield him, his whole inner life is nothing but a disguised love of power. This love leads him to compel others to promote his own happiness, forcing them ultimately into intellectual submissiveness. "Man does not really consider himself the master of others until he has enslaved their minds."[33] Society behaves in the same way as the individual; the state and religious bodies are inherently inclined to intolerance. "Opinion, they say, rules the world. No doubt there are instances where general opinion has overruled sovereigns. But what has this to do with the power of truth? Does it prove that general opinion is a product of the truth? No; experience shows, on the contrary, that almost all moral and political questions are decided by the powerful, not by the reasonable. If opinion rules the world, in the long run it is the powerful who rule opinion."[34] The theory of prejudice, then, led to the conclusion that Bacon had already been unable to deny: philosophy and politics, the intellectual power of knowledge and the social power on which institutions rest, confront each other like antinomies. Nor was their conflict limited to eighteenth-century France. Although the opposing po-

31. Helvetius, *De l'Esprit,* p. 551.
32. Ibid., p. 380.
33. Helvetius, *De l'Homme,* I:270.
34. Ibid., II:294. See Pascal, *Pensées sur la Religion chrétienne:* "C'est la force qui fait l'opinion."

sitions may change in history, their perfect reconciliation is impossible.

Prejudices, Helvetius continued, can only be uncovered and surmounted by the truth, but knowledge and communication of the truth require freedom. Freedom has two meanings. It means independence from the demands of the social and the individual will, which is possible because the human mind everywhere is basically sound and capable of knowledge. Freedom also means independence from the prejudices fostered and imposed by church and state, which can be gained by public criticism of these institutions. When both freedoms have been achieved, men will be able to know natural law and reason. This knowledge will enable them to act morally and thereby secure their true happiness. "All vice, the philosophers say, is an error of the mind. Crimes and prejudices are brothers, truths and virtues are sisters. But what are the sources of truth? Contradiction and dispute. Freedom of thought bears the fruits of truth."[35]

It was perfectly clear to Helvetius that his critical analysis of prejudice had political implications. Besides, he attacked despotism directly, though he put it back into a much earlier period to better expose its depraving effects. Despotism, he wrote, was basically concerned with "hiding the true principles of morality from the people." Their ignorance was then exploited by two types of men, religious fanatics who believed that nations must be blinded before they could be subjugated, and "half-politicians" who mobilized passion and prejudice against all who threatened their domination. The true principles of morality could be introduced only after such types were unmasked and their real intentions exposed. In this campaign Helvetius was joined by Holbach, who devoted his writings to a sociological, rather than a psychological, unmasking of state and church. His slogans never varied—"tear off the veil of prejudices," "unmask the impostures!" Both Helvetius and Holbach are tiresome in their repeated assertions that religions owe their origin to the fraudulent intentions of power-greedy priests. Two aspects of their thought deserve notice, however, for they were to reappear later in Hegel's early theological writings and again in the anthropologies of Feuerbach, Bruno Bauer, Marx, and Nietzsche. They concern the uses of religion. Religion, so Helvetius and

35. Ibid., II:276.

Holbach tried to show, created an imaginary world where men could satisfy their need for happiness which the social conditions and legal-political order of the real world denied them.[36] At the same time religion was a most efficient instrument of secular power because it invoked God's will as sanction for a concrete social order. Thus throne and altar conspired to keep men from the knowledge of a rational social morality which Holbach called "the only religion natural to man."[37] However, the trinity of the Christian faith was beginning to yield to the trinity of philosophical reason—freedom, truth, and utility.[38]

36. Ibid., I:172. "Always impatient with the satisfaction of their desires, men forever build castles in Spain. It is as though they wished to enlist the whole of nature on behalf of their happiness. But is not nature sufficiently powerful to bring it about? They really invoke imaginary beings, fairies, and spirits. If they wish that these existed, it is from the confused hope that, favored by some enchanter, they can with his help come into possession of the magic lantern, and nothing will then be wanting in their happiness. So it is the love of happiness . . . that . . . creates supernatural beings."

37. Paul Heinrich Dietrich Holbach, *Lettres à Eugénie,* II:163.

38. Holbach, *Essai sur les Préjugés,* p. 246.

III

Ideology and Ideological Consciousness in the Philosophy of Karl Marx

Hegel and the Practical, Revolutionary Beginnings of Marxian Thought

ON ENTERING the main part of this book, a word of explanation is in order about the purpose and limit of the various historical analyses and digressions that form an essential part of it. The preceding discussion of eighteenth-century philosophy was limited to identifying certain ideas taken up and developed by Marx; it did not aim to review all the intellectual sources to which his work is indebted.[1] The same limitation applies to the discussion in this chapter of the relation of Marx to Hegel and Feuerbach. Our primary interest is not in intellectual history per se, nor in the polemics Marx carried on with the philosophers preceding him. These are subsidiary to the main question: what was the importance of those philosophers for the concept of ideology as developed by Marx? The concept itself can be understood only with reference to certain philosophies from which it emerged and to which we put a number of specific questions: How must man be constituted, in-

---

1. Well informed is Sidney Hook, *From Hegel to Marx: Studies in the Intellectual Development of Karl Marx* (London, 1936). Unfortunately, the philosophy of the eighteenth century is not taken into account. To some extent Hook makes up for this omission indirectly by his discussion of Marx's relation to Feuerbach and Bruno Bauer, both of whom took up important elements of the Enlightenment's criticism of religion and of Christianity in particular. However, the religious criticism of both men has roots also in the historical and critical examination of the Bible, the begin-

tellectually and psychically, to produce ideologies and "false consciousness?" What sociological conditions, what political and economic systems, favor such production? What transforms a complex of ideas into an ideology? And how is ideology related to truth? We arrive at the answers by tracing the origin of Marx's conception of man and society back to his criticism of Hegel and Feuerbach in which his own concept of ideology began to crystallize.

Marx entered the university as a student of law and left it as a philosopher. He attempted, at the age of nineteen, a systematic review of Roman law, failed, and concluded that he could not

---

nings of which go back to the seventeenth century to Spinoza and Richard Simon. The following older, extensive works are not especially profitable for our problem: Thomas G. Masaryk, *Grundlagen des Marxismus* (Vienna, 1899); Ludwig Woltmann, *Der historische Materialismus* (Düsseldorf, 1900); Emil Hammacher, *Das philosophisch-ökonomische System des Marxismus* (Leipzig, 1909); and Georg Plechanow, *Die Grundprobleme des Marxismus* (Stuttgart, 1910). The same is true for Karl Kautsky, *Die materialistische Geschichtsauffassung,* 2nd ed. (Berlin, 1929), vol. 2. Much material about the general philosophical, ethical, and religious presuppositions is contained in Werner Sombart, *Der proletarische Sozialismus* (Jena, 1924), especially vol. 1:176 ff. and 291 ff. See also Hendrik de Man, *Zur Psychologie des Sozialismus* (Jena, 1927), a work which gives a good presentation of the scientific categories that occur in the later writings of Marx and Engels.

Marx's philosophical anthropology is contained in his early writings up to the *Communist Manifesto.* Any interpretation of his theory of history and his concept of ideology has to begin with them. Those who would gain an understanding of Marx only from his works on economic theory and history will be lacking the indispensable philosophic foundation. Philosophically oriented are the following works: Georg Lukàcz, *Geschichte und Klassenbewusstsein* (Munich, 1923); Siegfried Landshut, *Karl Marx* (Lübeck, 1932); Auguste Cornu, *Karl Marx, l'Homme et l'Oeuvre. De l'Hégélianisme au Matérialisme historique* (Paris, 1934); and Konrad Bekker, *Marx' philosophische Entwicklung: Sein Verhältnis zu Hegel* (Zurich, 1940); Stanislaw Warynski, *Die Wissenschaft von der Gesellschaft: Umriss einer Methodenlehre der dialektischen Soziologie* (Bern, 1944); Jakob Hommes, *Der technokratische Eros: Das Wesen der materialistischen Geschichtsauffassung* (Freiburg, 1955).

In reading interpretations of Marx, one always needs to bear in mind that there is such a thing as a Marx orthodoxy that deals in condemnation and heresy. The followers and believers generally nullify criticisms of Marx with the argument that the critic does not share his assumptions. In other words, only those who take the proletarian point of view are able to understand and apply the materialist dialectic, and it is this dialectic that tells us what the point of view of the proletariat is. Faith precedes knowledge, and objective examination becomes impossible. The circularity of the argument is deliberate and undisguised in Georg Lukàcz, and in August Thalheimer, *Einführung in den dialektischen Materialismus: Sechzehn Vorträge an der Sun-Yat-Sen-Universität in Moskau* (Vienna and Berlin, 1927).

succeed without philosophy. So it was "with a good conscience that he once more threw himself into her arms,"[2] as he reported in the illuminating letter to his father of 10 November 1837. The philosophy to which he returned was that of Hegel, whose "grotesque rocky melody" had on a first superficial acquaintance not been to his taste. This time he read Hegel "from beginning to end," with the result that he became increasingly attached to the very philosophy from which he had sought to escape. His first comments on Hegel are to be found in the Notes to his dissertation on *The Difference between the Democritean and Epicurean Philosophy of Nature*. They tell us what Marx demanded of philosophy and what he was able to get out of Hegel. Two questions required clarification: What did philosophy mean to Hegel, and what place did he assign to it in the system of knowledge and in the life history of a people?

Hegel answered as follows: "The task of philosophy is to comprehend what is, for that which is, is reason."[3] He asked his students to bring with them a faith in reason. In his Inaugural Lecture at the University of Berlin on 22 October 1818 he reminded them that "the courage of truth, the faith in the power of the spirit is the first condition of philosophical study. Man should honor himself and regard himself worthy of what is highest. He cannot think highly enough of the greatness and power of spirit. The closed essence of the universe is incapable of resisting the courage of cognition; it must open up and spread out its richness and depth before man to be enjoyed by him."[4] Since reason constitutes the essence of things, and since it is both objectified and estranged from itself in nature and history, the task of philosophy is to comprehend it in this bifurcation and thereby reconcile it with itself. For when spirit recognizes itself in its own creation, the disunion is overcome in thought.

Philosophy in such a comprehensive sense has not always existed. Spirit only knows what it is after it has made itself what inherently it has always been; it knows itself by externalizing its own essence.

    2. Karl Marx and Friedrich Engels, *Historisch-kritische Gesamtausgabe,* ed. D. Riazanov and V. Adoratski (Frankfurt/Main, 1927-Moscow, 1935), I/2, p. 217. Hereafter cited as MEGA.

    3. Georg Friedrich Wilhelm Hegel, *Werke,* 8:18. Unless otherwise noted, all references are from the Vollständige Ausgabe durch einen Verein von Freunden des Verewigten, 2nd ed. (Berlin, 1840).

    4. Ibid., 6:x1; similarly, his address in Heidelberg, 13:5–6.

"Spirit is only this fathoming of itself."[5] In this fathoming and perceiving, which occurs after spirit has divided into a knowing subject and a known object, the unity of spirit reveals itself. The separation is necessary, for otherwise spirit would remain in itself and never know what it is. What it is manifests itself in history. Consequently, spirit can know itself only at the end, not at the beginning, of history. Hence, "in time, philosophy as the idea of the world appears after reality has completed its formation and is fully actualized."[6] It is true that peoples already possess a religion at the very beginning of their history, and the content of religion does not differ from that of philosophy. What both contain is "the general Reason that is in and for itself." Philosophy differs from religion only in form. What religion presents in the form of feeling and imagination, devotion and cult, philosophy perfects by means of conceptual knowledge. The truth that appears to the believer in the inwardness of feeling, and is therefore inevitably subjective, philosophy raises to a level where it becomes compelling and general.

Hegel's conception of philosophy as the knowledge of the self-realization of spirit in history did not merely make philosophy a late cultural phenomenon. It also implied that its beginning coincided with a "period of ruin." Spirit is manifest in different ways—one constructive, the other destructive. In the first instance, spirit exists as a stable structure: it is that communal whole in which human life is ordered and bound together by genuine religious and ethical convictions. The claims of morality are there generally recognized as self-evident and require no philosophical justification. The individual consents to do what is required of him because the public law so determines his private life that he accepts its commandments as necessary and universally valid. Yet spirit also attacks what it has created. Thought, which is "life, activity, the power to generate itself," contains "negation as an essential element, in that production is also destruction. Philosophy, in order to appear, must annul the natural from which it departs."[7] "Thought is the negation of the natural way of life."[8]

5. Ibid., 13:88.   6. Ibid., 8:20.   7. Ibid., 13:65.

8. Hegel, *Vorlesungen über die Geschichte der Philosophie,* Einleitung: System und Geschichte der Philosophie, vollständig neu nach den Quellen herausgegeben von Johannes Hoffmeister (Leipzig, 1940), p. 151.

Philosophy flowers when cultures mature and lose their vitality, but natural age, Hegel emphasized, had to be distinguished from spiritual age. The first implied weakness whereas "the advanced age of spirit is its perfect ripeness in which spirit returns to unity with itself, but as spirit."[9] He explained further:

As spirit transcends its natural shape, it changes from concrete morality and vital power into reflection and comprehension. As a consequence, it attacks and makes uncertain the substantial form of its existence, manifest in concrete morality and faith, and so initiates the period of disintegration. As a further development, thought gathers itself up into itself. One may say that once a people has passed beyond the concrete stage of its life, the separation and difference of classes becomes a fact and the people approaches its end. When there is a break between inner aspiration and external reality, when the old religion no longer satisfies, when the spirit becomes indifferent or dwells with discontent in its living form and the concrete ethical life dissolves—only then do men philosophize. For then the spirit takes refuge in the realm of thought, there to fortify itself against the existing world. Philosophy is a reconciliation with the disintegration of that world which thought initiated. When philosophy with its abstractions paints gray in gray, the freshness and vigor of youth is already gone. The reconciliation it offers is not a reconciliation in the existing world but in the ideal world.[10]

Stated in simpler terms, in nearly all peoples philosophy originates "when public life no longer satisfies the citizens and holds their interest, when they cease to participate in the administration of the state."[11]

There is no evidence that Hegel excepted his own philosophy from the general law of this development. In fact, the end of the *Lectures on the History of Philosophy* confirms the impression that he looked upon his work as "the last philosophy."[12] That is, his

9. *Werke,* 9:134.   10. Ibid., 13:66.   11. Hegel, *Vorlesungen,* p. 152.

12. Hegel's contemporaries already considered his philosophy as the last. See the conversation reported by Adolf Hausrath, *Richard Rothe und seine Freunde* (Berlin, 1902), 1:61. Rothe was a student at the University of Heidelberg in 1818 when Hegel taught there. To the question "What philosophy could conceivably come after a philosophy that had comprehended all within the concept?" the theologian Daub, a colleague of Hegel, answered simply, "None."

philosophy contains the "totality of forms"; it is the logical product and result in which the truth of all previous stages of the spirit is preserved and duly recognized. Philosophy is itself a historical movement and exists, like life, only as process. But the philosophical process means both development and a judicial proceeding in which spirit sits in judgment over its own deeds and renders justice to what is rational and truly real. Spirit would not be spirit and "eternal life" if it did not reveal itself and know itself in the fullness of these self-revelations. It is not surprising that Hegel looked on his philosophy as the last since it was the "revelation of God as he knows himself."[13]

There is deep melancholy in this idea that philosophy flowers only in periods of social disintegration. Philosophy cannot change the world, and it cannot restore what has been lost. Philosophic thought corrodes the "simple custom" and the "simple religion" because there is no other way for spirit to progress toward self-understanding. At this point is revealed the problematic character of Hegel's role as the philosopher of the state who appears to justify existing political and economic conditions as rational. The attempt of the contemporary romantic philosophers to re-establish the original religious foundation of the state could elicit from him only a superior air of doubt or drive him, with his convictions about the ways and final end of spirit, to despair. The whole concept of the restoration of religion was foreign to his philosophy, and necessarily so. Spirit as eternal life meant forever producing and reconciling opposites. "Absolute knowledge is to know opposites as a unity and unity as opposites." Such knowledge appears as the result of the process in which spirit unfolds as knowledge of itself. Spirit remains the same, abstractly speaking, although it is also always saturated with its entire past and thus changes its concrete form, transformed and increased by the growth of its own history. When this pattern of thought is applied to the political situation, we find that the modern state triumphed over the church because the church lost its religious

13. Eberhard Fahrenhorst, in his valuable study *Geist und Freiheit in Hegels System* (Berlin, 1934), justifiably stresses the terminal, final aspect of Hegel's thought. His interpretation seeks to demonstrate that Hegel's philosophy, "rooted in a grave and truly tragic sense of the world," looked on itself as the last system and signified "the very evasion of reality." The same interpretation is given by Karl Löwith in his informative and solid study *Von Hegel bis Nietzsche* (Zurich, 1941).

vocation and was submerged in the secular power. Out of this ruin the modern state rose as "a higher form of the rational idea." Spirit "became capable of realizing the rational solely in the principle of secularity." Hegel's political theory thus enthroned the profane state. "The abstractly educated, rational consciousness," he declared, "is able to put religion aside."[14] But he also gave a gloomy prognosis of the future of religion in the Western world. Christianity—in his view the only religion that had inspired the inner life of Western man—was being dissolved and replaced by philosophy. Even though the ultimate aim of philosophy was to reconcile thought with reality, this reconciliation did not adjust reality to thought and so change the existing world. Reconciliation meant that the development of thought was interpreted and conceived as a rational, necessary progression.

As the Notes to Marx's dissertation show, he understood perfectly well Hegel's claim that philosophy contained the sum total of its forms. Marx's problem was to find some personal relation to a philosophy that achieved such a perfection. He asked himself whether men would be able to live with a total philosophy.[15] When he wrote his father that under the influence of idealism he was tempted "to search for the Idea in reality itself," he still sounded Hegelian. But at the same time he made a statement by which he is seen to move away from Hegel and to lay the basis for his critical opposition to him. This statement concerned the relation between theory and practice, between knowing the world and changing it. "It is a psychological law," Marx asserted, "that the theoretical spirit that has become free in itself is converted into practical energy."[16] This conversion into a practical relation to reality occurs when philosophy has withdrawn into a complete world of its own; and it is necessary because the Hegelian reconciliation of idea and reality takes place in the realm of the ideal but not in the world of the real. "The world is therefore a divided world and confronts a philosophy that is a totality by itself." "The development of philosophic thought is at times interrupted by phases of concentration when abstract principles coalesce to form a totality. At other times, philosophy turns outward upon the world, not to comprehend it

14. Hegel, *Werke,* 9:533.   15. MEGA, I/1, p. 132.   16. Ibid., L/1, p. 64.

but, like a practical person, to enter into intrigues with it . . ."
"When its heart is strong enough to create a world . . . philosophy,
having grown into a world of its own, turns against the phenomenal
world. This is what Hegelian philosophy is doing now." Total
philosophy, conceived as the self-knowledge of spirit in its historical
development, is transformed into total "practical energy" through
which philosophy itself is to be realized. Marx called this transformation "its transubstantiation into flesh and blood."

If one asks how a theoretical attitude to the world can turn into a
practical one, the answer must be that the practice of philosophy is
in itself theoretical: "It is the criticism that compares the single existence with the substance, and the particular reality with the Idea."
The theoretical spirit compares the real with itself. Such a comparison is possible because, according to Hegel, there is a contradiction "between the purpose or concept of an object and its
existence."[17] "Truth, in the philosophic sense, is a relation inherent
in the object as such; it is the identity of a content, the agreement of
the concept with its reality."[18]

According to Marx, the function of criticism consists simply in
ascertaining the discrepancy between the factual existence of a thing
and the role or task it is destined to fulfill. This discrepancy fur-
nished him with the motive for taking a hand in changing reality.
"What at first was an inner light becomes a consuming flame
directed outward." Philosophy discards its self-sufficiency, confronts reality as something that is in a bad way, and does not measure up to its immanent demands. Such a recognition transforms
philosophy into the will to remake the world according to the Idea
so that reality will become identical with itself.

It is not difficult to recognize in these early utterances the germ of
the notion of philosophy as an instrument for revolutionizing the
world. In this respect Marx was in agreement with Hegel, though he
could not have known the relevant passage in a letter Hegel wrote to
his friend Niethammer on 28 October 1808 while he was editor of
the *Bamberger Zeitung:* "Theoretical work, I grow more convinced
every day, accomplishes more in the world than does practical work.
Once the conceptual realm is revolutionized, reality will be unable

---

17. Hegel, *Werke,* 6:§24, Zusatz 2, p. 52.   18. Ibid., 7:2, 11.

to hold out."[19] Similar reflections on the relation of theory to practice occurred already in Hegel's early writings. Deeply impressed by the French Revolution and the Wars of Coalition which revealed the internal and external impotence of the old German *Reich*, Hegel wrote an essay on *The German Constitution*, in the introduction to which we read: "All phenomena of this age show that satisfaction can no longer be found in the old life." When idea and reality break apart and contradict one another, there arises a striving for a mutual rapprochement. Men "who in their inward life have transformed nature into the idea" want to change life and its concrete order accordingly. This change is completed when idea and reality again coincide. "The person whom the present time has exiled into an inner world may either persist in this state, which is a perpetual dying; or, if nature impels him into life, he must strive to abolish the negative side of the existing world in order to be able to find and enjoy himself in it." Hegel had enough historical realism to know that the abolition of the existing world required power. "The restricted, narrow life can be successfully attacked only when a better one has gained power and threatens to use force against it."[20] Marx, like Hegel, from early on allied philosophy with political programs and parties. That made him distinguish between two kinds of philosophy that were "extremely opposed to each other." One, attached to the liberal party, consisted in criticism and was "outward-directed." The other was inward-directed and suffered from the same deficiency as the world. The first, however, looked upon this deficiency as something that could be remedied by making the world philosophical.[21]

---

19. *Briefe von und an Hegel,* ed. Karl Hegel (Leipzig, 1887). I:194. Johann Plenge calls attention to this "concurrence" in his excellent work *Marx und Hegel* (Tübingen, 1911), p. 183. See also Siegfried Marck, *Hegelianismus und Marxismus* (Berlin, 1922). He, however, gives a one-sidedly positivistic interpretation of Marx.

20. The introduction to the essay on "The German Constitution" is quoted from Karl Rosenkranz, *Hegels Leben* (Berlin, 1844), pp. 88–90. Concerning ideological thinking in Hegel, see Peter Christian Ludz, *Dialektik und Ideologie in der Philosophie Hegels,* Archiv für Rechts- und Sozialphilosophie, (1961), 47:134 ff. In this connection, reference may be made to a passage in Hegel's political study *Die englische Reformbill,* that mentions ideas which run counter to the interests of certain classes and "therefore have not yet entered their heads." See *Hegels Schriften zur Politik und Rechtsphilosophie,* ed. George Lasson (Berlin, 1913), p. 320.

21. MEGA, I/1, p. 65

Any account of Hegel's relation to politics must also take note of the lasting impression left on his mind by the French Revolution. In spite of his criticism of its actual course and effect, he regarded it as a grand attempt to realize abstract rational principles in concrete social and political forms. In the *Lectures on the Philosophy of History,* he still celebrated the Revolution as an incomparable event in these words:

> Never before, so long as the sun stood in the heavens and the planets revolved about it, did it happen that man stood on his head, that is, on his thought, and built reality in accordance with it. Anaxagoras was the first to say that *nous* [mind] governs the world. But only now did man come to recognize that thought should rule the spiritual life. This had the effect of a magnificent sunrise. All thinking beings took part in celebrating it. A sublime feeling prevailed in that period, an enthusiasm of the mind thrilled the world as though it experienced for the first time a true reconciliation of the divine and the secular.[22]

Marx later reproached Hegel's philosophy for standing the world on its head, by which he meant that its system contained ideological or irrational elements. All that Marx would have to do to reinstate reason in its rights was to turn this topsy-turvy world around. But Hegel, with his assertion that in the French Revolution man for the first time had turned the state and social order upside down, had already defined the issue of Marx's philosophy of history. For Marx the issue was to make reason the criterion of the interpretation of history and the foundation of the future social order.

Philosophy as the Criticism and Ideational Supplement of Reality

The clarification of the meaning and scope of the problem of ideology in Marx and Engels must begin with a programmatic statement Engels made in his essay on *Ludwig Feuerbach and the End of Classical German Philosophy* (1888). The basic question of all philosophy, and especially modern philosophy, he said, was the relation of thought to being.[23] Now what Marx called ideology

22. Hegel, *Werke,* 9:535–6.
23. *Ludwig Feuerbach und der Ausgang der klassischen deutschen Philosophie,* Marxistische Bibliothek (Vienna-Berlin, n.d.), 3:27.

referred originally to a system of propositions by means of which knowledge of the real world is made communicable and valid. If, however, the cognitive value of such propositions is denied, that is, if they are asserted to be untrue or denounced as ideological, the question inevitably occurs why specific ideologies arise at all. One also wants to know why certain propositions are *not* ideological. There must be some criterion by which knowledge and ideology can be distinguished. Since Marx dismisses the overwhelming part of previous human knowledge as ideology—including philosophy, political and legal theory, ethics, religion, sociology, and economics—one is bound to ask whether the human mind is prevented from producing true knowledge by a condition that is as difficult to perceive as it is to remove. This problem cannot be solved by psychological and logical explanations of error. For to denounce a proposition or system as ideological is to exclude the avoidability of error. So the production of ideology seems to be subject to some secret compulsion. What is its nature? Is it simply psychological, causing man's subjectivity and his structure of urges to bias his acts of cognition? Or is the relation of thought to being so prejudiced by the way thought is constituted that the latter is capable only of ideologies, but mistakes them for knowledge? However one may try to answer the question, one thing is certain. He who would deny the truth inherent in all cognitive statements, betrays by his very denial that he possesses a criterion for distinguishing knowledge from ideology.

The young Marx had firsthand knowledge of the French ideologues. During his exile in Paris in 1844–45, he excerpted in part Destutt de Tracy's work, *Eléments d'Idéologie.*[24] He was well aware that the term ideology had changed from the description of a scientific discipline into a denunciation of politically embarrassing, theorizing critics. He, too, used it in the derogatory sense Napoleon had first introduced. But it should not be overlooked that the philosophical writings of the young Marx contain a theory about the origin of ideas, the same problem that the "science of ideas" had originally sought to clarify. Since he knew de Tracy's connections with the sensualism of Condillac and Locke, and with the sociology of ideas of Helvetius, one may presume that his own views incorporated considerable elements from his predecessors. This question

24. MEGA, 3:560 ff.

can be answered only after we have examined important aspects of Marx's system.[25] These include his views on the relation of philosophy to reality, the nature of his anthropology and sociology, and the function of his radical critique of religion in his definition of man. We do not intend to treat these matters exhaustively, but present them from the perspective of what Engels defined as the basic question of modern philosophy: the relation between being and consciousness. This relation is fundamental, also, to the problem of ideology, which in the last analysis is an epistemological problem. We need to discover whether the distinction between a "false," ideological consciousness and a "right," adequate consciousness is warranted, and what the corresponding social orders are that condition the two.

In his analysis of Hegel, the young Marx encountered two different notions concerning the nature of philosophy. According to the first, philosophy provided a measure or norm for judging reality, known as the idea. The idea is not a product of the philosophical consciousness, but an outgrowth of reality itself: it appears, in Hegel's words, as the contradiction "between the purpose or concept of a thing and its actual existence." The original unity of idea and reality, their separation in human history, and their final reunion at the end of history—these ideas are at the center of the Marxian anthropology and theory of history. The same pattern underlies the concept of human self-alienation in which the human essence becomes separated from the human existence. This disunion, which culminates in the period of capitalism, could not be recognized unless one had some concept of what man is like when he does not suffer from self-alienation. Philosophy provides that concept by projecting an image of man as he was before the bifurcation of the original unity occurred. Implicit in this idea of the original unity of man is the philosophic critique of his present existence and the summons to revolutionize the world in order to re-establish that unity.

But philosophy has not fulfilled its function by merely depicting an irreconcilable difference between idea and reality. Philosophy itself "belongs" to the world and to a particular period; it is their ideal completion.[26] In one sense, this is almost a truism, for phi-

25. Engels speaks of a "false consciousness" in a letter to Franz Mehring of 14 July 1893.

26. MEGA, I/1, p. 613.

losophers think about nature and history in categories and concepts that reflect their own cultural perspectives and assumptions.
Marx, however, intended more than this kind of "belonging" and so
did Hegel. Marx's conception of how philosophy was related to a
historical world is again best clarified by a comparison with Hegel's
view of the matter. Hegel was dissatisfied with the commonplace
idea that certain parts of a culture, such as politics or religion,
"influence" philosophy, and he went on to construct a different in-
terrelationship between them. "The essential category is the unity of
all of these different formations, one and the same spirit being
manifest and expressed in them all."[27] This implied that philosophy,
too, belonged to a certain period, as Hegel explained in the following passage.

Every philosophy, as representing a particular phase of development, belongs to its time and is caught up in its limitations. An
individual is the child of its people and of its world, whose substance he expresses in his own way. He may puff himself up as
much as he likes, but he can no more reach beyond his time than
he can escape from his own skin. He is a part of the one general
spirit that constitutes his substance. It is the same general spirit
that philosophy comprehends in thought. Philosophy is spirit
thinking itself, it is its particular, substantial content. Every
philosophy is the philosophy of its own time.[28]

Marx maintained this general conception while at the same time
shifting its emphasis, indicating thereby a characteristic difference
between Hegel's metaphysics and his own. Whereas for Hegel the
different cultural forms of spirit were related to each other as expressions of the same substance that characterizes a certain phase in
the development of spirit, Marx rated these forms according to the
power they are able to exert. On such a scale, neither philosophy nor
religion rated high.

It is true, of course, that even Hegel did not attribute to these
forms of higher culture the same historic moving force as to
passions and interests. Philosophy and religion were after all only
the forms in which spirit grasped and perceived itself. Still, he
assumed that behind the struggle of life by individuals and peoples
an autonomous development of spirit took place in which the ob-

27. Hegel, *Werke*, 13:65.   28. Ibid., 13:59.

vious passions and special interests of men became the means by which spirit achieved its own true aims. From this point of view, history, with all its struggles for food, power, and respect, and all its ups and downs, is degraded into a foreground masquerade concealing the meaningful march of the spirit that alone counts and is real. Marx rejected this strange "duplication of the world," but he held fast to the teleological conception of history. History for him, too, was a rational process whose end would coincide with the end of philosophy, that is, the realization of philosophy would be identical with a reality transformed by philosophy. In this respect, Marx always remained a Hegelian; allegedly a representative of scientific positivism, he was a metaphysician at the core. For Marx, too, philosophy and culture, including political and economic conditions, form a whole. But whereas to Hegel all parts of a culture were equal manifestations of the same spirit, Marx made certain parts of the culture dependent on others. Philosophy and the economic and political system are declared to be dependent on the material conditions under which men earn their living. From his point of view, a cultural unity still exists in the sense that philosophy and religion, and also economic and political theories, are intellectual reflections of the actual conditions of life as prescribed by the social power of the ruling classes. But this unity takes the form of the dependence of the superstructure on the base. When Marx wrote about pauperism in Great Britain, he referred to English economic theory as the "scientific reflection of the national economic conditions of England."[29] There is no reason why the same metaphor should not be extended to other products of the mind, so that philosophy, religion, and especially theories of law and the state are also turned into "scientific reflections" of the prevailing political and economic conditions of a people. In that case, however, philosophy ceases to be an instrument of criticism. All it can do as a reflection of reality is to articulate what exists in fact. "My general consciousness," Marx wrote, "is merely the theoretical structure of the living communal form."[30]

Philosophy, it would appear, is here being charged with two functions that are difficult to reconcile. A solution can only be attempted later after we have examined Marx's theory of history, but the dilemma presented may be summed up thus. On the one hand,

29. MEGA, III:9.   30. Ibid., III:116.

philosophy performs a critical function by comparing the political-economic reality to an ideal norm. The comparison reveals a disparity between the two, giving rise to a demand for changing the world. On the other hand, philosophy reflects, expresses, and represents in ideational form the actual prevailing conditions. This dual role of philosophy is of fundamental importance for Marxian thought, and it raises two questions of concern to this inquiry. What does the ideal norm or measure presumed by Marx's critique consist in? And how must the relation of being to consciousness be constituted so that philosophy and other intellectual products can be understood as reflections or expressions of the existing material conditions? Philosophy makes social criticism possible and helps justify the demands for revolution. It is oriented toward what ought to be and rests on a dynamic anthropology that distinguishes three evolutionary phases: the original unity of man's essence and existence; the separation of his existence from his essence; and their final reunion, which occurs at the end of mankind's "prehistory." But, again, this conception of the role of philosophy comes into opposition with another which, since Marx, we are used to designate as ideology, that is, as the ideational expression of actual political and economic conditions.

Hegel and the Dissolution of the Christian Religion

At the very beginning of the *Critique of Hegel's Philosophy of Right,* Marx wrote: "The criticism of religion is the premise of all criticism." The full force of this assertion becomes apparent once we understand Marx's concept of religion. He thought that the religious conduct of man, his ties to a supernatural power in control of human destiny, expressed a specific human deformation conditioned by political and economic circumstances. His criticism of religion thus offers an early clue to his anthropology. It is a first step in his criticism of the traditional economic and social system whose removal will open the way for a knowledge of the human essence. Marx's criticism of religion grew out of his reading of Feuerbach, whose critical principles he adopted and carried forward. But

Marx and Feuerbach also had important elements in common with Hegel, whose relation to Christianity was problematic in more than one respect.

Hegel's statement that philosophy and religion had the same content, namely, the knowledge of God, was in itself a threat to religion. For philosophy expressed in rational terms, and thus in a higher form, what religion grasped only by subjective, incommunicable feeling and by the imagery of myths of chance historical provenance. Hegel further did not conceal from himself that the Christian religion had entered a critical phase of its history. The fact that church dogma no longer provided the spiritual foundation of the state—its place being taken by a secular ethics derived from reason—was an unmistakable sign that the power and inviolability of the Christian religion were in question. In a way that left no doubt about his own position, Hegel expressed his insight into this tragic situation of the Christian forms of life at the end of his lectures on *The Philosophy of Religion*. True, philosophy also served to justify religion by showing that religious ideas and cults corresponded to certain stages in the development of spirit, and were therefore necessary. But the time had come when the truth of religion, conveyed and revered in images, had to be transformed into the truth of the concept, and this was the task of philosophy. Thus, philosophy was equally a justification of the intellectualism that "made inroads into religion" and "was hostile to the imagination and concrete content of religion."[31] This encroachment of thought upon the articles of faith was unavoidable. It demonstrated that the contents of religion, too, were included in the developmental stages of the world-historical process by which spirit explicates itself.

But "this all-dissolving consciousness" did not play the same role in Hegel's thought as in the Enlightenment. The philosophic consciousness was not to accept the conflict of faith and knowledge as final, but to assume the work of reconciliation by showing that religion, too, had a philosophical content. This reconciliation, however, by no means signified a restoration of the religious feelings and myths already undermined by rational thought, nor could it protect them from further attacks. Philosophy was merely concerned to do religion an historical justice by showing that its con-

31. Hegel, *Werke*, 12:351.

ceptions corresponded with the general development of spirit in time. "Since thought is set in motion by coming into opposition with what is concrete, it must pass through and beyond this opposition until it is reconciled with the concrete. Philosophy is this reconciliation; it is, in this sense, theology. For it depicts the reconciliation of God with himself, with nature as His own divine otherness, and with finite spirit that is destined in part to educate itself to this reconciliation, in part to achieve it in world history."[32] Self-estrangement and self-reconciliation together constitute the nature of spirit. The self-realization of spirit generally follows a trinitarian pattern that is repeated in the development of religion. Religion first appears in the form of absolute, naïve faith. Then faith is destroyed by critical reflection or enlightenment when religious dogmas are denounced as contrary to reason, and hence untrue. This conflict is overcome in the third phase when philosophy demonstrates that faith, too, is a manifestation of the truth of spirit, although in a nonconceptual, subjective form.

Yet the end of *The Philosophy of Religion* made it clear that such a recognition of religion could do nothing to arrest its virtual decline. The following passage expresses Hegel's tragic sentiment about the inevitable process by which a religious community is transformed into a secular community, and faith replaced by philosophic reason. "Having considered the origin and existence of the community, we now observe its final realization and spiritual actuality fall into inner dissension so that, it would appear, its actualization coincides with its decline. But can one really speak here of a decline since God's realm is eternal and the holy spirit as such lives forever in its community, the gates of hell being powerless to overwhelm the church? To speak of decline would be to end on a discordant, pessimistic note." "And yet," Hegel continued, "what is the use? The discord is there . . . When the time has come and the justification of religion by conceptual thought is felt as a need, then the unity of the inner and the outward no longer exists in the immediate consciousness and in reality, and nothing is vindicated by faith alone anymore. Then stern commands, official enforcement, and the power of the state are of no avail because the decay has gone too deep."[33] Philosophy likewise has no remedy. Though it resolves the

32. Ibid., 12:354.   33. Ibid., 12:354–5.

"discord" and reconciles reason with religion by recognizing in revealed religion truth of a kind, it cannot arrest the actual decay. For "this reconciliation is but a partial one and does not extend to the external, public world. For philosophy dwells in a secluded sanctuary whose servants form a separate priestly caste that must not become involved with the world, but stand guard over the truth. How the contemporary practical world is to extricate itself from its dilemma and what shape it will take is its own affair, and not the *immediate* concern of philosophy."[34]

Feuerbach's Reduction of Theology to Anthropology

Feuerbach's criticism of religion, and that of Marx as well, easily followed the path opened by Hegel. By his identification of theology and philosophy, and by making the philosophizing subject the agent and medium of the self-realization of spirit, Hegel had prepared the ground for Feuerbach's turn to anthropology. The autonomous position of theology was already nullified when its content was presented as a preliminary form of philosophy. Moreover, the nature of religion was radically changed when, having been identified with philosophy, its content ceased to be a matter of faith and became an object of knowledge. Since, finally, the self-knowledge of spirit throughout history was accomplished in the philosophizing human subject, the conclusion easily suggested itself that man himself was the autonomous center of the world. Hegel, too, had conceived spirit essentially as activity, so that if one wanted to know what spirit was, one looked at what it did. In the same way, the productions of religion and art, law and the state expressed what man was. And so, with man as the creator of culture, anthropology seemed entitled to become the fundamental science.

In Feuerbach's criticism of religion, man is returned from God to himself. Philosophy, he said, was the critical reduction of all articles of faith to "their internal origin,"[35] which was to be found in simple truths natural to man. It was therefore necessary "to explain that

34. Ibid., 12:355–6.
35. Ludwig Feuerbach, *Sämtliche Werke,* ed. Wilhelm Bolin and Friedrich Jodl (Stuttgart, 1903–11), 6:141, 63.

theology is nothing but a combination of pathology, anthropology, and psychology,"[36] and to write "the history of God's sickness." Feuerbach attempted to show that the attributes of the divinity, such as prescience, providence, goodness, love, justice, and holiness, are really reifications of human attributes. Man, not God, is the real subject matter of theology. God exists only because we so think or believe. "If I never think or believe God, then I have none; He exists for me only because of myself, and He exists for reason only because of reason. Therefore, what exists a priori and prior is not what is being thought, but the being who does the thinking—not the object, but the subject."[37] The foundation of theology is man, the sensual and desiring being, active in the here and now, constituted through, and fulfilling and exhausting himself in, the community of I and Thou. "Religion abstracts the powers, qualities, and essential traits of man and deifies them as objective entities."[38] "Every being . . . has its God or highest being within itself." "God is the human self expressed, its internal life made manifest." Since God is really the reified essence of man, and the role of God in human history demonstrates that man himself is not what he would be in a state of complete self-realization, Feuerbach concluded that the invention of God is a pathological phenomenon. The past transfiguration of anthropology into theology is nothing but the "history of God's sickness;" and by the same token the reversal of this process, the reduction of theology to anthropology, is the beginning of a universal recovery of health.

The question arises, however, why man in the first place should have projected his own being onto God and objectified his essence in Him. Since God is in man, and in fact man by himself is God, it is hard to understand why this projection of his inmost being onto a personified object that is adored and endowed with redemptive power should have occurred. Such religious behavior requires a philosophical explanation. Why does man objectify himself in the form of a divinity? A preliminary answer might be that it is in his nature to seek self-objectification, and that we know man only by the productions resulting therefrom. Religion, however, does present a special case because man is at first unaware that in it he is portraying himself. It is this "lack of awareness that constitutes the

36. Ibid., 6:107.   37. Ibid., 2:270   38. Ibid., 6:4.

peculiar nature of religion,"[39] its childlike character. It is the "mystery of religion" that man should first feel compelled to objectify his own essence in a divinity, and then turn this relationship around so as to view himself as the object and creation of that same personified being. But, so Feuerbach observed, the difference between the divine and the human being is "illusory"; it simply "conceals a difference between the universal human essence and the particular individual."

Still, the question posed above had not really been answered, and Feuerbach continued to probe further. Having dismissed the difference between divinity and humanity as specious, he had still to explain why man's essence differs from concrete, historical man, and why the latter falls short of what he ought and would like to be. The fact is that concrete man affirms in God what he finds wanting in himself. The essence of man is in effect the exemplar of his truth, goodness, and happiness, and consequently God signifies "the moral law personified," or the fully "realized idea." "God is at work," Feuerbach wrote, "so that man may become good and blessed, for without goodness there is no blessedness." Divine activity is thus a "means to human salvation."[40] "God is the being that acts *in* me, *with* me, *through* me, *on* and *for* me; He is the principle of my eternal welfare, my benevolent dispositions and actions; in short, He is the goodness of my own nature."[41] Man thinks of his essence as his own perfection, with God serving as the measure of what he could and should be. *Could* and *should* are complementary notions; to stipulate "an *ought* without the corresponding *can* would be a ridiculous chimera."[42]

We have now arrived at a more satisfactory answer to the question of why man turns his own essence into an external object. God represents what man ought to be, but in fact is not. As Feuerbach put it: "God is born in the misery of man."[43] The divine being is an *Ersatz* for the actual ungodliness of man and his world. By creating God, man laments the loss of his true idea of himself, but at the same time feels exhorted to so put his hand to his own existence as to embody that idea in it. Generally speaking, philosophy is being

---

39. Ibid., 6:16.   40. Ibid., 6:38.   41. Ibid., 6:35.
42. Ibid., 6:257.   43. Ibid., 2:292.

credited with "an act of universal demystification" by its reduction of theology to anthropology and by revealing God as the essence of man. It puts an end to human self-deception and to the schism between the "lord of heaven" and the "lord of the world." The divine being is repatriated in man, where it was born, and it is now incumbent upon him to realize the true idea of himself in the here and now, in the state and in the family. This realization is preeminently the task of politics; in Feuerbach's words, "Politics must become our religion."[44] What began as a criticism of religion ends in a practical urge to change the world. Man, who is social by nature, is led to realize his true being by creating the conditions that will allow him, jointly with others, to satisfy common wants and needs. "The negation of the other world entails the affirmation of this one. The abolition of a better life in heaven implies a challenge to improve the human lot on earth. A better future ceases to be a matter of idle faith, it becomes an object of duty and human responsibility."[45]

Marx's Passage from the Critique of Religion to Politics

Marx expressed unqualified appreciation of Feuerbach's work. From now on, he confessed, he saw "no other way to truth and freedom . . . than through the Fire-brook."[46] Positive humanistic and naturalistic criticism began only with him. Marx regarded Feuerbach's books, notably *The Essence of Christianity* (1841) and *Preliminary Theses for a Reform of Philosophy* (1842), as "the sole treatises since Hegel's *Phenomenology of Spirit* and the *Logic* that contained a true theoretical revolution."[47] This recognition, which is all the more remarkable because it puts Feuerbach on a level with Hegel, is, however, followed by a typically Marxian reservation. The stumbling block proved to be that the revolution was merely theoretical. "For Feuerbach, only theoretical behavior is genuinely human, whereas practice appears only in its sordid Jewish fashion. That is why he does not understand the importance of 'revolutionary,' 'practical-critical' activity."[48] Marx conceded that Feuerbach's theoretical revolution led to a number of important insights,

---

44. Ibid., 2:219.   45. Ibid., 8:358.   46. MEGA, I/1, p. 175.
47. Ibid., III, p. 34.   48. Ibid., V, p. 533.

which have been described, and he accepted his challenge to eliminate the "duplication of the world into a religious and a secular
one." But Marx objected that Feuerbach's reduction of theology to
anthropology was not radical enough. The mere knowledge of how
and why human beings adopt a religious attitude does not put an
end to religion. This only happens, and here Marx went beyond
Feuerbach, when the conditions for the production of religion have
been abolished. The difference in the position of the two men was
well defined by Rudolf Haym in his study, *Ludwig Feuerbach und die
Philosophie:* "To have explained the objectivity of God as a phantom was something; but to explain the objectivity of this phantom
was something else, and equally necessary."[49] Marx never doubted
that God was an illusion or that religion was a "phantastic realization of the human being owing to his having no true reality." For
Marx the crucial question was: "How did it come about that men
got this illusion into their heads?"[50] Neither the political revolutionary nor the sociological observer could ignore the fact that the
phantom had grown into a spiritual, historical power. It was real, it
peremptorily demanded an explanation, and Marx tried to provide
one. He attempted an "analysis of the mystical consciousness that is
unclear to itself," and one that had assumed both religious and
political forms. Marx called this consciousness unclear because it
did not, and could not, explain to itself the causes of religion. "The
reform of consciousness is accomplished by making the world self-
conscious, by awakening it from its dream about itself and by explaining its own actions to it."[51] Such self-enlightenment is the first
step to world change.

Though Marx agreed with Feuerbach that "man makes religion"
and that its existence demonstrates a human deficiency, he went
beyond him when he probed into the causes of this phenomenon.
For Marx the decisive fact was that man is a social being who lives
in a certain political and economic order. To speak of man is always
to imply the existence of a state and a society. Therefore, it is "this
particular state, this particular society which produces religion,"[52]
and because state and society are perverted, religion is a perverted
consciousness of the world. Marx clearly suggested that man is not

---

49. Quoted by Otto Westphal, *Welt- und Staatsauffassung des deutschen
Liberalismus,* Historische Bibliothek (Munich, 1919), 41:59.

50. MEGA, V, p. 215.   51. Ibid., I/1, p. 575.   52. Ibid., I/1, p. 607.

inherently disposed to seek an illusionary satisfaction of his desires; only his social and economic conditions lead him on to it. The bifurcation of the world into a religious and a secular realm has to be explained by the self-contradictory character of the secular base, that is, state and society. The diremption of the world cannot be derived from the nature of man. On the contrary, the deficiencies of his existence have their root in circumstances outside him, in the state and society that corrupt him. If the world were rational, the conditions that give rise to religion would not exist. But "the religious reflection of the world can disappear only when the conditions of practical workaday life allow men daily to be in rational relations with each other and with nature."[53] So-called transcendental powers personified in God simply testify to the fact that man has not yet acquired the power to dispose over certain areas of the production and reproduction of life. The idea of the creation of the world, which is central to Jewish and Christian religion, vanishes as soon as man "owes his existence to himself,"[54] that is, when he not merely thinks but directs, and transforms the world into a rational whole. Marx did not doubt that reason has always existed, "only not always in rational forms." "The critic may therefore start from any form of the theoretical and practical consciousness and develop from the forms of the existing reality themselves the true reality, that which ought to be, its final end."[55] Marx's criticism of religion, then, ends in the conclusion that religion is antirational because the order of the existing world is antirational. This conclusion anticipates Marx's theory of history; like Hegel, he thought of it as the realization of reason.

It is apparent from this discussion that in Marx's view religion, like philosophy, performs a dual role. It is both an expression of, and a protest against, "a real misery." This view also announces the practical, revolutionary character of his philosophy, which already appeared in his criticism of Hegel. Enlightenment by itself is incapable of putting an end to religion. The real problem consists in making impossible the very production of religion. By examining the method by which Marx sought to arrive at this goal, one gains

53. Karl Marx, *Das Kapital,* ed. Friedrich Engels, 10th ed. (Hamburg, 1922), 1:46.

54. MEGA, III, p. 124.   55. Ibid., I/1, p. 574.

an insight into his idea of the nature of mind and the function of consciousness. These are precisely the questions that concern us. Before we proceed to them, we must point out, however, that his criticism of Feuerbach was not entirely fair.

It is not true that Feuerbach paid too little attention to politics. As a matter of fact, he expected his reduction of theology to anthropology to have definite political consequences, including a democratic reorganization of German political life. He by no means ignored the practical bearing of his philosophy, which by aiming "to dissolve God in man," was bound to undermine the kind of political conservatism that sought support in the idea of a timeless revealed order. Conservative political theorists were misled into identifying the existing order with one that is eternally valid because they excluded historical time from their considerations, and to this Feuerbach strongly objected. "A people that excludes time from its metaphysics and idolizes an eternal, abstract existence also excludes time from its politics and so idolizes the principle of stability contrary to right and reason."[56] Marx endorsed this view, but it failed to satisfy him because he wanted the criticism of religion to culminate in the recognition that the dependency of man on a transcendental power concealed from him his real dependency on the existing socio-economic order. We return to this point later in the discussion of the division of labor and the concept of the "alien social power." For religion finds its ultimate support in this power, which man, even though it is the product of his own activity, does not control but rather is controlled by.

The other problem in which Feuerbach's solution seemed inadequate to Marx was the relation of theory and practice. In Marx's view, the alliance between philosophic criticism and politics was the only means "by which contemporary philosophy could be made true."[57] The unity of theory and practice, postulated by Marx, meant that the practical and the theoretical revolution require one another. Without the practical revolution of the existing political and economic conditions, the theoretical revolution—meaning the complete understanding of the historical, social process—could not be achieved; and, deprived of such understanding, the practical revolution lacked the necessary knowledge of its aim and means.

56. Feuerbach, *Werke,* 2:233.   57. MEGA, I/1, p. 613.

The end for both is the same, and it is reached when the world has become philosophical and philosophy has become worldly. This is what Marx meant when he said that "it is impossible to abolish philosophy without actualizing it."

Finally, Marx differed from Feuerbach's anthropology, and this is because he placed the origin of religion into a sharper focus. The reason why man produced the illusions of religion, Marx argued, is that the world in which he lives is itself inverted, or, more precisely, the relation of being to consciousness is inverted. Religion acts like opium, producing those "mystical veils" that prevent man from perceiving the world as it is and from taking a hand in changing it. Feuerbach's philosophic formula—"the dissolving of God into man"—implied a restoration of man. His philosophy, to use his own term, is "anthropotheism", it deifies man. Marx, too, occasionally echoed such a view, as when he wrote: "Religion is an illusionary sun which revolves around man only as long as he fails to revolve around his own axis." But to do just that, "to revolve around himself and so about his real sun,"[58] is his philosophical and political task. Both expect the criticism of religion to result in the recovery and restoration of man, but Marx places the emphasis on specific reforms of social life: "The critique of heaven issues into a critique of the earth, the critique of religion turns into a critique of law, that of theology into a critique of politics."[59]

History Viewed in Terms of the "Loss" and "Recovery" of Man

Our investigation has now advanced to the point where the problems of Marxian sociology and theory of history can be analyzed insofar as they are relevant to the concept of ideology. But one preliminary question needs to be answered first. It concerns Marx's anthropological assumptions and his view of the nature of man.

Marx viewed history and society in terms of struggle. "The history of all previous society is a history of class struggles."[60]

---

58. Ibid., I/1, p. 608.   59. Ibid., I/1, p. 608.   60. Ibid., VI, p. 525.

Because this struggle is total and inevitable, one suspects from the outset that it is not restricted to political and economic decisions, but involves the entire intellectual world as well, including religion and art, man's reflection on history and himself, and the science of law, the state and the economy. One may assume also that the intellectual activity of man, including his apparently presuppositionless search for knowledge, is colored by the position he takes in this universal struggle. It is not a matter of indifference where the knower stands—for he, too, is compelled to make practical decisions—what class he belongs to, what material interests he represents, and what kind of political institutions he therefore upholds. If these assumptions are correct, it means that the problems of knowledge are drawn into the practical political struggle, and theoretical activity is affected by the socio-political reality. The nature of this influence will occupy us later. For the moment, we wish to stress merely the universality and totality of the struggle. Marx does not accept this struggle as being "natural" and "inevitable," but sees it as the reflection of a certain deformation of human nature. This deformation characterizes all previous history and societies and consists in what he calls the "complete loss of man." The end and meaning of history should be, however, the "complete recovery of man." Once this goal is realized, social struggle comes to an end, and so does history. More precisely, as stated in the preface of "To the Critique of Political Economy," "the prehistory of mankind" concludes with the establishment of a social order in which social antagonism has ceased. This conclusion of the historical process is intelligible only as a secularized version of Jewish-Christian eschatology; the epoch in which the complete recovery of man is fulfilled represents the realm of God made real. The realm of necessity is finished, and the realm of freedom begins, when the production and distribution of goods is socially controlled and has, as a "blind power," ceased to dominate man. Man at last returns to himself, his reintegration becomes a fact.

At this point, the following questions arise. How do we recognize the deformation of man? What are the conditions of its appearance? What are the consequences of the historical necessity that subordinates man to a superior power during the whole course of history? What is the meaning of man's self-alienation, the process that compels him to objectify himself and to surrender his freedom since he must eat, be clothed, and sheltered? Why does Marx reject as possible explanations of the antagonistic forms of social production individual strife and an, allegedly, evil human nature? For Marx, as for Rousseau before him, the intellectual and moral condition of men is a function of the social order in which they happen to live. Up to the present, this dependency has resulted in human disintegration and self-alienation. But the concepts of reintegration and recovery with which Marx thinks, and which will become reality when social and economic antagonism is resolved, presuppose the idea of an original human wholeness. The beginning of history appears to signal also the beginning of self-alienation, which has reigned through the entire course of what Marx calls "prehistory." Obviously, then, self-alienation plays an important role in Marx's understanding of human nature. We will return to it after we have examined J.J. Rousseau's contribution to the problem of human self-alienation.

The Idea of Self-Alienation in Rousseau

We embark on this historical digression fully aware that it is an endeavor only, and one not without risk. What we attempt is a clarification of the early history of the concept of self-alienation, antecedent to the role of an organizing principle it came to play in the philosophy of Hegel and Marx. The risk derives from the nature of Rousseau's work, which abounds in paradoxes and contradictions. He himself once remarked to David Hume that his theories were full of extravagances. These difficulties notwithstanding, we will try to clarify the concept of self-alienation by an analysis of Rousseau's cultural criticism and social philosophy. At the same time we hope to show, with the help of this concept, that there is a basic unity in Rousseau's work despite its inner tensions.

That unity is still, however, very much in question. Scholars who know Rousseau well argue whether his writings are in basic agreement with each other, are relatively unrelated, or even contradictory. There is the further question of Rousseau's relationship to his own period. Is he inseparable from the Enlightenment, its rationalism and natural-law theories; or did his subjectivism and irrationalism force him into opposition to it, making him appear as a forerunner of romanticism? It is, indeed, difficult to imagine another writer who puts before the reader so many annoying, tormenting, and challenging paradoxes without the slightest concern of how to resolve them. Rousseau confessed to have been born with a longing for solitude that grew the better he got to know people; and that he preferred the creatures of his dreams and his imagination to the company of men. But this is the very man who, more than almost anyone before him, is interested in justifying the compulsory unity of the state. The fervent apostle of freedom espouses a state religion to which every citizen must conform or suffer the penalty of expulsion, and he advocates education by and for the state. He poses as the great detractor and accuser of reason: it is the "great vehicle of all our foolishness;" and "the man who thinks is a depraved animal." At the same time, he feels he must play the great defender of reason. Thus, the fundamental difference drawn in *The Social Contract* between the "general will" and the "will of all" rests on the fact that the "general will"—itself the very epitome of rationality—is accessible to reason.

Intellectual honesty requires that we state our own assumptions. They are, to begin with, only assertions, but we hope that they will be substantiated in the course of the inquiry. We hold, first, that the concept of self-alienation is crucial to the understanding of man. It plays a dominant role in the philosophy of culture and society, much as the actual process of self-alienation does in civilized social life. The second assertion concerns the interpretation of Rousseau's work and requires a lengthier statement.

Nobody disputes that Rousseau's writings contain a criticism of culture. One may argue, however, over whether his criticism contains a measure of objective validity, or whether it must be regarded as a purely subjective response. Let us consider the second interpretation first. It would regard Rousseau's criticism as nothing more than the personal rebellion of a man deeply in conflict with his time. It would grant, of course, the mastery and passion of his language, which moved and enchanted even his bitterest enemies and lent his personal suffering an impressiveness that stirred deep revolutionary unrest all over Europe. Rousseau possessed the power to excite human longing for a simple, uncomplicated life in peace and happiness by naming a guilty party, society, on which all corruption could be blamed. At the same time, he consoled man with the conviction that his original goodness would unfold if only the social order were changed. It would further be granted that Rousseau suffered the hard fate of exile and had his most significant books burned and proscribed in both Geneva, the city of his birth, and in Paris. In the light of his many misfortunes, his work could accordingly be seen as the personal justification of a perpetual revolution, which would terminate only when conditions favorable to the free unfolding of human nature were established. In support of assigning only a subjective value to his work, one could even quote Rousseau himself. For example, in a letter written 12 January 1762 to his friend and patron Malesherbes, who was then president of the Censor's Office in Paris, he said: "Embittered by the injustices I had to suffer or whose witness I was, often deeply saddened by the derangement into which example and the force of conditions had thrown me, I held my century and contemporaries in contempt. Because I felt that I would never find a place among them that would satisfy me, I detached my heart from human society and in my imagination found another, which delighted me all the more as I could dwell in it without any effort or danger and which was always safely at my disposal in any shape I might desire." Such a confession would make it appear as if the zealous hatred with which he pursued the arts and sciences, and the accusations he hurled at social institutions, were but the reverse of his flight into the world of his own illusions. If we settled for this sort of subjective interpretation of Rousseau's work, the only question still remaining would be to explain why it could have such an extraordinary impact on posterity. Such an explanation might resort, among other things, to an analysis of the psychological and socio-political conditions of Rousseau's life.

For our part, we find this kind of interpretation both cheap and unsatisfactory. It is wanting in the respect due to the work itself because it denies it that objective significance to which the mind producing it intrinsically aspired. Rousseau wanted to understand. Merely to express and promote himself did not interest him in the least. The two *Discourses* of 1750 and 1755 have, by his own account, no other aim than a knowledge of man. He feared that such knowledge was put in jeopardy by the development of culture and society. In the preface to the *Discourse* of 1755, he wrote: "It is still more cruel that as every advance of the human race removes it farther from its primitive state, the more knowledge we acquire, the more we deprive man of the most important knowledge of all. So, in a sense, it is by our very study of man that we make it impossible for ourselves to know him."

Let us, therefore, consider the other interpretation, according to which Rousseau's social and cultural criticism contains a measure of objectivity. It, too, would have to make a number of concessions to the other side, such as that his criticism reflects subjective traits of an eccentric author; that his historical knowledge of the structure of social relations was defective and afforded too slim a base for his vehement assault; and that he worked with certain untenable assumptions, including the idea of a paradisical state of nature. Despite these undeniable faults, we are inclined to accept this second interpretation as basically correct, which does not, however, commit us to the various philosophic views and moral judgments contained in Rousseau's work. We think that an objective basis of his criticism is to be found in the concept of self-alienation that has remained central to the philosophy of history down to the present. If this assumption could be substantiated, we would find ourselves in agreement with the view of Lord Acton, who may have exaggerated very little when he wrote to Mary Gladstone: "Rousseau produced more effect with his pen than Aristotle, or Cicero, or St. Augustine, or St. Thomas Acquinas, or any other man who ever lived."

Rousseau is the first thinker in the eighteenth century to describe some of the constitutive elements of self-alienation in the two essays he submitted to the Academy of Dijon in 1750 and 1755. These essays contain not merely accusations against society, they also reveal the grounds and the criteria of his criticism. The criteria are derived from the original nature of man, and from the process of self-alienation that seems to be part and parcel of man's life in culture. The question answered by the first prize essay was whether the "restoration of the arts and sciences has had the effect of purifying or corrupting morals." Rousseau took the latter side. Culture not only made man unhappy, it also made him evil. "Before art had shaped our behavior, and taught our passions to speak an affected language, our morals were rude but natural; differences in behavior proclaimed at the first glance differences in character. Not that human nature was at bottom better then; but men found their security in the ease with which they could see through one another, and this advantage, of which we no longer feel the value, spared them many vices. In our day, when more subtle study and a more refined taste have reduced the art of pleasing to a system, there prevails in modern manners a base and deceptive conformity, so that one would think every mind had been cast in the same mold. Politeness requires one thing, decorum commands another. We always follow custom, never the promptings of our own nature. We no longer dare seem what we really are. Under this perpetual restraint, the herd of men, which we call society, all act under the same circumstances exactly alike, unless more powerful motives deter them."[61]

This passage contains the crucial elements of Rousseau's criticism of culture. Culture is an artificial world. It requires, in the interest of a common life, that men submit to certain forms of behavior. Its mark is uniformity embodied in a complex of agreements and conventions that prescribe how men should act. Culture obliges man to renounce his original autonomy and individual idiosyncrasy. It creates a world of appearance that conceals man's authentic being, whose reality it in fact denies. This essentially is the view Rousseau held to the end of his life. He expressed it for the last time in the third dialogue of *Rousseau the Judge of Jean-Jacques:* "All seek their happiness in appearance, but no one cares about reality. All put their being into seeming. Slaves and dupes of vanity, they do not live for the sake of living, but merely to make believe they have lived." These few words compress Rousseau's final critique of culture, which remained for him an hypocrisy, a lie, and an actual corruption because it demanded the renunciation of self and self-determination. The critical flaw of culture lay in the discrepancy it created between being and seeming, a discrepancy synonymous with the opposition between nature and culture. To summarize, Rousseau's concept of self-alienation is defined by his description of men as living and acting under the compulsion of external models and patterns of behavior, in a world in which they cannot be themselves but are other-directed.

The second prize question of the Academy of Dijon of 1755 concerned the origin and conditions of inequality among men. Rousseau's reply contained no less than a critique of society, but we

---

61. Jean Jacques Rousseau, *Discours sur les Sciences et les Arts, Oeuvres complètes* (Paris, 1825), 1:10–1.

here restrict our attention to the way in which this second discourse further illuminated his concept of self-alienation. According to Rousseau, man is by nature good and becomes evil only under the influence of social institutions. In the state of nature men enjoy unrestricted equality because nature in its inexhaustible wealth grants to all what they need in order to sustain themselves. Admittedly, men are unequally endowed physically and mentally. But this natural inequality remains uninstitutionalized as long as they continue in the state of nature. Only the civil state puts an end to natural equality, and the inequality it initiates is such as to make men dependent on one another. They now no longer provide for their own physical needs with their own hands, but divide their labor so as to produce things collaboratively. This signifies the loss of their natural liberty. "As long as men were occupied in work they each could do by themselves, and practiced arts that did not require the collaboration of many hands, they lived a free, healthy, good, and happy life." When the state of nature is exchanged for the social state, man suffers a loss of freedom and happiness. What are the consequences of this associated life?

In view of his preceding criticism of culture, Rousseau's answer will hardly come as a surprise. The discrepancy between being and seeming is renewed and intensified, the difference between nature and culture sharpened. "The natural man," he wrote, "who lives a truly human life and for whom the opinion of others means nothing, follows solely his inclinations and his reason, without regard for public approval or blame." Natural man is what he seems, he is at one with himself, whereas social man is divided within himself. This inner break is the cause of his misery, and all the differences between the social man and the natural man in the end reduce themselves to this existential difference. In Rousseau's words, "The savage lives within himself whereas sociable man, forever outside himself, only knows how to live in the opinion of others, from whose judgment concerning him he receives the sense of his own identity." As our being is reduced to appearance, we are driven to ask others what we are, never daring to ask ourselves. "We have nothing to show for ourselves but a frivolous and deceitful exterior, honor without virtue, reason without wisdom, and pleasure without happiness."

In these memorable words, which occur near the end of the second *Discourse,* Rousseau compresses the essence of self-alienation. In the social state, man dare not and cannot be himself; he must submit to certain codes of behavior and let himself be directed by others. But such other-directedness and the submission to the law of others make men unfree, whereas obedience to a self-given law would allow them to maintain their autonomy and freedom. The natural man is autonomous, the social man, heteronomous. To this difference, Rousseau adds another important one in Book I of *Emile,* where he writes:

> The natural man is a whole unto himself, he is a unit, an integer, dependent only on himself and his like. The citizen is but the numerator of a fraction, whose value depends on its denominator. His value depends on the whole, that is, on the community. Good social institutions are those best suited to denature man, to take from him his absolute existence and replace it with a relative one, to merge his self into the group so that, no longer regarding himself as one, he thinks of himself as a part of the whole and is conscious of being only that.

This passage, too, is extremely significant for Rousseau's idea of self-alienation, but to take it as such does not commit us to the other convictions he expresses. We need not adopt his cultural pessimism or his natural optimism, nor are we obliged to follow his doctrine concerning the conflict between nature and society. It is in fact impossible to imagine a natural, non-social condition of human life, for even the performance of its physical functions requires the existence of structured social communities. What solely concerns us is to understand the condition of associated human life that may appropriately be termed self-alienation. In such a mode of life, conflicts are indeed inevitable because social man is subject to two different types of law that determine his conduct. On the one hand, he is impelled to conduct himself according to his particularity and individual character, for he experiences himself as a unique, even irreplaceable being who follows his own inner law. On the other hand, his conduct is ruled by the sum of expectations with which the social environment confronts him. Since everyone has different tasks and different functions to fulfill, functions that necessarily arise from his having a family, a vocation, and a place in politics, he is compelled to adapt himself to quite different systems of order and sanction. The emotional and intellectual uniqueness of the individual is thereby thrust into a highly charged field of forces that both attract and repel him. These forces, which manifest the will of groups and institutions and tend to their own self-preservation, affect the individual in various ways, sanctifying, censoring, and sanctioning his actions. The more powerful and direct this influence, the greater the threat of the loss of self. In other words, society insists on the surrender of individual autonomy, and demands instead the unconditional acceptance of its own system of norms because it sees itself, and wants to be seen, as the whole of which the individual is but a part. From society's point of view, the individual has, in Rousseau's words, only a "relative existence." Society is so constituted as to inherently deny the natural wholeness of man. It deprives him of the original and essential characteristic of being "an absolute unit related only to his like."

If the reader accepts the preceding statement of Rousseau's concept of self-alienation, he will have no difficulty in perceiving the close internal relationship that exists between Rousseau's critique of culture and society and his political philosophy, set forth in the article on "Political Economy" written for the Encyclopedia of Diderot and d'Alembert, and *The Social Contract.* Both these works have identical aims which can best be stated with reference to the idea of self-alienation. The problem Rousseau confronts is that of finding a way to avoid the loss of self and self-determination and its destructive consequences. More specifically, his problem is to conceive of a form of state community in which man is not condemned to be "outside himself," but can remain at one with himself. It is the central question of Rousseau's political philosophy. In trying to answer it, he faced—so at least it seemed—an alternative. One choice led back to the past while the other pointed to the future.

In view of his social and cultural criticism, Rousseau might have been tempted to proclaim a return to nature, that is, the restoration of the natural state of man, the recovery of his "original simplicity." He might have promised human salvation by dismantling culture through the dissolution of social bonds and legal institutions. This is what Voltaire thought Rousseau had in mind when he wrote derisively—expecting to win the public to his side by a frivolous joke—that never had so much intelligence been wasted on the effort to reduce the human race to donkeys. After reading the *Discourse on the Origin of Inequality,* one felt, said Voltaire, like walking on all fours again. Actually, the author of the *Discourse* had expressly and unmistakably disclaimed in the text any intention of wanting to restore the natural state. He knew it was impossible to return to a condition of natural equality and freedom once men had established themselves in the civil state. And once Rousseau had gained insight into the irreversibility of the historical process, he never again abandoned it. Perhaps the most telling evidence for that is to be found in a passage of the third dialogue of his late work *Rousseau the Judge of Jean-Jacques,* a work of self-examination in which the embittered, lonely, and excessively sensitive man who was prone to paranoia sought to justify and defend himself against the reckless attacks and suspicions of his contemporaries. The passage, bare of illusion and filled with resignation, reads as follows.

> Human nature never regresses, and once the time of innocence and equality is passed, it is impossible to return to it. This is another of the principles he [Rousseau] has always maintained. His aim, therefore, could not have been to lead large populations and great states back to their first simplicity, but only to arrest, if possible, the rush toward social perfection and human degeneration of those states whose small size and particular situation have so far preserved them from an equally rapid advance. People have persistently accused him of wanting to destroy the sciences and arts, theaters and academies, and to plunge the world back into primitive barbarism. He, on the contrary, has always insisted on preserving existing institutions because their destruction would not abolish the underlying vices, but merely remove their cloak and replace corruption with brigandage. He has served his country and the small states that resemble it.

The road back being closed, there remained only the way forward into the future. It is true, of course, that Rousseau longed ardently for a paradisiacal past and continued to see the natural man in a glorifying light. But this longing and this glorification derived their power, perversely perhaps, from his very knowledge that we cannot go back again. The myth of revolution, not the myth of restoration, was therefore the only possible conclusion to his thought. All the same, his profound pessimism compels one to admit that, in the last resort, all he hoped that he might be able to do for the human race was to help slow down its inevitable degeneration. And this seemed to him to be possible only in the smaller states. The famous "Letter to Mr. Philopolis," which incidentally contains a criticism of Leibniz's optimism, explains his position on this subject. Rousseau there writes: "Pray remember that in my view society is as natural to mankind as decrepitude is to the individual. Nations need arts, laws, and governments as much as old folk require crutches. The only difference is that old age in individual man proceeds solely from the human constitution, while that of society derives from the nature of mankind—though not directly, as you say, but, as I have shown, with the help of certain circumstances which may or may not be present, or which at least may occur at an earlier or a later date and so accelerate or slow down the process as the case may be. To establish complete parity between the two processes, I had to assume that since some of these circumstances depend on human will, the individual is capable of accelerating the coming of old age and the race of slowing it down. Since the social state has a terminal phase, and it is in the control of men to decide how soon they want to arrive there, it is worth pointing out to them the danger of getting there so fast, as well as the wretchedness of a condition they mistake for the perfection of the race."

This pessimism notwithstanding, however, Rousseau attempted to construct a political order in which the conflict between autonomy and heteronomy would cease and the individual would be relieved of paying the price of self-alienation. This could be achieved if he submitted to a law he gave himself. Being the expression of his steady will and clear reason, unclouded by individual passion and prejudice, this law would also be recognized by others. The individual would then no longer be other-determined or be "outside himself;" he would have returned to himself and be his true self again. In short, self-alienation would be eliminated.

Here, it seems to us, is the core of Rousseau's political philosophy. As far as *The Social Contract* is concerned, it is to be found in the dialectic between the two principles of the "general will" and the "will of all." In order to understand Rousseau's political philosophy correctly and to guard against the kind of misunderstandings from which it has suffered in the past, it is important to know the kind of social union Rousseau had in mind. In the manuscript first published in 1896, he wrote: "There are a thousand ways of binding people together, but only one of uniting them. That is why I present in this work only one method of forming political societies, even though there exist among the large number of groups in this category perhaps scarcely two that were founded in this way, and not a single one exactly as I have stated. However, I search for right and reason and have no quarrel with the facts." It must further be borne in mind that Rousseau distinguished sharply between "subjecting a multitude" and "governing a polity." To subject a multitude of men to the rule of one or a few does not make a people or establish a "body politic." In other words, an aggregation is not the same as an association. It is the latter alone that interests him. *The Social Contract* investigates solely the process by which an association is brought into being; it does not, it should be emphasized, present a general doctrine concerning the origin of states and constitutions, nor does it describe the historical growth of any particular state. Rousseau's concern is to define the kind of social union from which self-alienation is constitutionally excluded. The social contract represents an agreement by which each associate places his own person and power under the supreme direction of the common, or general, will. It is important in this connection not to fall into a fairly common misunderstanding concerning the scope and nature of the general will that could prejudice fatefully the whole interpretation of Rousseau's political theory. Though the social contract creates a viable and sovereign political community, it does not prescribe the content of the general will itself. Or, to put it more concretely, men may express the will to organize a political union and act accordingly, but they cannot will that the nature of this union should be determined by the accidents of time and circumstance. They must recognize that there is something over which they have no power, and that is the general will. This will alone legitimizes their union as a body politic. Independent of their likes and arbitrariness, its content is to be sought in a spiritual and ethical reality that exists antecedently to the establishment of any political union and provides it with a measure of its internal order. One may say, therefore, that if men wish to found a society, they must be willing to submit themselves without reservation to the supreme power of the general will. Such action is morally justifiable because the general will contains exactly what every man seeking to unite with others must will, namely, reason and justice. To affirm the power of the general will is, therefore, to affirm that a rational and just will shall be the foundation and general rule of the body politic.

That this is what Rousseau really meant, one need only recall the original purpose of the social contract: to establish a form of human association in which each, while bound to all, obeys only himself and so remains as free as he was before. Freedom consists in obeying the law one has given to oneself.

The concept of the general will may be further clarified by an examination of the criticism Hegel directed against it in his *Philosophy of Right*. There Hegel first praised Rousseau by saying that the merit of his contribution was to have established the will as the principle of the state, a principle which unlike the gregarious instinct, for instance, or divine authority, has thought as its content. Hegel continued:

> Unfortunately, however, Rousseau, as Fichte did later, takes the will only in a determinate form as the individual will and regards the universal will not as the absolutely rational element in the will. It is for him only a 'general' will which proceeds out of the individual will as out of a conscious will. The result is that the union of individuals in the state is reduced to a contract, to something based on their arbitrary wills, their opinion, and their capriciously given express consent. As a further consequence, common reasoning proceeds to draw inferences which destroy the divine principle of the state, together with its absolute authority and majesty.

When, Hegel continued further, Rousseau's abstractions attained political power, "they produced for the first time in history the prodigious spectacle of the overthrow of the constitution of a great actual state, involving the destruction of everything existing, and its complete reconstruction on the basis of pure thought," (*Philosophy of Right,* § 258). The question arises, however, whether Hegel here fairly represents Rousseau's true intent. His principal objection is that Rousseau does not allow the general will to proceed from a will that is inherently rational. The general will is thereby reduced to being merely a common will that results from the conscious individual wills of a multitude of men. This objection appears to be based on a certain passage in Chapter 3 of Book II of *The Social Contract,* where Rousseau does indeed say that the common will in the end always emerges as the "grand total" from the great number of the small differences between individual wills. Hegel's interpretation seems to overlook, however, all the characteristics the general will possesses a priori and by definition. For example, the general will is, according to Rousseau, always right; it provides a reliable criterion for deciding between right and wrong; it necessarily and unerringly tends to the public advantage and common good; it is always *droit,* a word difficult to translate, connoting as it does such meanings as fair, obligatory, correct, reasonable, authoritative, and generative of order. In short, the general will, because it precedes any particular will and restrains human arbitrariness, fulfills the very same task Hegel assigned the will that is the founding principle of the state.

We turn, finally, to a crucial difficulty in Rousseau's political philosophy. It arises from the dialectic between the general will and the particular will, from the fact that every individual is both a man and a citizen. As a man, he has a particular will that may differ from, or even come into conflict with, the general will he represents as a citizen of a state. The particular will manifests subjectivity, it is influenced by circumstances of time and place, and moved by individual passion and interest. The general will, by contrast, represents objective reason, the content of which everyone in his capacity of citizen may discover when, undisturbed by the calculations and whisperings of others, he perceives what he truly wants and deems right and useful. From this point of view Rousseau also defines what he means by virtue. It is defined, in the article on "Political Economy," as "the conformity of the particular will to the general will." When subjective reason agrees with objective reason and the two wills merge into one, then man is in a position to obey himself and to follow his own law, which is the only law he has really got. As Hegel put it afterwards, man is then "with himself and therefore free." But when the general will and the particular will are in opposition, then, Rousseau says, "man contradicts himself," or "he is outside himself" and hence alienated from himself. Conversely, self-alienation comes to an end when subjective reason unites with objective reason. By this union man is made whole because he is determined by what he himself can and ought to be.

These assumptions also make intelligible Rousseau's theory of political force or compulsion. The body politic is granted the power to compel all who unintelligently or wickedly insist on having their own particular will. This power has no other purpose than to lead men back to their own true selves. In Rousseau's words: "Whoever refuses to obey the general will shall be forced to do so by the whole body politic, which only means that he will be forced to be free." The idea of forcing people to be free, which was later taken up by Robespierre and the German philosopher Fichte, is obviously very dangerous. To Rousseau, however, it was justified on the ground that people were only led to do what in truth they want, and indeed must want if they have insight into objective reason and are clear about their own true will. No one, he apparently believed, could seriously object to being forced to desire what he really ought to desire; and no one could seriously wish to renounce his freedom as Rousseau had defined the state of being free. This idea of compulsion is also his reason for instituting a public system of education and a secular state religion: both are to guarantee the spiritual unity of the body politic.

We have stated that the dialectic between the general will and the particular will forms the crux of Rousseau's political philosophy. But in addition to contrary particular wills, the polity will have to reckon also with the will of special interest groups, classes, estates, and the like. *The Social Contract* lumps all such special wills together under the designation *volonté de tous* or the "will of all," distinguishing them clearly from the general will. A most important question now arises. If occasions and events occur in the internal and external development of the state that are not covered by any pronouncement of the general will, how and by whom is the general will in such cases to be ascertained? The question is a crucial one because only such compulsion as may be exercised in the name of the general will and objective reason is morally justified and certain of universal acceptance. It is certainly conceivable, in the framework of Rousseau's political philosophy, that a majority may enact a law and claim for it the rational authority of the general will, whereas in fact it merely represents the "will of all." Strictly speaking, Rosseau has no answer to this question. Neither his trust in the people as speaking with the voice of God, nor his faith in the individual's insight into the essence of the general will can resolve the problem. In the end he retreats to a position he has often taken before: that he never planned to construct a political theory applicable to large states, but had in mind only small communities where differences in wealth were insignificant and customs simple, where people knew each other and the general conditions of life were clear and manageable.

If the preceding presentation of the basic notions of Rousseau's anthropology and political philosophy is valid, it will help to explain why nearly the entire social philosophy, as well as the philosophy of history, from the late eighteenth to the end of the nineteenth century came under his spell. The reason was that Rousseau confronted certain problems that had, and will continue to have, their source in the human condition itself, even though his solution of these problems rather resembled the cutting of the Gordian knot. His influence could not have been so powerful were his work simply the lament of a dreamer seeking refuge in the world of his imagination to escape clashing with the real world, or the product of a maladjusted man bringing wholly unjustified accusations against culture and society in order to defend himself against the charge of being an irresponsible *promeneur solitaire*. In his second *Discourse* of 1755, Rousseau asserted that to write the history of human maladies was to record the sicknesses of human society. This epitomizes the theme to which he owes his great influence. Diagnoses, prognoses, and therapies similar to his recur with an oppressive monotony in contemporary philosophies of culture and technology. To an ever growing extent, man today feels himself the victim of the autonomous workings of the economy, technology, and bureaucratic organizations. As an American sociologist has written, "The feeling of helplessness is a consequence of the enormous increase in the power of social groups and of the insertion of their authority into the character of the individual." Central to all such recent diagnoses is the desperate state of self-alienation at whose liquidation the corresponding therapies are directed.

In closing this section, we wish briefly to illustrate from the work of Kant and Schiller Rousseau's historical influence. In one of his magnificent small essays on the philosophy of history, entitled *Conjectural Origin of the History of Mankind,* Kant proclaims as the ultimate aim of the moral development of man that "perfect art should become once again like nature." It is an idea which, in the way it is put, reveals how steeped it is in the spirit of Rousseau. Schiller's *Letters on Aesthetic Education* revolve, as the author put it, about the wounds culture has inflicted on modern man. "Not merely some individuals, but whole classes of men develop only a part of their capacities and, like stunted plants, show barely a feeble trace of the rest." Is it not Schiller's concern, too, that man become again an expression of "all-unifying nature?" In the sixth letter he laments: "Forever tied to a small separate fragment, man himself becomes a fragment. With the monotonous noise of the wheel he drives in his ear, he can never unfold the harmony of his being; and instead of making his nature representative of mankind, he merely becomes a reflection of his occupation or science." State and society abet this fragmentation because they stress the training of separate skills, promoting their perfection with an intensity that is proportionate to the loss of extension or breadth in the individual.[62]

62. Heinrich Popitz, *Der entfremdete Mensch: Zeitkritik und Geschichtsphiloso-phie des jungen Marx* (Basel, 1953), gives an excellent presentation of the concept of alienation in Marx in relation to the philosophy and poetry of German idealism, with special emphasis on the idealists' criticism of their age. The older study by Richard Fester, *Rousseau und die deutsche Geschichtsphilosophie* (Leipzig, 1890), is still instructive. Also good is Iring Fetscher, *Rousseaus politische Philosophie: Zur Geschichte des demokratischen Freiheitsbegriffs* (Neuwied, 1960). Helmuth Plessner in *Das Problem der Öffentlichkeit und die Idee der Entfremdung* (Göttingen, 1960), lays much emphasis on the change in meaning that the concept of alienation has undergone in the present. The concept, according to Plessner, is nowadays concerned with the characteristics modern society "has acquired in its struggle against proletarianization and the class struggle: its high degree of organization and its rational structure for the purpose of a smoothly functioning system. In literary usage, the figure of the alienated man applies today to the individual whose social role is dictated to him by a bureaucratized world, to man as the performer of functions" (pp. 12–3). "Our ancient German, troubled relationship to society which is supposed to support state and community, finds renewed justification in the idea of alienation, this time as it is employed by the two philosophies of proletarian Marxism and late bourgeois existentialism. The latter devalues public life to an insipid, inauthentic type of human existence by equating inwardness with authenticity; the former does so by regarding public life in its present form as a reflection of man who has not yet succeeded in mastering his own alienation. In our situation, there can be nothing more disastrous than to put one's trust in the consolations held out by the idea of alienation. To seek freedom and authenticity within, as existentialism bids us do, promotes the reification of man in public life no less than Marxist eschatology which, its eye fixed on the end of history, puts man in a state of waiting" (p. 20). One may agree with Plessner in regard to the German situation; and yet one may ask whether the original meaning of alienation, as in Rousseau, does not expressly aim at man's inescapable responsibility for actively determining the quality of public life. Taken in this sense, the idea of alienation decidedly favors the struggle for a social and political order that is cut to human measure.—The analysis of the American situation, as presented by William H. Whyte in *The Organization Man* (New York, 1956), makes it clear how group pressure on the individual and the idolatry of a smoothly functioning system make the rehabilitation of individual creativity and responsibility imperative. See also Ralf Dahrendorf, *Homo sociologicus: Ein Versuch zur Geschichte, Bedeutung und Kritik der Kategorie der sozialen Rolle* (Köln und Opladen, 1961).

Self-alienating Work and the
Division of Labor

In one of Marx's early writings concerned with the question of man's essence, he frames the answer in the form of praising Hegel. Hegel, he says, stood on the ground of modern political economy and grasped work as the human essence. "The outstanding thing about the *Phenomenology of Spirit* is . . . that Hegel grasps the self-creation of man as a process, grasps objectification as externalization together with the removal of this externalization. He understands the nature of work and conceives actual man as the result of his own work."[63] Marx is correct in this, for Hegel says of spirit that it is essentially active, it is "pure activity" and "absolute restlessness." But having rendered his tribute, Marx proceeds to add a critical qualification. Despite his familiarity with modern economic theory, Hegel nevertheless failed to recognize the nature of work because the only kind he knew and recognized was "abstractly intellectual." Marx is right here, too, for according to Hegel, the inherent law of spirit is "God driving toward knowledge of himself," and "the development of spirit attains its aim when spirit has become completely conscious of its own concept," comprehending "what it has produced as identical with the act of producing." As compared with this abstractly intellectual notion, Marx sees the work that constitutes the nature of man as being distinctly different. At stake is "the production of material life itself."[64] He singles out three basic conditions or aspects of work "that have existed since the beginning of history and since the first men, and which continue to be present today":[65] labor, the creation of new needs, and the family. Labor is the sum of all efforts, primarily practical though theoretical, too, that man must make to survive. He at first seeks to satisfy only his immediate needs but then also produces tools and artifacts that aid his survival. The second aspect is the creation of new needs. Man is "led" to discover them by the satisfaction of his primary needs and by the instruments already acquired.[66] The third aspect arises because men "begin to produce

---

63. MEGA, III, p. 156   64. Ibid., V, p. 17.
65. Ibid., p. 19.   66. Ibid., p. 18.

other men, to procreate, which entails relations between man and wife, parents and children, the family."[67] These three aspects of human activity involve both a natural and a social relationship, for several individuals collaborate in each. From the fact of collaboration, Marx concludes that "a certain method of production, or industrial stage, is always connected with a certain method of co-operation, or social stage."[68] To acknowledge these three sides of man's original social activities is tantamount, for Marx, to giving historiography a materialistic basis.

Human energy is objectified in the products of labor; and labor being man's essence, man himself becomes objectified, too. Marx calls this objectification self-externalization *(Selbstentäusserung)*, or self-alienation *(Selbstentfremdung)*. Through work, man shows what he is and what he can do. Work produces objects that have a kind of existence of their own. Since, however, these objects do not exist for themselves but as means for sustaining life, they fulfill their purpose by being destroyed in the form of human consumption and so serve man's reproduction. Work and satisfaction thus belong together. The process of self-alienation by which goods are produced is thereby cancelled, at least as long as man lives in "natural conditions." Man constantly renews and repeats the process of creating himself. Driven by the relative scarcity of the livelihood nature puts at his disposal, he sets himself off from himself as worker and objectifies himself in a product which he then consumes or uses to provide himself with more goods. Within this closed circle man naturally and constantly moves, negating or abolishing his self-alienation along the way.

Man is always forced "to struggle with nature," and no social system, no order of production can relieve him of it. Working physically and mentally, responding to his mounting needs while forced to reckon with scarcity in the material basis of existence, he remains in the power of the "realm of necessity," so Marx emphasizes, "under all possible methods of production." Yet even under simple conditions there are signs that the labor process does not always remain the same. Because of differences of the sexes and possibilities inherent in the parent-child relationship, a quantitative as well as a qualitative differentiation occurs which is the beginning

67. Ibid., p. 18. 68. Ibid., p. 19.

of the division of labor. This division is promoted by an increase of the population, which in turn leads to "increased productivity" and augmented needs. Not that the division of labor itself institutes the collaboration of men, for man is originally a social being necessarily dependent on others; but its intensification brings into being social institutions that appear to make individual existence for the first time possible. Men's natural endowments, their physical strength and mental abilities, as also the demands and eventualities of life, all bring about an increasingly elaborate division of labor so as to make a specialization of activity imperative. But as soon as men specialize in certain types of work, mutual dependency results. The individual no longer produces all he needs but leaves it to others, according to their qualification, to contribute to the preservation of the whole. Thus the division of labor, although it is of course not the exclusive factor, forms social institutions with rules that cannot be disregarded without causing immediate disturbance in all individual lives. The existence of all now depends on the particular contribution of each. According to Marx, this whole development of the division of labor "makes itself"; it is "natural."[69]

The system of mutual dependencies appears as the very essence of a social formation which, even though single individuals remain its supporters or "members," claims to be something more than the sum of its parts. The social structure begins to acquire a life of its own, largely independent of its parts, and also develops an autonomy that tends to ignore the will of the "members." This claim to autonomy further promotes a disposition, on its part, to consider itself independent of its substratum, even as a "body" superior to it. The social formation appears two-faced as it responds to and represents all individual interests while at the same time asserting an existence and special character of its own. Though the common interest is founded on individual interests, the collectivity as a whole adds a feature of its own, namely, an interest in its own continued existence. The representative bearer of the common interest, objectified in a legal system, is of course not to be conceived in terms of a special social Reason. Man himself always remains the "organ" of the common interest; his will becomes, for certain reasons, representative of the will of all. All social formations,

69. Ibid., p. 21.

whether large or small, ephemeral or permanent, are made up of men—an obvious fact that nevertheless requires some emphasis in view of certain phenomena that tend to obscure it. Language, for one, because of its inherent anthropomorphizing tendency seduces us to conceive of such indispensable concepts as family, friendship, community, state, people, and nationality in terms of active, effective subjects. For another, because social configurations possess, as we have said, a certain autonomy over and above the sum of individual wills, they give rise to a grave misunderstanding of them as "bodies" analogous to natural organisms. These obscurities are dispelled by reminding ourselves that only concrete men in the here and now are able to sustain a society, because it is they who preserve the vitality of a historic tradition and make political and legal institutions real by actualizing their claims and content in personal conduct. Still, society exists independently of these actualizing agents, and in fact can exist only if the members submit to its inherent requirements. These requirements, which at first do not take the form of moral imperatives, result from the nature of the mutual relations into which men have entered. But as these relations solidify into a social community, it becomes evident that they turn into a system of moral rules involving mutual duties and rights. No society exists that is not founded on moral obligations. Yet it would be wrong to regard interhuman relations solely in terms of ethics. Friendship, the family, or a professional organization come into existence when certain objective conditions have been fulfilled. Every relation has both an optimum and a minimum, the first being determined by the purpose for which it is intended, the second indicating the lower limit of its existence beyond which dissociation sets in.

Marx regards the division of labor as the "riddle of history." When we know its conditions and, more especially, its effects, we shall have found the key to his philosophy of society and history. But first, since the division of labor is something "naturally" given, it must be accepted as a simple fact. To put any sort of moral valuation on it would seem to be out of place because what happens from natural necessity generally precludes evaluative judgments. Yet the plain fact is that Marx treats this natural necessity not at all as if a positive or negative evaluation were irrelevant. The division of labor holds so central a place in his philosophy as to grant decisive insights into history and the destiny of mankind, and to promote an understanding of social systems. More concretely speaking, according to Marx, the division of labor allows us to understand the structure of the family, the origin of social classes, the development and organization of the state, and the phenomenon of "exploiter" and "exploited." It sheds light on the notion of historical necessity and the "blind" powers that subjugate man, degrading him from a free subject to a mere object in the movement of history. Its significance is greater yet. The origin of ideologies and of the "false" ideological consciousness appears to be a direct consequence of the division of labor, just as the entire teleology of history, too, hinges on it. It signifies nothing less than the Fall, the original act of sin with which history commences, and with whose abolition history, or more precisely the "prehistory of mankind," comes to an end. The liquidation of the division of labor assumes for Marx the meaning of the salvation and the restoration of man.

To return to human material production and reproduction, we have shown that the process is circular in the sense that man first externalizes and alienates himself in the products of his labor, but by consuming and enjoying these products cancels òut his self-alienation. The essential characteristic of this constantly renewed movement is that man freely disposes over what he produces. His freedom consists in having practical power over the results of his work. "The producers," so Engels wrote, "know what becomes of their produce: they consume it, it does not leave their hands, and as long as production is carried out on this basis, it cannot grow over the producers' heads and create ghostly alien powers opposite them as is regularly and inevitably the case in civilization."[70] Or to let Marx explain it: "So long as the work process remains individual, one and the same worker unites all the functions that later become separate. In individually appropriating natural objects for the purpose of his livelihood, he controls himself. Later on, he is controlled."[71]

The actual history of social life makes it evident, however, that the cyclical process of production and consumption breaks down, and man loses control over his product. But if appropriation be-

70. Friedrich Engels, *Der Ursprung der Familie, des Privateigentums und des Staats.* 23rd ed. (Berlin, 1928), p. 183.

71. *Kapital,* 1:472.

comes doubtful, the negation of self-alienation is also imperiled. What is the source and nature of the obstruction? From the moment the original, natural work process is disturbed, an "objective world" begins to be erected outside man, "alien to him, and an independent power opposite him." In his first manuscript on Alienated Labor, Marx wrote in 1844: "The more the worker expends himself, the more powerful grows the foreign world of objects he creates in face of himself, the poorer he becomes in his inner life, and the less he can call his own. It is the same as in religion. The more man attributes to God, the less he has left for himself."[72] The crucial question Marx puts as follows: "Individuals have always acted out of themselves and they still do. Their relations are the relations of their actual life process. Why is it that their relations become independent of them and the powers of their own life acquire domination over them?"[73] Why is it that "man's own deed, namely, the production of the means of life, turns into an alien, opposite power that subjugates him, whereas it is he who should control it?"[74] To put the question in our own words, how does a historical-social configuration come about that exerts compulsion, degrades man from a subject to an object, and deprives him of control over his life and work? Why does he become a mere function of the historical-social movement? The answer is to be found in the problems connected with the division of labor. The latter destroys the original, natural cyclical movement whose various aspects have already been described. As a consequence, a contradiction arises "between the interests of the single individual and the common interest of all." Secondly, work and satisfaction, production and consumption, self-alienation and complete reappropriation become separated and are distributed among different individuals. Thirdly, it becomes possible to dispose over the working power of others and to acquire private property. Fourthly and finally, mental and physical labor become separated.

The division of labor creates "the unequal distribution of labor, both qualitatively and quantitatively." This fact, Marx assumes, is a consequence of the original family order where the wife and children are "slaves of the man." The relation of domination and submission is, accordingly, a natural one. It turns one part of humanity into usufructaries who, even though they also work, primarily enjoy life,

72. MEGA, III, pp. 83–4.   73. Ibid., V, p. 537.   74. Ibid., p. 22.

and another part into exploited people who, though they too enjoy themselves, primarily work. The power to dispose over the labor of others is, therefore, "a natural growth." Even in these initial stages of the division of labor, a "contradiction of interests" appears between the single individual and the common interest of all, creating the condition for the rise of social classes and the state. For, as Marx argues, the classes, conditioned by the division of labor, lead to a situation in which the opposition between special and common interests solidifies so as to let "the common interest assume, in the form of the state, an independent existence that is separate from the real interests of either the individual or the whole." True, the "common interest," which the state pretends to be that of all the citizens, always rests on the "real basis of the bonds to be found in every conglomerate of family and tribe." But this basis represents only an "illusory commonality" because the interests of the state are simply the interests of the class that "rules all others." The state, for Marx, is merely the form "in which the members of a ruling class assert their common interests."[75]

As a further consequence of the division of labor, work becomes concentrated upon the sort of occupation that appears to suit the intellectual capacity and psycho-physical dispositions of the individual. An inevitable result is the one-sided development of man. "As soon as work is divided, each man is assigned a particular, exclusive sphere of activity which he is unable to leave: he is a hunter, a fisherman, a herdsman, or a critic, and must remain one in order not to lose the means of his livelihood."[76] The division of labor also makes men collaborate, transforming them into members of a social system that has an order and momentum of its own. The individual loses the power to dispose over what he produces because not only must he exchange his product for others he needs, but he must submit to the legal order controlling the market in which goods are exchanged, or bought and sold. As the division of labor becomes advanced, man loses his independence and his freedom, for "a being is regarded as independent only when it owes its existence to itself."[77] To employ the earlier phraseology, the division of labor and its unequal distribution give rise to a political order that bestows final sanction on the condition of self-alienation, and does not

75. Ibid., p. 52.   76. Ibid., p. 22.   77. MEGA, III, p. 124.

provide for a compensatory reappropriation or elimination of alienation. The relations of production "must" find expression in "political and legal relations."[78]

The Division of Labor and the Origin of Ideological Consciousness

Marx maintains that there is a connection between the division of labor and the rise of ideological consciousness, the former having a decisive effect on the latter. When, he writes, "physical and mental labor become divided, consciousness can really imagine itself as being something other than the consciousness of existing practice, as *really* representing something without representing anything real; from then on, consciousness is able to emancipate itself from the world and to pass over into the formation of 'pure' theory, theology, philosophy, morality, and so on."[79] This emancipation of consciousness from the actual world, which leads to the rise of philosophy and theology, become intelligible only after we have clarified, at least provisionally and roughly, how Marx defines the relation between being and consciousness. Consciousness is for him "from its very inception a social product and remains so as long as men exist." It arises, as he explains in one passage—though he did not maintain this position—"from the need, the necessity of human intercourse."[80] The content of consciousness "can never be anything other than being become conscious of itself"; that is, it can never be anything but the factual relations, raised to consciousness, in which men find themselves when they reproduce their existence through the production of goods. "The being of human beings is their actual life process."[81] "It is not conciousness that determines life," so Marx states contrary to the kind of German philosophy that descends from heaven to earth, instead of ascending from earth to heaven, "but life that determines consciousness."[82] What we find in consciousness are the rules and conditions under which men produce and reproduce their lives.

78. Ibid., V, p. 342.   79. Ibid., p. 21.   80. Ibid., p. 20.
81. Ibid., p. 15.   82. Ibid., p. 16.

This relation of consciousness to being is altered by the division of labor into physical and mental, a change that is of basic significance for the world of "objective mind." The moment the original unity of physical and mental labor is dissolved, consciousness loses connection with being, giving rise to the fiction that it is now independent of being even though the latter is its necessary condition. The division of labor leads consciousness to substitute its own creations for "real being." A split occurs and results in man no longer realizing that his consciousness is nothing more than conscious being, that is, being become conscious of itself. This process is greatly advanced when, owing to the division of labor, the product of labor is withdrawn from the producer's power of disposal and transformed into an autonomous alien power. This alien power takes effect as a necessary economic order, into which man feels himself incorporated. In this way, the division of labor leads to a "consolidation of our own product into an objective power over us that escapes our control, crosses up our expectations, and confounds our calculations."[83] It is this power that has been a major factor in previous historical development. By "dehumanizing" man, by making him feel historically impotent, and by degrading him to an object or function of the existing social order, this power creates at last the condition for the rise of religious and philosophical consciousness. Such a consciousness affirms a world order that is theologically or philosophically derived from an immutable, eternal divine will, or from a spiritual principle active in man and nature alike.

The resulting bifurcation of the world into a secular and a religious-philosophical one has its source in the dissociation of being and consciousness, which in turn is a consequence of the division of labor. The separation of mental from physical work causes the human consciousness to create for itself an object of its own, the world of essences and ideas, which it now regards as the moving forces and ultimate aims of history. This bifurcation of the world was a fault with which Marx reproached the philosophy of Hegel. The self-movement of spirit postulated by Hegel, which uses the passions of individuals to arrive at self-knowledge, was for Marx simply an "expression" of the sense that man does not make his own

83. Ibid., p. 22.

history, but rather suffers it to be made over his head. Though man remains, of course, the organ of spirit, he is all the same implicated in the world-historical process through which spirit comes to comprehend itself. Because men have been tyrannized by the division of labor as though by an alien power, they think of this oppression as a "chicanery of the so-called world spirit."[84] When, therefore, traditional philosophy or theology represents political constitutions, judicial systems, and national codes of ethics as the manifestations of some metaphysical principle or divine being, it is simply testimony of man's inability to recognize that the superhuman power, whether it be God or the world spirit, is merely an expression of human self-alienation. What the alleged autonomy of those "mysterious powers" reveals is, again, man as the object rather than the subject of history. Since actual conditions are outside his control and authority, he believes in a supernatural being as the source of the political order and motor of history. Yet this "higher being," Marx asserts, is "merely an idealistic intellectual expression for the decidedly empirical fetters and limits within which the mode of the production of life and the relevant forms of communication move."[85] To cite another passage: "Social power, that is, productive power multiplied by the collaboration of individuals under the division of labor, is not recognized by them as their own united power because their collaboration is not an act of volition, but is something naturally grown. That power instead appears to them as foreign, outside themselves, something whose whence and whither they do not know. They therefore are no longer able to control it as it runs through a certain series of phases and developmental stages, independent of men's will and movement and actually directing them."[86] "Social power" is the real substratum of what unsuspecting man conceives as metaphysical principle or world spirit. "Just as in religion man is dominated by a fiction of his own mind, so in capitalistic production he is ruled by the work of his own hand."[87] For Hegel the concept of historical necessity meant the personified world spirit affirming and explicating itself in ever ascending levels of self-realization. But for Marx historical necessity meant human

84. Ibid., p. 26.   85. Ibid., p. 21.
86. Ibid., pp. 23–4.   87. *Kapital*, 1:585.

self-alienation, that is, a condition of material production in which man no longer controls but is controlled. He writes:

> The realm of freedom only begins, "with the cessation of work determined by need and external expediency; it lies, by the very nature of things, beyond the sphere of actual material production. Like the savage who must struggle against nature to satisfy his needs, sustain life, and procreate, so civilized man must also do, in all social systems and under all possible modes of production. As his development advances, the realm of necessity grows along with his needs; but at the same time the forces of production that satisfy his needs grow, too. Freedom in this realm can only mean that socialized men, the associated producers, regulate their material traffic with nature by putting such dealing under their common control instead of letting it dominate them as though it were a blind power; and, further, that they carry it on with a minimum expenditure of energy under conditions most adequate and worthy of their human nature. But a realm of necessity there will always be. Only beyond it begins the development of human power that is its own end, the true realm of freedom, which can blossom, however, only if grounded in the realm of necessity.[88]

According to Marx, such philosophic notions as the Hegelian concept and the Platonic idea are products of a mystical consciousness, "phantoms" that engender a "history of phantoms and spirits," which "exploits empirical history for the single purpose of obtaining bodies for those phantoms."[89] Marx refers to the notions of those philosophers as phantoms because the mystical consciousness—or its equivalent, the ideological consciousness—is unable to comprehend that their existence results from the socio-economic reality having become independent of man. The ideas of self-alienated man are spirits that dwell "outside nature and man." The nature of language points in the same direction. As Marx says:

> All conditions including the conditions of material production and of political and social relations that take form as the state

88. MEGA, III/2, p. 355.   89. Ibid., V, p. 110.

constitution and legal system of civic life find linguistic expression only in concepts. That these generalities and concepts should be regarded as though they were mysterious powers is due to the autonomy of the real conditions whose expression they are.[90]

Because man no longer disposes over the autonomous real conditions, he has lost control also over the intellectual "reflex" of this situation, and is compelled to interpret religious and philosophic ideas as autonomous beings or mysterious forces. Man's dependency on the social power, which has moved beyond him and set itself against him, becomes transformed in consciousness into the assumption that history, the legal system, and moral order of society are dependent on those intellectual ideas. Since, however, the autonomous social power is perpetuated by the class system, that is, by domination and submission, man's relation to the intellectual order, to ideas and concepts, is likewise one of submission. As a reflection of the material order of production, the social power possesses an order that is compelling: any transgression of it is punished by the state as the representative of the interests of the ruling class. Translated into conscious being, this means that under the condition of self-alienation, intellectual creations such as the contents of religion, morality, and law lay claim to being autonomous. There is an ideological correspondence between the historic inevitability of social life and the alleged autonomy of the intellectual world. In either realm, man has no choice but to submit to powers outside him. The whole content of what Hegel called "objective spirit," including religion, law, the state, family, science and art, is for Marx only a special mode of production and subject to the general law of production. This law, which rules the entire prehistory of man from the inception to the elimination of the division of labor, determines the production of all goods during the period of human self-alienation. It signifies that whatever man produces as a member of a specialized society, he produces in the form of a commodity, externalizing and objectifying himself in the process, but in such a way as to lose control over and surrender his product to an alienated world.

90. Ibid., p. 342.

Marx's criticism of traditional philosophers, and of Hegel especially, that they "stand everything on its head," can be properly understood only in this whole perspective of the division of labor. A knowledge of the real relations between being and consciousness is obscured, indeed it becomes impossible, if, like Hegel, one regards thought as the demiurge or creator of the real. This is an illusion, according to Marx, because such ontological entities as God and ideas are nothing but the "intellectual reflex" of man's secular self-alienation. Philosophy treats the various cultural contents of consciousness—religion, law, morality—as realities. But though these play an important role in the psychic economy of human beings, they are in fact illusions that simply help man bear the misery of his social existence.

Since Marx has assigned primary responsibility for human self-alienation to the division of labor, its abolition can be expected to have equally far-reaching consequences. This abolition is the aim of history and the realization of reason, it is the meaning of the teleological process in terms of which Marx conceives history. When that aim has been reached, man will be at liberty "to do one thing today, another tomorrow." A social order will prevail in which "there are no painters, but at the most men who among other things also paint."[91] Whereas the specialization of labor deformed and impoverished man, the new society in which it is abolished will produce man in the "full plenitude of his being, and make his inner wealth, his depth, and many-sidedness its own permanent reality."[92] The socio-political system to realize this promise is communism. Communism "is the true resolution of the conflict between existence and essence, objectification and self-activization, freedom and necessity, individual and species. It is the solution of the riddle of history and knows itself as such."[93] In this society, the "creative and free development of the individual will not be an empty phrase;" for many-sided self-realization, or "total man," becomes possible once the division of labor has ceased to exist. "Real human life is vindicated when it takes possession of itself," and that would signify the "beginning of a practical humanism."[94] It is clear that Marx views history as the restoration of man. This view derives in part from his anthropology, to which we now turn.

91. Ibid., p. 373.   92. Ibid., III, p. 121.
93. Ibid., p. 124.   94. Ibid., p. 166.

Man—the Natural Being, Free, Conscious, and Social

In Marx's anthropology man appears at first as an "immediate natural being" who possesses "natural powers," along with dispositions and capacities, in the form of urges. He is a "passive, dependent, and limited creature similar to animal and plant." "That is, the objects of his urges exist outside him, independently, but they are the objects of his need"[95] which activates and confirms his inherent powers. This, however, is not an exhaustive description of human nature, for it does not sufficiently differentiate man from other organisms. "Man is not simply a natural being," as Marx says, "he is a human natural being."[96] What this specifically human element is, Marx first tries to show in comparison with the animal. "The animal is immediately at one with his life activity" and therefore essentially unfree: its psychic actions and reactions are exhausted in the nexus of motivations. The animal lacks the possibility of reflection "by which the sensual, given world is first transformed into an object." The kind of things that enter the animal's horizon, and the way they are perceived, are conditioned by its own vital interests and physical constitution. It perceives as much as is required for its orientation in the world, for its sustenance, and procreation. Man behaves differently: he "makes his own life activity the object of his will and consciousness. His life activity is conscious."[97] He has, as Marx says, a mind. What the animal does instinctively, man turns into acts of will and reflection. Though he, too, must provide himself with food and seeks to preserve his species, he is no longer immediately at one with his life activity. Rather, he mediates it, and the mediation is reflection. To

95. Ibid., p. 160.
96. Ibid., p. 162.
97. Ibid., p. 88. It is significant that in a draft of the *German Ideology,* Marx distinguished spirit as the essential trait of man. We note, he writes, "that man has 'spirit' and that this 'spirit' becomes manifest as consciousness." This sentence was then crossed out and changed into the statement, "that man has also consciousness." Marx apparently sought to avoid using the concept of spirit because of its theological and Hegelian bias. See *Marx-Engels Archiv* (Frankfurt a. M., n.d.), 1:247. The passage quoted is correctly interpreted by Ernst Lewalter in "Wissenssoziologie und Marxismus," *Archiv für Sozialwissenschaft und Sozialpolitik,* vol. 64 (1930), pp. 80ff.

have "conscious life activity" means that he possesses freedom and universality. Whereas the animal is determined by its psycho-physical organization and "forms" its world under the pressure of immediate physical need, man produces also when "free of physical need," and he produces "truly" only when he is generally free from it. Moreover, man knows "how to produce like any other species," or "universally," whereas "the animal's production is one-sided." By drawing these distinctions, Marx lifts man out of the sphere of exclusively natural determination. He, of course, remains a natural being, but in his particularly human way. What animals do, he must do, too, but he does it through the mediation of planning foresight. What to animals merely happens, appears in man as his own work, as the realization of purposes and aims. Hence the difference between animal and man is not one of degree but of kind. The essentially human characteristic is "conscious life activity," which involves freedom and universality. Were man a purely natural being, it would be impossible to understand why he produces free of physical needs, or indeed, as Marx declares, why he "produces truly" only in a state of freedom from these needs. This freedom implies two things. First, man does not produce exclusively in order to satisfy immediate needs and to survive. He produces over and above his needs and—this is the specifically human element—without regard to need, "universally," because his life activity is conscious. He also knows how to apply the appropriate measure to the object. Second, man is capable of perceiving the material his senses present to him as objects, and of knowing the attributes and laws of such objects.

This anthropological description does not, however, define man exhaustively. He is, for Marx, a basically social being, a species being, who realizes himself in community, through I-and-you relationships. The character of the species finds expression in mutual dependency. The I-and-you relationship is a "natural growth," for man is, of course, a part of nature; yet at the same time it is also specifically human because it is realized through conscious life activity. The social configurations in which his human essence is made manifest are objects of his conscious will. For man is a "conscious species-being who relates to his species as to his essence."[98] Man relates to his own kind in the same way as he relates

98. MEGA, III, p. 88.

to his material production, as a reflective spiritual being. Human existence is a social existence, and only in society can it find completion. Still, this completion deserves to be called wilful in the sense that it is also a manifestation of conscious life activity. Social bonds are naturally grown and given, but on the human level they are realized by conscious beings whose activity is for that very reason free activity, too. The form of human activity is not naturally determined, and this distinction raises man above the level of animals. It follows that the social tie, too, is a product of conscious activity. Marx defines the relation between society and individual as a mutual involvement: "As society itself produces man, so it is produced through him."[99]

Just as the division of labor had destructive effects on the life of the individual, so also in the life of the species. Mankind that carries on production under permanent socio-political conditions of self-alienation makes "species life the means of individual life." In other words, social existence is degraded to a means of individual existence, with the direct consequence of "man's alienation from man." He begins to use his peer as a mere means or instrument for the satisfaction of his own needs. Society, too, is dehumanized because a relation between men arises that in some respects is analogous to the relation between the individual's work and its product. As a man's labor is set against him as an alien power, so too one man becomes an alien power for the other. "When an activity is not my own, but alien and forced, to whom does it belong? To another being? But who is that being? . . . The alien being to whom labor and its product belong . . . can only be man himself."[100] What Marx means is that one man gains power over another, a sign that society is split into classes. The individual's self-alienation in labor leads to the alienation of man from man, and in such a relation man is treated as a means or a commodity. It has been the stigma of the economy till the present time to transform human relations into object relations, thereby subjecting everything man does and creates to the law of commodity production. The material of real history consists of two objective conditions: the individual's own work takes on the shape of an alien, independent power that sets itself up against him, and the bearer of that power is man himself, or a certain class of men.

99. Ibid., p. 116.   100. Ibid., p. 90.

We are now able to understand what alienation in the final analysis means. According to Marx, free and conscious activity originally characterizes man's species-being. Merely material production does not fulfill the meaning of human life but enables man to lead a "higher" spiritual life. Self-alienation through work, however, reverses this original situation because alienated work obviously is not a condition for the higher life; on the contrary, it even damages the human essence, "causing man, just because he is a conscious being, to degrade his life activity and his *essence* into a mere means of his existence."[101] In other words, he cannot fulfill his higher vocation because all his energies are concentrated on securing his material existence. He loses his essence through the division of labor, and this is why Marx speaks of the "loss of man" which, to his mind, marks the beginning of history. In that state, man "does not develop any free psychic and intellectual energy, but mortifies his body and ruins his mind."[102] To repeat, the production of material life and the satisfaction of needs are natural, necessary activities. "Eating, drinking, and procreating are genuinely human functions,"[103] but they do not completely occupy a truly human life. "As abstractions, separated from the remaining round of human activity and made into final, sole purposes, they are beastly."[104] As soon, and as long, as a social condition prevails where, in order to live at all, man looks on eating, drinking, and procreation as the exclusive goals of his desire, he "feels," according to Marx, like an animal. That happens when the division of labor has advanced to the point where we lose control over our own production and are controlled by it instead.

The Philosophy of Art

The principles of Marx's anthropology just reviewed were set forth in his economic and philosophical manuscripts of 1844. The same work, though it remains a fragment not easily

---

101. Ibid., p. 88.   102. Ibid., p. 85.
103. Ibid., p. 86.   104. Ibid., p. 86.

penetrated, affords certain other supplementary insights. It contains some brief and incomplete references to those human capacities that go beyond the sphere of the natural functions and therefore constitute man's true being. Marx entertained the idea of a real humanism, by which he meant the development of a "deep and all-round man," the unfolding of his essential powers, and the realization of human freedom. The creations of which this "total man" is capable on the level of his fully developed nature do not include religion and philosophy. Both will have lost their existential basis when the state of perfect humanism has been reached—religion because it is a reflection of human self-alienation, philosophy because it criticizes reality by means of a comparison with the ideal. Marx envisages a world that has itself become philosophical in the sense that idea and reality coincide. Nor will that ultimate humanistic creativity be concerned with the problems of the social order: justice and the classless society having been realized, law and the state, at least in so far as they are organizations of the ruling class, will have become superfluous. Thus, of all the creations of the human spirit, only one remains, and that is art.

It is striking that Marx should assign such a distinguished position to art, and that he should do so in the passage of the economic and philosophical manuscripts that presents his anthropology in a nutshell. "Man," he says, "forms things also according to the laws of beauty." Man differs from the animal, we recall, by his ability to produce "truly" only when free of physical needs. Since even scientific knowledge is largely a response to physical needs, there remains, strictly speaking, only one activity representative of, and appropriate to, that state of freedom. This statement about aesthetic creation is remarkable because Marx's theory of ideology, in which the intellectual superstructure is clearly determined by the material base, comes into obvious conflict with the idea of perennial beauty. Marx was aware of the problem and referred to it, albeit very briefly, in a later passage on the timeless beauty of classical Greek art. "The difficulty," he writes in an incomplete draft of an introduction to *The Critique of Political Economy,* "is not in understanding that Greek art and epic poetry are tied to certain forms of social development. It lies rather in explaining why they still afford us aesthetic enjoyment and in certain respects are accepted as standards and unattainable models."[105] If, as Marx's theory of history assumes, the entire higher culture is conditioned by the constantly changing material base, then it is difficult to understand why Greek art should still mean so much today. Long after the mode of production prevalent in the Greek city states was superseded by capitalist economy, that should not really be the case.

Now it might be said that the difficulty derives from Marx being the captive of an outdated, unhistorical aesthetic doctrine about classicism. But even if we grant that the idealization of Greek art was peculiar to a certain time and to the Germans especially, the objection is irrelevant to the argument. Nor would it help to prove, though it might perhaps be possible, that the economy of the Greek city states differed little in principle from that of the petty German states in the early nineteenth century. The point at issue is not the enduring influence of classical Greek art, or the oddity of such a phenomenon in intellectual history, interesting as it may be, but the fact that certain creations of the human spirit prove to be relatively independent of the corresponding stage of material production. Marx was quite right to recognize that this difficulty touched the nerve of his theory of ideology. At stake was nothing less than the truth of his assertion that the "social existence" of men "determines" their consciousness. From this determination, which was not difficult to demonstrate for legal and political institutions, art had not been expressly exempted. It belonged, like law, political theory, philosophy, and religion to the "ideological forms."[106] This whole system of dependency is, however, put in question when certain aesthetic standards are shown to outlast fundamental historical changes in the economic structure of society.

The crucial problem Marx here encounters really derives from the phenomenon of the autonomy and independent life of the mind. It is

---

105. Karl Marx, *Zur Kritik der politischen Ökonomie*, p. 248. For a recent English edition and translation of this work, see David McLellan, *The Grundrisse* (New York, 1971). It is remarkable that Wilhelm Hausenstein's instructive outline of a sociological theory of aesthetics, presented at the beginning of his book *Der nackte Mensch in der Kunst aller Zeiten und Völker* (München, 1931), takes no notice of these views of Marx. Marx, it seems, would have questioned the possibility of a sociology of aesthetic forms because he defended the timeless character of beauty, and thereby contradicted the principles of historical materialism which Hausenstein sought to apply to the history of art.

106. *Zur Kritik der politischen Ökonomie*, p. 5.

important, for our purposes, that he himself made a breach in his theory of ideology. "It is well known," he writes in the introduction to *The Critique of Political Economy,* "that certain periods of the flowering of art are not at all directly related to the general development of society, to the material basis or skeletal structure of its organization." We may grant therefore that Marx at least reduced to an acceptable, demonstrable measure the dependency of intellectual forms and contents on socio-economic conditions. Still, the critical fact is that he himself raises the question of the timelessness of the "idea." Though changes in productive relations and consequent changes in social structure are indisputable facts, they are unable to explain either the origin or the autonomous life of certain creations of the human mind. We do not in the least deny that such matters as the choice of artistic subjects, means of expression, and technique may be conditioned by the form and stratification of society. Yet we do not think that the sociology of art can tell us why a work of art is called beautiful. Precisely this, and only this, is what is here at issue. The philosophy of art uncovers the defectiveness of Marx's theory of ideology while restricting its validity to its proper scope. Marx confirms this view in a passage following immediately on the one just quoted concerning the difficulty of explaining the continuing enjoyment of Greek art.

A man cannot become a child again unless he becomes childish. But does he not take pleasure in the naiveté of the child, and must he not strive to reproduce its truth on a higher plane? Is not the character of every epoch revived in its original truth in the child's nature? Why should not the childhood of mankind exert an eternal charm in the unique historic age where it obtained its most beautiful development? There are ill-bred children and precocious children, and many of the ancient nations belong among them. The Greeks, however, were normal children. The charm their art has for us does not conflict with the immature stage of the society in which it had its roots. That charm is rather the product of the latter. It is inseparable from the fact that the immature social conditions under which that art arose can never return.[107]

107. Ibid., p. 248. See Peter Demetz, who arrives at the same conclusions in his book *Marx, Engels und die Dichter: Zur Grundlagenforschung des Marxismus* (Stuttgart, 1959).

The metaphor about childhood that does not return and adulthood that takes pleasure in it, is to the point only because both youth and maturity are stages in man's life, and because both transformation and preservation are at work in the course of an individual life. Since Marx applies this metaphor to world history, he is all the more compelled to assume that above and in spite of the radically changed relationships of production that condition intellectual life, something is being preserved. And what else could that be but the identity of the intellectual structure of man.

Ideology and Ideological Consciousness

We have shown that Marx conceives of history as the dissolution of man into idea and reality, followed by his restoration and final realization. We must now clarify how man's dissolution and decay take effect, anthropologically, economically, and sociologically, during the so-called "prehistory of mankind." This is a period marked by a general degeneration of the original conditions of life. It is characterized anthropologically by the loss of freedom and rise of an ideological consciousness; economically, by the involuntary division of labor, the introduction of compulsive labor, and private property; and sociologically, by the origin of classes, the class struggle, and the state.

The ideological consciousness brings forth two things—a supernatural, religious *ersatz* world that affords man an illusory compensation for his real misery; and a philosophy whose sole purpose is to offer an apology for existing social conditions and to declare the legal and political order underlying them as God's will or the manifestation of reason. The substratum underlying religion and philosophy is the alien power that has come into being through the self-alienation of man. Both of these intellectual enterprises are ineffectual in the real world. Such effect as they do have is limited to man's imaginings. Marx usually employed this term when investigating the influence of mythologies and philosophies. Thus, through philosophy man imagines he knows history as a process by which ideas or spirit find realization, while through mythology he imagines that he controls nature. "Since absolute spirit . . . appears as creative spirit only *post festum* in the philosopher's consciousness, it manufactures history only in consciousness, in the opinion and speculative imagination of the philosopher."[108] About mythology Marx writes similarly: "All mythologies command and shape natural forces in the imagination; therefore, they vanish with man's real control over nature."[109] This is not to say that the imaginary control over nature, the illusory consolations of religion, and the pretended knowledge of historical reality lack all significance in the intellectual and psychic life of man. Marx does not mean to assert that men have never attempted to shape their lives in accordance with religious and philosophical ideas, only that these lack both cognitive value and the power to change the world. Where religion or philosophy appeared to effect revolutionary changes in social conditions, the actual motive force was the regrouping of interests within society. For in the last analysis, the "production and reproduction of real life" is always the determining factor. Of course, the struggle between different social interests has its repercussions on the ideological superstructure. For example, proclamations about freedom of conscience only reflect the basic power of free competition.[110] And Calvin's doctrine regarding the elect as chosen by divine grace was simply a "religious expression of the fact that success or bankruptcy in the commercial world does not depend on individual action or skill, but on circumstances outside man's control."[111] "Man plans, but God (that is, the alien power of capitalist production) runs the show."

This way of arguing rests on the distinction Marx draws between object-related and ideological consciousness. This is clearly illustrated by the charges he levels against mythology. Its alleged influence over the forces of nature is a pretense and due to self-deception. Still, man has no choice but to control these forces in order to make them serviceable to himself. This control depends, however, on his knowledge of nature, hence one is driven to the assumption that he is capable of such knowledge. The implication is that in regard to nature, the ideological consciousness is incapable of exerting its usual power to conceal reality, which accords perfectly with the theses of Marx's anthropology.

108. MEGA, III, p. 258.
109. *Zur Kritik der politischen Ökonomie,* p. 247.
110. MEGA, VI, p. 544.
111. Friedrich Engels, "Über historischen Materialismus," *Auswahl,* 1:407.

The situation is similar in respect to man's understanding of history, economics, and society. The philosophy of history and society does not yield reliable knowledge of the motive powers and true causes of historical change. Its pronouncements, like those of religion, have no truth content. Stated differently, man's consciousness during the entire period of "prehistory" is ideological and false in the sense that it mistakes the appearance of things for their reality. Man's attitude is unscientific *par excellence,* for "science consists in reducing visible, apparent movement to inner, real movement."[112] The ideological consciousness is not sufficiently acute to make this distinction. It lacks such concepts as true and false, and what it terms knowledge has therefore no relation to the object itself: the historical social reality remains concealed and eludes its grasp. It is important to note that economic theory, too, is afflicted by this failure. In Marx's view, history is first of all a matter of economics because the original and primary activity of man is economic. But if the ideological consciousness is denied any knowledge of reality, it cannot even penetrate as far as the laws of economics. "Common economic theory accomplishes, indeed, nothing more than a doctrinaire translation, systematization, and justification of the ideas entertained by those who are enmeshed in bourgeois productive relations."[113] But since economics forms the substance of history, the ideological consciousness is also denied a knowledge of history. It is a deluded consciousness. It confounds objective situations by transforming mere ideas into corporeal beings. "It generates within itself a world of palpable, tangible phantoms. That is the secret of all pious visions, as of folly generally."[114]

Even if the claims to truth of the ideological consciousness are declared void, *some* relation to reality it has all the same. Marx characterizes this relation by such various terms as "expression," "intellectual reflex," "ideological echo," and "symptom." Ideas, he also says, are "ideally expressed conditions of existence." "Economic categories are merely theoretical expressions, they are abstractions from the social relations of production." "The same men who establish social relations in conformity with their material pro-

112. *Kapital,* III/1, p. 297.   113. Ibid., III/2, p. 352.   114. MEGA, III, p. 361.

duction also produce principles, ideas, and categories in conformity with their social relations."[115] This kind of lawful correspondence applies not only to specifically economic concepts, but to the ideological superstructure as a whole.

The epistemological possibility of comprehending ideas as the expression of the material relations of production is based on the assumption that consciousness is determined by being. It is evident that this view contradicts Marx's anthropological assumptions. Even the view that consciousness is nothing else than conscious being—and this thesis forms the point of departure for his theory of ideology—cannot be brought into agreement with the basically correct idea that man is able to discover the inherent truth of things. For, if consciousness can give us only a theoretical representation of the living form of the actual community, and if the form and content of consciousness are made to depend on the material conditions of life, man's capacity to relate to the world objectively, as knower, is put in question. It is exactly man's distinguishing characteristic, his "free, conscious activity" separating him from the animal, that is hereby abolished. If the material relations of production "determine" consciousness, then man merely exchanges his own social determination for the natural determination of animals, and he is degraded to being a function of prevailing conditions. Yet, according to Marx's anthropology, nature as well as the individual and social life of man are suitable objects of his free, conscious activity. This view implies a certain epistemological and behavioral position. To say that man does not produce exclusively according to the measure of his own species but rather "universally," is to imply that, within certain limits, human behavior, and especially cognitive behavior, is free of the natural drives of man's psycho-physical nature. In order to discover the objective truth of things, knowledge presupposes a minimum of freedom. We may conclude, therefore, that the world appears to consciousness not exclusively in the perspective of the struggle for existence, but in its own inherent lawfulness.

Marx's theory of ideology incorporates the psychology and the theory of ideas as developed especially by Helvetius in the

115. Ibid., VI, pp. 179–80.

eighteenth century. In this perspective, ideas appear as the expression of interests, and they change in accordance with the social-class membership of their authors. "The ruling ideas of an epoch have always been the ideas of the ruling classes."[116] At the same time, ideas represent the revolutionary aim of the exploited class. They express the "necessity of individuals, classes, and nations to maintain their position," and they reflect the "conditions of life of the ruling class in the form of moral laws." These laws are held up to the oppressed "as a standard of conduct, partly to varnish, partly to provide moral support for, domination."[117] One easily recognizes Helvetius's theory of ideas in these statements. Incidentally, Hegel, too, was familiar with this train of thought. Ideas, he says, that run counter to the interests of a certain class of people do not enter their heads.[118]

To pass now to a general appraisal of the theory of ideology, we acknowledge first its sociological importance. There is no disputing the fact that judicial systems, moral codes, and religious commandments always reflect certain interests. The sociology of ideas is, therefore, a legitimate scientific pursuit as important to man's understanding of himself as it is to his knowledge of the ideational content of the will of groups and classes. It is also an indispensable means of scientific self-criticism because the concepts of the social sciences still contain remnants of an earlier mythological and religious interpretation of the world, and because the entire framework of those concepts always rests on a system of historically conditioned principles deeply influenced by intellectual traditions and pragmatic considerations.

Having acknowledged the importance of the sociology of knowledge, we state, secondly, a serious limitation of the theory of ideology. Neither a psychological nor a sociological analysis by which the mechanism of the formation of ideas is evidenced can undermine the objective content of ideas. The meaning of the idea of truth or justice is not invalidated by any evidence that what was accepted as true or just in certain cases was only an expression of political or economic utility to a particular social group. Even though it is possible to demonstrate that personal and social interests undeniably

116. Ibid., p. 544. Marx uses the expression "bourgeois prejudices" in the same sense as it was used in the period of the Enlightenment.
117. Ibid., V, p. 398.
118. Hegel, "Über die englische Reformbill 1831," *Schriften zur Politik*, p. 320.

influence man's criteria of truth or justice, the dependency of the ideological superstructure on such interests does not alter the fact that a social order believed to be just was intended to be truly *just*. But what happens if, like Marx, one assumes a direct correspondence between ideas and concrete conditions of life so that ideas are taken to be nothing more than an "expression" of the material basis of existence? To put the question in another way: does consciousness, which is determined by social existence, produce nothing but ideologies? Marx returns a qualified answer. He expressly limits the ideological coloration of intellectual forms to the products of religion, the humanities, and the social sciences; it never occurred to him to include the concepts of mathematics and the natural sciences. Had he done so, he could not, with "scientific faithfulness," have distinguished the revolution in the conditions of economic production from "the juridic, religious, artistic, philosophical—in short, ideological—forms in which men become conscious of this conflict and fight it out."[119] Leaving aside the fact that Marx here treats the scientific method as nothing less than exemplary, the contrast drawn between the scientifically faithful description of social phenomena and their ideological disguise permits one to conclude that the dependency of consciousness on being is limited. Indeed, given Marx's assumption—since become untenable—that the natural sciences are devoid of ideological elements, one may go further and conclude that the structure of the knowing consciousness is a constant one as long as it is directed toward nature and its laws.[120] In that case, the dependency on social being would assert itself only in so far as consciousness concentrates its attention on the productive process of historical social life. This conjecture is especially suggested by Engels when he credits Marx with having discovered the evolutionary law of history, that is, the "natural law of capitalism," a discovery comparable to Darwin's law of the evolution of organic nature.

It is possible by yet another argument to defend the autonomy of the intellectual world against the dependency Marx asserts. One

119. *Zur Kritik der politischen Ökonomie*, p. 5.

120. Engels knew that concepts employed by the natural sciences may contain ideological elements. In *Dialektik und Naturwissenschaft*, he writes: "The Darwinian doctrine of the struggle for existence simply transfers Hobbes's theory of the war of all against all and of bourgeois economic competition from society to organic nature," *Marx-Engels Archiv*, 2:190–1.

may grant that the content of religious, moral, and legal views is subject to change, and at the same time maintain that the idea of religion, of morality, and justice is itself timeless. Marx himself took note of this objection, but his reply aimed at the complete destruction of the autonomy of the mind. In a passage which sets forth and then dismisses all objections against communism, he writes:

> It will be said that religious, moral, legal, and philosophical ideas are of course modified in the course of historical development while religion, morality, philosophy, politics, and law themselves are preserved through all change. It will be charged, moreover, that there are eternal truths such as freedom and justice common to all social conditions; that communism abolishes the eternal truths, abolishes religion and morality instead of reshaping them, and thereby contradicts all previous historical developments.

Marx then replies to this accusation with the following analysis: "The history of all previous society moved in class antagonisms that took different forms in different epochs. But whatever form they assumed, the exploitation of one part of society by another is a fact common to all past centuries. No wonder, therefore, that in spite of all variety and difference the social consciousness of all centuries moved within certain common forms—forms of consciousness that are going to dissolve only with the disappearance of class antagonism."[121] According to Marx, we are, therefore, in error when we designate the common elements preserved through all historical change by such locutions as the idea of justice or the true state, timeless moral precepts, or natural religion transcending all historical prejudices. The identical element in all these manifestations of the mind is rather that formally they belong to the ideological superstructure, and materially they reflect the social facts of oppression and suppression, that is, the class struggle. This means that the problems of the intellectual life are reduced to a mere difference in the possession of social or political power. For if the unity and permanence of intellectual "forms" consists in their representing sim-

---

121. MEGA, VI, p. 544. Karl Korsch, in his study *Marxismus und Philosophie,* 2nd ed. (Leipzig, 1930), p. 121, shows that Marx's theory of social development was interpreted as a "merely theoretical expression" of the "working-class struggle for liberation;" thus, Marx's doctrine was understood to be merely the form of the historical struggle for power.

ply the permanent state of class antagonism or inequality in the distribution of real social power, then they are only ideological antagonisms. Distinctions between good and evil, true and false, just and unjust, beautiful and ugly are thereby reduced to a function of the struggle for social power.

To conclude this discussion, we summarize, in the light of Marx's anthropological and sociological assumptions, what are for him the essentials of the ideological consciousness and its products. The question he attempts to answer is what circumstances of human existence entitle us to designate law and morality, religion and philosophy as ideological constructions. The principal mark of the ideological consciousness is its general delusion. Every one of its constructions has a certain alleged significance and concrete meaning. Thus, a legal doctrine is intended to represent a just social order; moral commandments are guided by the idea of the good; religion is alleged to contain man's "knowledge" and "experience" of God; and philosophy, his understanding of nature and himself. To accuse these constructions of being ideological is to assert that their alleged sense rests on a radical misunderstanding and is the result of a fundamental self-deception. The alleged sense is just a front for concealing a wholly different relationship of meaning existing in reality. Consciousness here evidently fails to carry out its knowledge function because it is directed to an aim of its own conceit not grounded in the objective world. The latter is replaced by a substitute world fitted out with the claims and badges of reality. Given this situation, we need to ask whether consciousness is perhaps *compelled* to turn away from concrete reality, and for reasons lying in the very structure of consciousness itself. The answer to these questions has already been indicated in our earlier exposition of the division of labor. The reader will recall that according to Marx, the separation of mental from physical labor created the condition under which man hypostatizes the products of his mental activity into autonomous Platonic ideas or Hegelian concepts and then mistakes these for the true reality. Owing to the division of labor and his self-objectification in work, man also produces the hostile social power that controls him and so creates what is the real substratum of the apparent autonomy of the mind.

The essential trait of the ideological consciousness thus emerges as its unfitness to know its own historical and social situation, its origin and workings. This unfitness has its cause in the concrete conditions of production that constitute the prime reality of human life. What the ideological consciousness presumes to be true knowledge is only the expression of the political and economic conditions under which men always reproduce their own existence. But how, exactly, is consciousness conditioned by being? Marx's answer, to be found in the summary of his critical discussion of Hegel and post-Hegelian philosophy in the Foreword to the *Critique of Political Economy,* is contained in the following oft-quoted classical passage: "In the social production of their livelihood, men enter into definite, necessary relations that are independent of their will, productive relationships that correspond to a definite stage of development of their material productive forces. The sum total of these productive relationships constitutes the economic structure of society, the real basis on which a juridical and political superstructure arises, and to which definite forms of social consciousness correspond. The mode of production of the material means of existence conditions the entire process of social, political, and intellectual life. It is not the consciousness of men that determines their existence; on the contrary, their social existence determines their consciousness."

In arriving at a critical appraisal of the concept of ideology, it is of the utmost importance to ascertain what precisely is meant by saying that the intellectual life is conditioned by the mode of production of the material means of existence, or that men's consciousness is determined by their social existence. Viewed in the light of Marx's anthropology and theory of history, such determination implies an impairment of human life during the "prehistory of mankind." If history is defined in terms of the loss and restoration of man, the determination of consciousness by social existence must be regarded as a temporary deformation, but not as the final destruction of man's essential powers. This interpretation is suggested, also, by Marx's meaning of the term "social existence": it signifies the sum total of the concrete political, economic, and juridical conditions of an age. Men's being, Marx has said, is to be found in their real life process, which is primarily taken up with the production of the means of existence. The latter always takes place in some association with a legal and political constitution adapted to prevailing productive relations. Within such an association, everyone occupies a special social position where his particular interests are brought into relative harmony with the interests of others in similar positions. Together with his place in the social hierarchy, the individual takes on the prejudices, the moral standards, and aesthetic preferences appropriate to his class and occupational group, his family, and his nation. A common social position breeds common perspectives on life in which interests solidify into relatively permanent forms.

According to Marx, man's whole vision and interpretation of the social-historical environment is conditioned by the class system. Both the selectivity of his impressions and the pattern guiding his explanation and construction of social-historical phenomena are undeniably dependent on the interests of man's social position. This places his knowledge of the social world into permanent jeopardy. Interests tied to social position mislead him into approaching reality with prejudicial opinions which, because they are useful to him, he accepts unexamined. What he apprehends of the social world and how he interprets and organizes these perceptions are all determined by the expectations that guide him in the struggle for existence. These expectations are keyed to a plan whose realization promises the kind of success that is desired. Thus, theoretical behavior does not primarily aim at explaining the facts in a concrete case, but rather at yielding some practical return. It is controlled by the impulses and direction of the will. Still, the economic facts and possibilities of social class play only a restrictive, not a constitutive role in knowledge.[122] Marx explains: "The question whether human thought has objective truth is not a question of theory, but of practice. It is in practice that man must prove the truth, that is, the reality, power, and worldliness of his thought."[123] Consciousness is ideological whenever knowledge is related not to objective fact, such as the social-historical reality, but to the anticipated success of life plans, which derive their orientation chiefly from the perspectives and value system of a certain group or class. Political, practical behavior moves within a conceptual framework put together to suit concrete interests, fitting reality only partially or not at all.

But this is not the whole of Marx's concept of ideology. It comprehends far more than the insight that to every position in the social hierarchy there corresponds a certain value system and per-

122. Fritz Medicus, *Von der doppelten Basis des menschlichen Daseins* (Zürich, 1943), p. 13. We make the distinction between constitutive and limiting in the sense suggested by Medicus.

123. MEGA, V, p. 534.

spective on life. It also includes, as already shown, a critique of religion and philosophy that culminates in the destruction of their traditional subject matter. Generally speaking, the comprehensiveness of Marx's concept of ideology appears in the configuration of the "ideological superstructure" rising above the base of the material relations of production as its "expression" or "symptom." Religion, morality, metaphysics, and all other ideological forms lose every "semblance of independence" if they are merely "inevitable sublimations" of a material life whose process is empirically verifiable.[124] Taking Marx's concept in this more inclusive sense, consciousness is defined as ideological when occupied with its own creations, mistaking them for independent entities as though ideas could have claims on man apart from the constantly changing conditions of production.

The critical implications of this train of thought, too, were anticipated by Marx himself. They are to be found in his interpretation of history as the self-alienation and restoration of man, as well as in his conception of philosophy, which derives the need for revolutionary change from the diremption of idea and reality. In both cases Marx uses ideas for his point of departure and as his criterion. Underlying his political and economic criticism of contemporary German conditions is an idea of man and of social justice; and history, too, insofar as it culminates in the self-restoration of man in classless society, is the realization of the idea of justice and of a real humanism. Were one to treat this idea in the same way as Marx treated the political and philosophical ideologies of feudal and bourgeois society, then the ideology of the proletariat, too, would have to be unmasked as the interest-conditioned ideology of a single class. Thus, Marx's theory of ideology turns back against him. His claim to have transformed socialism from a utopia into a science appears to be purely a concession to the idolatry of science characteristic of the latter part of the nineteenth century. To go against that powerful current would earn one a

---

124. Ibid., p. 16. Hendrik de Man, in *Die sozialistische Idee* (Jena, 1933), pp. 167–8, calls attention to the ideological content of Marxism. "Neither the proletarian fate nor the Marxist doctrine provides immunity against ideologizing." "What the Marxist worker believes to be true knowledge is also largely ideology." Marx's bourgeois intellectual background, on which de Man lays particular stress, may explain these facts.

reputation for regression and ignorance. In Marx's case, claiming for socialism the character of a science may perhaps have helped ward off attempts to uncover the interest bias of his own economic and philosophic views. But if he really wanted to avoid the charge that his philosophy and economic theory were just another class ideology, he had to adhere to the idea of justice as something more than the expression of concrete power relationships: it had to be a postulate that is part of the original nature of man. It was necessary to uphold this idea if the ultimate classless society was to be justified, not simply *de facto* in terms of sheer power—because the proletariat became the sole power within the state—but in moral terms as the realization of humanism, which Marx does in his early philosophical writings. After all, Marx, as well as Hegel, conceives history as the realization of reason, and reason for them means two things: it guarantees a knowledge of the historical-social reality, and it also contains the idea of what is just and good.

History Viewed as the Self-Negation of the "Alien Power"

To understand Marx's philosophy of history, it is helpful to distinguish in what ways it differs from, and in what ways it agrees with, that of Hegel. Though Marx accuses him of standing everything on its head, it is a fact that Hegel's construction appears recast in Marx's own work.

According to Hegel, history is the realization of the Absolute or spirit. It is the nature of spirit to be active, to reveal itself. "The realization of spirit consists in getting to know what it itself is. Spirit is essentially only what it knows about itself."[125] Spirit obtains this knowledge by comprehending nature and history as revelations of itself. "The history of the world shows how spirit gradually becomes conscious of, and wills, the truth . . . spirit finally becomes fully conscious of itself."[126] This process occurs in and through historic individuals and nations, and it poses a problem. How can the realization of the world plan accord with the autonomy of individuals, and how can their freedom coexist with the necessity under which

125. Hegel, *Werke,* VII/2, p. 34.   126. Ibid., IX, p. 66.

spirit realizes itself? The realization of the divine world plan, which is really a theodicy, is accomplished by means of a grand deception. Hegel writes in the Introduction to the *Philosophy of History:*

> This may be called the cunning of Reason, that it lets the passions work for itself, and makes those through whom it enters existence pay the price and suffer the damage . . . The Idea pays the price of existence and transience not out of its own pocket, but with the passions of individuals.[127] This immeasurable mass of wills, interests, and activities are the means and instruments by which the world spirit accomplishes its purpose, raises it to consciousness, and realizes it: it has no other aim than to find itself and to gaze upon itself as real.[128]

It should be observed that Hegel does not eliminate the individual from the workings of the world spirit, whose organ he after all is. Still, the individual, while satisfying his own passions and realizing his own purposes, always remains in the service of the world spirit. "Reason," Hegel says, "is as cunning as it is powerful. The cunning consists generally in assuming a mediating role that allows objects to act on each other according to their proper nature without directly interfering in this action while yet carrying out only reason's own purpose. In this sense one may say that divine providence behaves toward the world and its course as absolute cunning. God grants men the satisfaction of their particular passions and interests, but what materializes in the process are *His* intentions, and these are different from what men originally had in mind."[129] That is why Hegel calls man the "material in which the rational final purpose is carried out." "In the material of human knowing and willing, the rational obtains its existence."[130] Passions, particular interests, and the satisfaction of egotism are mighty forces, but not mighty enough to carry any weight against the world spirit. The individual "comes out short." Empirical particulars may well differ and "be better or worse because chance and particularity have here been authorized by the Concept to exercise their immense right."[131] Greater than the power of chance and particular interests, however, is the power of ideas and divine reason "to consummate themselves." "For one

127. Ibid., IX, p. 41.   128. Ibid., IX, p. 34.   129. Ibid., VI, p. 382.
130. Ibid., IX, p. 47.   131. Ibid., IX, p. 45.

thing, ideas do not at all exist only in our heads. Nor is the Idea so impotent that its realization must wait upon our bidding. On the contrary, it is that which is both absolutely active and real. For another, reality is not so corrupt and unreasonable as debased practitioners, barren of mind and despairing of thought, pretend."[132] States, nations, and individuals are "unconscious tools and organs of that internal transaction" in which they themselves pass away whereas spirit moves on to the next higher level.

Like Hegel, Marx too believes in a "world law" that achieves realization. For him, too, history is an orderly process oriented toward a rational final end. In Hegel's philosophy, understanding and realization of the world law are one and the same thing. This identity is made possible because complete knowledge of spirit comes at the end of its self-revelation: the philosophy of spirit is the last and also the highest revelation. But whereas Hegel finds this world law written in the course of human history, Marx abstracts it as a rule determining future history. For him, world history has not come to an end because the social agent of an unfinished secular movement, the proletariat, is still in the process of formation. Hegel, too, was familiar with the proletariat, but did not treat it as a separate social class. In his *Philosophy of Right,* he refers to it as the rabble and an appendage of the third class.[133] His whole social philosophy centers around the middle class, that of Marx around the proletariat. In Hegel's system, the full development of bourgeois society coincides with the last phase of philosophy when spirit grasps itself in its totality, whereas for Marx philosophy comes to an end simultaneously with the prehistory of mankind, a conclusion signaling the beginning of the classless society. The abolition of the proletariat coincides with the end of philosophy.

Marx seeks to escape from the "cage of the Hegelian perspective," especially where the philosophy of history is concerned. He raises two objections to the "Hegelian ideology." He first takes exception to the personification of the world spirit, which he dismisses as a theological, religious leftover from a time when men explained actual events in mythical terms; and, second, he objects to the role Hegel assigned to the idea in history. Marx rejects the "German

132. Ibid., VI, p. 283.
133. Ibid., VIII, §§240–246. See also Sven Helander, *Marx und Hegel* (Jena, 1922), pp. 8–9.

philosophic conception of history" which, by declaring the speculative ideas as the driving force of history, deteriorates into a mere history of philosophy devoid of informational value concerning actual history. In this philosophy man's true being is identified exclusively as spirit. Yet Marx is able to moderate his criticism because Hegel makes spirit differentiate and realize itself in a cycle of self-alienation and return. He thus grants the *Phenomenology of Spirit* the distinction of "containing *all* elements of criticism and often anticipating and elaborating them in a way that goes far beyond Hegel's own point of view."[134] But he also demurs, calling that work an "unclear and mysticizing critique" that fails to take man for what he really is, a conscious natural being compelled to keep struggling for his existence. Still, setting aside Hegel's one-sided definition of man as spirit, Marx praises his insight into the nature of human self-alienation. He acknowledges and accepts from Hegel the trinitarian pattern of the development of spirit. By going through the process of self-alienation and repossession, spirit makes itself into what it inherently is. By externalizing and objectifying itself, spirit learns to know itself, and with this knowledge its alienation is overcome. Hegel looks upon this process as necessary, dictated by the very nature of spirit. What Marx balks at is the quasi-theological definition of man as finite spirit through which infinite spirit becomes conscious of itself. In his view, this definition is ideological in the sense that it consolidates the self-alienation of real man into an autonomous alien power to assume control over him. In contrast, Marx insists on man as a natural, suffering, urge-driven being, though also equipped with an object-directed consciousness and hence with spirit, who objectifies himself in work and alienates himself in the products of his mental and physical efforts. The meaning of history, as we have seen, consists in the removal of the alien power that reigns over him.

For Hegel, too, world history takes the form of self-alienation and self-reconciliation. Spirit is satisfied and finds peace only when it finally knows what it is. Self-alienation is overcome when spirit learns to know itself as alienated, comprehends this state as necessary, and so achieves self-reconciliation. To accomplish this is the work of philosophy, whose task, Marx agrees, is "to recognize necessity concealed under the appearance of contingency."[135] Yet

134. MEGA, III, p. 156.   135. Ibid., VI, p. 290.

Marx differs from Hegel in that he shifts the reappropriation and repossession of man from the sphere of knowledge to revolutionary practice. He objects to the postulate of an "abstract and absolute spirit whose development the mass of mankind, whether consciously or unconsciously, supports."[136] Marx here echoes his now familiar complaint about man being the object and not the master of history. He further repudiates Hegel's personification of the world spirit which makes history appear to be fashioned by a person standing apart. This for Marx is plain mythology unsupported by any historical evidence. "History itself does *nothing,* 'possesses no immense wealth,' 'fights no battles!' It is man, real living man, who does all this, who possesses and fights. It is not 'history' which—as though it were a separate person—uses man as a means to work out its purposes; rather, history is but the activity of man in the pursuit of his purposes."[137] "Man is both the actor and author of his own history."[138]

Contrary to Hegel, Marx does not attribute to ideas the power to form and transform reality. The operant and real power in history is the unified and organized interests of men. "The 'idea' separate from 'interest,'" says Marx, "has always been an object of ridicule."[139] It is possible to make a revolution with a "political idea" if it is backed by "real interests." But when these two do not accord, any revolutionary change is doomed to failure from the start. "Ideas can never lead out of a former state of the world, but only beyond the ideas of that state. Ideas cannot execute anything at all. That requires men who use practical force."[140]

In Marx's theory of history, the polarity of the author's mind reveals itself as a contradiction. The scientific understanding of bourgeois economy and the resultant discovery of the "natural laws of capitalist production" clash with the eschatological prophecy of the politician and the revolutionary practitioner. A paradoxical union of these two poles is brought about in the belief that the

136. Ibid., III, p. 257. On Marx's theory of history see Werner Heider, *Die Geschichtslehre von Karl Marx* (Stuttgart und Berlin, 1931). Marx's philosophy of history as guided by a transfigured idea of the realm of God is the topic of Fritz Gerlich, *Der Kommunismus als Lehre vom tausendjährigen Reich* (Munich, 1920). For another contribution to the same question, see Louis Rougier, *Les Mystiques politiques contemporaines et leurs Incidences internationales* (Paris, 1935), pp. 57 ff.

137. MEGA, III, p. 265.   138. Ibid., VI, p. 184.
139. Ibid., III, p. 253.   140. Ibid., p. 294.

promised paradisaic epoch will occur with the necessity of a natural event. The perfectly correct idea that men make their own history, men "endowed with consciousness, acting from reflection or out of passion, and working toward definite purposes," is invalidated by Engel's assertion—which is quite in keeping with Marx's own thinking—that "the course of history is controlled by general inner laws."[141] If it is true that in the history of society "nothing happens without conscious intent," then it remains to be shown how and through what means these general inner laws take effect. In his role as revolutionary and prophet promising the dawn of a new and final social order to include all mankind, Marx has to appeal to the political will of the proletariat. But as the discoverer of a "great evolutionary law of history" by which, in Engel's opinion, socialism is transformed from a utopia into a science, Marx must maintain that history unfolds lawfully, automatically.

Both Marx's scientific pretension and revolutionary practice go back to the same roots: Hegel's Christian theological metaphysics, on the one hand, and, on the other, the radically secularized hope of a realm of God unmistakenly derived from Judeo-Christian thought. The theological conception underlying Hegel's *Logic,* described as the "presentation of God as in His eternal being He is before the creation of nature and finite spirit," returns in the work of Marx in another form. His materialistic theory of history and society, dressed in the habit of nineteenth-century science, conceals an eschatology. The traditional faith in the redeeming and liberating power of God is replaced by the "knowledge" of the evolutionary law of human history, which restores the original state of man and brings about his real redemption and liberation from the curse of the division of labor. Just as Christ could not justify himself before God or hasten the coming of God's realm by his own work, so economic man cannot influence the necessary course of history that issues in a social state from which class antagonism is excluded. This antagonism is only a characteristic of the prehistory of mankind, whose various concomitants of private property, state power, and embellishing ideologies have been discussed. The realization of a classless society means that the "truth of this world"—the unprejudiced, real knowledge of nature and her laws—will be es-

141. Friedrich Engels, *Feuerbach und der Ausgang der klassischen deutschen Philosophie,* p. 56.

tablished once otherworldly truth—ideologies and the ideological consciousness—has disappeared.[142] Thus, the realm of God takes the form of the classless and stateless condition of the human community; it is the realm of freedom, where free common control over the production and distribution of goods makes possible the realization of many-sided "total man." Engels tries to lend support to this theology of history by findings from modern ethnology. Even if his description of aboriginal communism among primitive peoples were correct, it could hardly do more than give empirical confirmation to what is an essentially metaphysical construction of history.

The law by which the classless society comes into being is based on the dialectical nature of the historical-social process. Every social class necessarily breeds its own negation by developing according to the law inherent in the conditions of its own existence. It creates the economic and political conditions for the rise of a new class that aims at the destruction of the old. This rise and decline of social classes in history is, however, only a special case of the dialectical structure of all life. Like Hegel, who regards the dialectic not as a method of thinking alone, but as a law of being, Marx and Engels assume "in nature the universal presence of a movement of opposites."[143] Every living being is said to exhibit the principle of negation along with the principle of self-preservation. "Negation," to quote Engels, "is of the nature of life itself."[144] Everything is in a state of becoming that includes both affirmation and negation. Applied to the institutions of society and the state, the dialectic, in Marx's words, assumes a function "critical and revolutionary," dissolving things into processes and immersing crystallized forms in the "flux of movement." More specifically, all ideas and institutions, such as justice, the state, and religion claiming general validity and permanence are shown to have a necessary rise and decline. This

142. MEGA, I/1, p. 608.

143. Engels, *Dialektik und Naturwissenschaft*, 2:189. History passes through three stages as defined by the dialectic: the thesis, as represented by original communism; the antithesis, by its negation through private property; and the synthesis, by the negation of the negation, in "communism on a higher level." If the dialectic were the basis of history and nature, the negation of communism would have to be the necessary next step. This, however, is not the case because the classless society is designated the final social state. But the classless society is an illusion because a new aristocracy or leading group arises in the form of a single party with exclusive political power.

144. Ibid., 2:159.

alleged dominance of the dialectical principle in both nature and history is responsible for Marx's belief to have shown in *Capital* the "natural laws of capitalist production."[145] Comparing his method to that of the physicist, he describes "trends that occur with iron necessity"; economic developments are treated as analogous to the processes of natural history. What is surprising in Marx is not that he should assert the inner necessity and inevitability of past history, for Hegel had already done so, but that he should espouse the same thesis about the future development of man.

Marx constructs history from the point of view of a final state of mankind. His method is voluntaristic and dogmatic in that he postulates a certain aim and a will to realize it. For a politician, an agitator, or a revolutionary this is a perfectly natural and legitimate thing to do. Yet Marx, the economic theorist and social historian, claims to have discovered the law according to which the bourgeois social and economic order must necessarily disintegrate and lead to the classless society. Thus, a social state willed by the political agitator because it fulfills the highest ethical requirements, para-doxically realizes itself with "iron necessity," following the evo-lutionary laws of bourgeois society. According to this view, the dialectic must eventually put itself out of action because new societal forms beyond the classless society are inconceivable. The law by which every previous class produced its own negation would cease to operate once the economic and political conditions of proletarian existence were destroyed, for all class rule would then have ceased to exist. This means that the great law of history Marx discovered had run its course—the law according to which "all historical struggles, whether they occur in politics, religion, phi-losophy, or any other region of ideology, are in effect only the more or less distinct expression of struggles of social classes, and the ex-istence and conflict of classes are conditioned in their turn by the degree of development of their economic situation, the manner of their production, and of the exchange associated with it."[146] Here is a law whose very nature consists in doing away with itself by necessarily producing a social state to which it no longer applies. Paradoxically, the law of the movement of history is a law of nature that eliminates itself.

145. *Kapital,* I VI.
146. Friedrich Engels, Foreword to the 3rd ed. of Marx, *Der 18. Brumaire des Louis Bonaparte* in *Auswahl,* 2:323–4.

By the inner polarity of its author who wanted to be a theorist of society and history as well as a political revolutionary and prophet, the Marxian theory of history is condemned to unite two wholly disparate views. This difficulty becomes evident when we investigate the relation between necessity and accident, between lawful occurrence and freedom in history as Engels presents it in the light of Marx's criticism of Hegel's philosophy of history. History, as we have seen, is a process that leads with natural inevitability to a predetermined state. It also exhibits signs of a teleology by realizing a rational purpose; and finally, viewed as the realm of necessity, history is the sum of those political and economic revolutions whose meaning is revealed by the eventual establishment of the realm of freedom. But who, we need to ask, makes up the fabric of this process? The stuff of history, we are told, is "all men endowed with consciousness, acting with reflection or passion, and working for definite purposes." Nothing in history happens "without conscious intent, without desired aim." "Men make their history, no matter what the outcome," Engels writes, "by each pursuing his own consciously willed purposes, and the result of these many wills acting in different directions is what we call history."[147] It may be assumed with a high degree of probability that the variety of particular interests on the part of individuals, groups, classes, and nations will produce a fabric full of tension and conflict. Hence the critical question: how is it that the end result of this multitude of conscious, conflicting wills is predictable and expresses only the general laws that rule human society? Is it possible that an infinite number of individual purposes, which may supplement or cancel each other, can bring about a certain social state and make this appear to be a necessary result? "By and large," so Engels says, history is ruled by chance, at least at the surface. But, he continues, chance is "always governed by hidden inner laws." Still, the object of these hidden laws, and the medium in which they become operative, can only be man. No social institutions or organizations exist independently of man; they are what concrete human beings make of them.

Yet history is made to appear lawful in spite of the accidental and conflicting nature of individual and social wills because Marx and Engels, following Hegel, reduce to practically nothing the impor-

147. Engels, *Feuerbach und der Ausgang,* p. 56.

tance individuals have in the actual historical process. Marx conceives of individual man as a mere function of economic conditions when he writes: "The figures of capitalist and landowner I by no means present in a rosy light. But persons are here treated only as the personification of economic categories, as representatives of certain class relationships and interests. My point of view, which comprehends the development of the economic formation of society as a process of natural history, can, less than any other, hold the individual responsible for the conditions whose creature he socially remains, regardless of how much subjectively he may raise himself above them."[148] It is difficult to rid oneself of the suspicion that this conception of history as a process of natural history and the asserted autonomy of economic conditions so functionalize man that the history-making power Marx ascribes to him becomes wholly illusory. For economic categories are not here used like conceptual schemes that aid in the organization and understanding of the historical-social reality. They represent instead real relations that are subject to continual transformation. Like Hegel, Marx falls into the error of hypostatizing real forces and institutions. As in Hegel the world spirit uses an infinite number of individual wills, interests, and activities for its own special purpose, so in Marx economic categories take their own predictable development over the heads of people. The economic category of private property, for example, is turned into the subject of a development that proceeds on the principle of the dialectic. Like everything else in existence, private property must create its own negations, just as bourgeois society necessarily generates from within itself the proletariat that negates it.

The hypostatizing and mythologizing Marx so severely criticizes in Hegel are easily perceived in his own work, as, for example, in this passage. "Private property," Marx writes most graphically, "drives itself through its economic movement to its own dissolution, but through a development that lies in the nature of the thing, is wholly independent of it, unconscious, and takes place against its will."[149] Even the metaphors of this sentence are odd and raise grave objections. Private property is a social and legal institution that cannot be said to have a will. Economic relations are always relations among men. In the same way, institutions exist because and as long

148. *Kapital,* I, VIII.   149. MEGA, III, p. 206.

as concrete men orient their practical behavior by them. If we finally ask what really is the substratum of this whole automatic development, the answer will have to be that it is the "social," "alien" power generated by human self-alienation. This power, which allegedly forms the real content of religious conceptions and of the autonomy of the mind, and which is also the real condition for the origin of private property, classes, and the state, Marx now makes the sole carrier of the socio-economic movement. The bifurcation and duplication of the world he has previously condemned reappears in a curious form in his own theory of history. True, Marx says that conscious, economically active men make their own history even though they find themselves faced with conditions to whose constraining force they are obliged to adjust. Yet the real object of history, which unrolls according to the immanent dialectic of its substratum, appears to be the hypostatized socio-economic relations, which transform man into a mere product, and turn his consciousness into a mere function, of themselves. It is only on the basis of this hypostasis that Marx is able to construe history as a process of natural lawfulness: above the real world of social-historical conditions, another world is constructed that consists of autonomous conditions born out of man's self-alienation. This bifurcation has all the characteristics of a product of ideology. To point this out is not to deny the real power or efficacy of social conditions, but rather to put us in the way of a true understanding of the historical process.

Some Reflections on Social Philosophy

Marx attempted to comprehend history, economics, and society in terms of man, but he lost sight of this fruitful possibility because his thought got diverted into the dead end of hypostatization through the concept of self-alienation. His basic error, it seems to me, was to find in man's necessary self-objectification through work and in the natural division of labor the source of the hostile alien power that directs itself against him. The state and the hierarchical order of a society are thereby given a negative value from the very moment of their origin. Yet the fact is that men at least partly affirm both self-alienation and the division of labor, just as they do not under all circumstances look upon the state, law, and the hierarchical order as the reflection of an alien order. A consistent application of the principle of the dialectic, especially to the fundamental problems of social philosophy, would have promised considerable success. Marx made some beginnings in this direction, but they remained undeveloped because he spoiled the foundation of his social philosophy and, to a lesser extent of his anthropology, by the introduction of specifically political aspects. From the very start, his social philosophy construes man's relation to state and society in terms of absolute opposition. Social relations are without doubt the products of human self-alienation, but they are not such that man is unable to recognize himself, or feel himself at home, in them. The radical separation between the two assumed by Marx is unable to support any philosophy of society. The relation of the individual to society and the social order is neither one of radical opposition, nor of total agreement.

Though all social relations are conditioned and formed by history, they are also marked by the way they point to the future. Expectation is one of the conditions of the existence of social relationships. The moment men join in permanent communities or meet in relatively fleeting encounters, their behavior is oriented toward aims, be these fixed or vaguely defined, felt or rationally postulated. A social structure may be said to fulfill its inherent meaning if the expected aim is realized.

All social relations have a polar structure because each side lives and acts in the expectation of a certain performance by the other; and because of this, each side is prepared to exhibit the kind of behavior the other counts on. The possibility of exercising dominion, for example, corresponds to the readiness to obey. Whatever particular motives may lie behind the attitudes of either side, it is certain that both attune their behavior to the other side's expectation. Thus, a system of mutual obligations is created in which the claims of both sides are acknowledged. This system is always fluid because the expected fulfillments are never satisfied fully, but find a solution in compromise. The decisive fact, however, is that each side gives relative affirmation to the performance and claim of the other. Thereby it partially identifies with the opposite side, and this participation may run all the way from passive toleration to active consent. The important thing in social relations is the recognition of the reciprocity of services and entitlements. In every social relationship, a person is both obligated to perform a service and entitled to exercise a certain authority. Neither the service nor the authority is a one-sided, simple "compulsion" or "demand"; both rest on mutual recognition. This fact also legitimizes force by which a person who owes a service is compelled to render it. Compulsion is the consequence of the original and presupposed acknowledgement of the service. Terror is a borderline case in which a certain behavior is exacted that is no longer legitimized by even a partial affirmation of what is demanded. That is why in terror a society reaches the point of radical dissociation. Terror exemplifies barbarism because under it man no longer exists as the bearer of authority and services which he himself acknowledges, but solely as the object of a totally alien will.

Authority, even when legitimized by the relative affirmation and the recognition of the person obligated, has an irremovable limit. The forms of recognition change; it may be given habitually, tacitly, or expressly. Affirmation, however, has been qualified as relative because absolute obedience—to refer once more to this example —would mean that a person extinguishes himself as a human being, and also because absolute dominion would extend no longer over man, but would mean the disposal over things. In that case, man would be "denatured." But social relations are relations among men, and social formations are formed with men. Therefore, social formations exhibit not only the lawfulness inherent in themselves, but also another that is inherent in the very nature of man. For this reason, the concrete shape any social formation may take must reckon with the idea of man that sets a limit to it. This is not to say that this limit has never been transgressed in the course of history. Indeed, the history of political constitutions and economic systems records nothing but the unceasing struggle to preserve this limit.

To understand what this boundary means, it is necessary to reflect on the nature of man. Human existence has always been a social existence. That is, the possibility of a social order is coeval with man himself, and this order is based on the idea of justice. Social existence presupposes the possibility of mutual understanding concerning human affairs, and also concerning the events of the world and the phenomena of nature on which human survival depends. Such understanding is based on the idea of truth. Man is the only living creature that makes its whole life the object of conscious, free activity. Because of his own essential instability and his dependence on the outside world, he is infallible neither in the realization of justice nor in the knowledge of truth. The possibility of error and guilt are rooted in his freedom. For this very reason, his freedom must be preserved; for the fixation of what was once, or what is presently held to be, true or just includes the danger of perpetuating falsehood and injustice. He can hope to avoid this only by remaining in motion and orienting his movement by the ideas of justice and truth that are like fixed stars. Freedom, which is essentially political, is the indispensable condition if these ideas are to assume a concrete and verifiable form in human life. Every proposition with a claim to truth and every legal rule with a claim to justice is politically relevant because it must take effect within a certain social order. Men think out loud. An idea that is not expressed, that is not or cannot be communicated, is no idea at all and no knowledge, for knowledge implies communicability. Every idea that is articulated becomes a political idea because it is always objectified within an existing community. That is why the knowledge of justice and truth is tied to freedom. Anyone who thinks, or strives for justice, must assume and affirm freedom as a constitutional right. He must affirm, insist on, and personally defend the legal institutions of the state granting him such freedom. If we want people to think, we must also want their thoughts to be communicated; and we must support a political constitution that confirms the public nature of thought. The argument is unavoidably circular, though this is but another way of describing the indissoluble link between the ideas of truth and justice and the freedom and political constitution that grant them realization. All four elements must come together to build the kind of intellectual and social domicile in which men can at least try to do justice to the idea and vocation of man.

Freedom is indispensable lest a settled social order and a body of received scientific and philosophic opinions frustrate men's adjustment to changing economic conditions and new scientific insights. History is a struggle between the "old" right that intended to be just and the "new" that promises to be. This struggle, which involves suffering and sacrifice, is carried out within the framework of the ideas of truth and justice. Violence and brutality could be avoided or greatly reduced if men were to remind themselves that the loss of freedom of action and moral responsibility puts an end to man's humanity. In this connection we call attention to a grave defect of Marx's work. The formulation of practical social and moral ends implies certain means by which they are to be achieved. The correlation between the two restricts the seemingly infinite number of available means. Marx proposes a social state in which man will be able freely to develop all his capacities, and his means to this end is the social revolution that will destroy, if not the state itself, its use as a political instrument of one class. What he overlooks is that the classless society cannot renounce educating a new elite, and that new class conflicts arise, "only in a different form," whereby the possibility of the misuse of state power on behalf of special groups is reintroduced.[150] Besides, a socialist economy entails an increase in state power that easily bears comparison with any historical experience of theoretical and practical state omnipotence. The realization of freedom, which is for Marx the aim and meaning of history, is thereby reduced to an illusion. It is also clear that the modern development of technology, with its growing requirement of highly specialized work skills, is unable to remove the curse of the division of labor and to allow the development of all-sided man. The inconsistency between Marx's formulation of the end of history and the political, economic means to achieve it results from the contradiction between freedom and compulsion.[151]

All social structures and organizations are the products of men whose physical and mental labor, emotional and intellectual needs they embody. At the same time, every social formation develops, from the moment it is constituted, a momentum and autonomy of its own that is not subject to the individual's arbitrary will. But this autonomy does not imply the existence of a separate, self-realizing social substance. On the contrary, the lawfulness of a social body is actualized in and through the individual when he accepts, consciously or emotionally, the conditions of society's existence as a criterion of his own behavior instead of manipulating society for his private ends. Unless the individual incorporates the life and law of

150. See the valid observations by Valentin Gittermann, *Die historische Tragödie der sozialistischen Idee* (Zürich, 1939), pp. 84–8.

151. On this contradiction, see Elie Halévy, *L'Ere des Tyrannies: Etudes sur le Socialism et la Guerre* (Paris, 1938), pp. 213 ff.; and Wilhelm Röpke, *Die Gesellschaftskrisis der Gegenwart* (Erlenbach-Zürich, 1942), pp. 131 ff.

society into his own life plan, societies could neither exist nor endure. They are always something more and other than the sum of individual wills. Though society rests upon a consensus, its content is not arbitrarily determined or changed. It is in the nature of society to secure and defend the conditions of its own existence even against its members. Its autonomy usually attracts special notice only when individual transgressions and violations occur.

The thesis of the partial identification of the individual with his society runs, however, into some practical difficulties. The question is how, in concrete cases, social organizations and institutions possessed of considerable autonomy and power may convincingly be represented as being actualized in and by individuals. The question arises *vis à vis* enforcible state law, the varying influence of churches and sects, the impact of social classes and political parties, and the ostracism and distinction meted out by various groups. It is equally relevant in the face of the power of cultural tradition and custom, the tyranny of fashion, and the apparent autonomy of bureaucracies. All these institutions and organizations seem to exist independently, without regard to the individual and his will. In the case of the state itself, finally, the attempt to conceive its actions as realized and actualized in individual life appears completely hopeless. The autonomy of the state is so great as to suggest a permanent will wholly independent of the will of individuals who are its current members. Its geographical location dictates political principles that permanently control its position and options in the international field of forces. The emotional and intellectual dispositions of its people form another enduring component of its politics. And there are other collective forces that derive from the state's history and social change which also transcend the individual.

Yet, despite all this evidence of the power and autonomy of social bodies, it cannot be denied that social forms of life without exception are realized in concrete men. So far as they act as "members" of the social body, it is they who incorporate its autonomy into their own conduct. Whenever decisions must be made, in the interpretation and application of the law or in the administration of the state through the bureaucracy, they are made by concrete men on the basis of their partial identification with the idea of the society to which they belong. The decisive and deciding authority of man in all problems concerning the social order stands out most clearly in times of insecurity and crisis. The soundness of a state is tested when the identification of the acting individual with the state is put to its severest test, namely, when he risks his life. Those times in which the existence of the state is threatened demonstrate most vividly the truth of what we have been saying, that only in individuals do societies find their actualization.

IV

Schopenhauer's "True Critique of Reason"

ARTHUR SCHOPENHAUER broke radically with a century-old tradition in Western philosophy that had hardly been impugned before. He abandoned two principal ideas that had dominated philosophic thought about such subjects as God, the world, and man: the Christian, theistic notion of the creation and the rationalist view of human nature. Schopenhauer was well aware of the radical difference of his own thought. With characteristic intellectual honesty, he remarks that his philosophy stands "in undeniable contradiction to the Judaic-Christian doctrine of faith, even though this is nowhere explicitly stated."[1] Proudly conscious of inaugurating a major philosophic change, he also denounces as an error the attempt that goes back to Greek thought "to prove in all natural beings something analogous to human cognition and intellect."[2] "After millennia of philosophy," he thinks he is the first to rectify the relation between will and intellect so as to present the latter as a function of the former.[3] He characterizes as the "ancient and universal basic error" of "all" philosophies the view "that the

1. Letter to F.A. Brockhaus, 3 April 1818.
2. Letter to Julius Frauenstädt, 16 September 1850.
3. Arthur Schopenhauer, *Sämtliche Werke,* ed. and rev. Arthur Hübscher, from the first ed. of the complete works, ed. Julius Frauenstädt (Leipzig, 1937–41), 3:222.

whole of things originated in mind."[4] He maintains, on the contrary, that "nature has produced mind," and that nature is essentially will, "a blind urge, a wholly irrational, unmotivated drive."[5]

Schopenhauer rejects the Christian idea of creation and with it the view that man is made in the image of God. He renounces, too, the view that man is originally endowed with, and guided by, reason. His analysis of the human mind destroys the dogma of the "original rationality of our nature;" and reason, so we remind ourselves, used to imply not only a reliable faculty for knowledge, but an inviolable law of moral behavior. Schopenhauer's philosophy, which reached its final form already in the 1820's, treats human intellect and reason in a way that was to have great significance for his successors, especially for Nietzsche. Reason is for him merely a "tool."[6] That is why he opposes Kant's *Critique of Pure Reason,* which in his opinion should have been entitled "Critique of Occidental Theism," with his own "Notes toward a future, true critique of reason."[7]

The point of Schopenhauer's "true critique" is that it denies reason any competence in matters of religion and morality. Reason does not contain any timeless, universal principles of ethics and affords no insight into the origin of the world. It is nothing but the "capacity to form concepts," the power to abstract from concrete images ideas of a higher, more general order. These permit man to make plans for future action and to anticipate behavior, both his

---

4. *Werke,* 6:101.

5. Ibid., 3:407. Schopenhauer's metaphysic of the will, which is influenced by Fichte and Schelling, must, however, be related to that aspect of intellectual history concerned with the problem of the connection between intellect and will. On this, see Heinz Heimsoeth, *Die sechs grossen Themen der abendländischen Metaphysik* (Berlin, 1934), pp. 249, 304.

6. *Werke,* 7:91. Concerning Schopenhauer's opposition to the post-Kantian metaphysics of the rational foundation of the world, see the following works: Georg Simmel, *Schopenhauer und Nietzsche,* 3rd ed. (Munich and Leipzig, 1923), p. 28; Johannes Volkelt, *Arthur Schopenhauer,* 5th ed. (Stuttgart, 1923), pp. 170 ff. Volkelt follows Simmels' excellent analysis. Ernst Troeltsch, *Der Historismus und seine Probleme* (Tübingen, 1922), pp. 136–7. Troeltsch is correct in saying that Schopenhauer began the destruction of the older concept of humanity by moving his value system "out of the tradition of European humanity, which was still taken for granted by Kant, Goethe, Hegel, and Comte. See also Erich Frank, "Schopenhauer und Nietzsche," in *Wissen, Wollen, Glauben* (Zurich and Stuttgart, 1955).

7. *Arthur Schopenhauers handschriftlicher Nachlass,* ed. Eduard Grisebach, 2nd ed., rev. (Leipzig, n.d.), 4:34. Hereafter cited as *Nachlass.*

own and that of others. They also serve mutual understanding and the communication of knowledge. Concepts are indispensable tools of science and philosophy; they help to store knowledge, but do not create it. Because of reason's instrumental nature, it is neither good nor bad; moral qualifications derive from the uses to which it is put. At first, Schopenhauer did not distinguish clearly between intellect and reason. In notes made during his student years at Berlin, he compared the intellect to a predatory beast that should be killed because once it is fully developed, it will not be appeased and encroaches on domains over which it has no claim. "What lies outside the intellect's domain has no relation to it, it is nothing, and has no power over it; if the intellect is to be killed, it will have to be a suicide. [Kant calls this 'setting a limit to itself.'] The suicide of the intellect is—the critique of reason."[8]

According to Schopenhauer, will is the essence of the world. Will "urges and drives toward existence, to organic existence or life if possible, and after that, to the highest possible enhancement of it."[9] Will is the original power—nonrational, unconscious, never satisfied, and ever restless—which always and everywhere aims at asserting, increasing, and propagating life. Since man, too, is essentially will, through which he becomes conscious of himself, "everyone wants everything for himself, wants to possess or at least to dominate everything, and what resists him, he wants to destroy."[10] It is this will that constitutes the true, indestructible nature of man, taking precedence, in consciousness, over the intellect "which appears throughout as secondary, subordinate, and conditional."[11] Though manifest in all parts of nature, will develops a cognitive capacity only on the animal and human level. The need for knowledge arises with mobile organisms that must orient and maintain themselves among a multitude of living things. Intellect is therefore primarily and originally an instrument of the struggle for existence, a "weapon" required by the will. It does not form any part of the essence of the world, which is without reason, but is solely an accidental property of human nature. Intellect is produced by will, our essential nature, and being "a product, it is a parasite on the organism because it does not directly enter into its internal functioning, but serves its self-preservation by regulating its relations to

8. Ibid., p. 17.   9. Ibid., 3:399.
10. Ibid., 2:391.   11. Ibid., 3:222.

the outside world."[12] "As a rule," Schopenhauer writes, "knowledge remains at the disposal of the will, which it was born to serve, having grown from it like the head from the rump."[13] As the will is without knowledge, so the intellect is without will. The apposite metaphor to describe the relationship between the two is "the strong blind man carrying the lame man on his shoulders."[14] Since will is the master and intellect the slave, it is evident that the latter can properly fulfill its knowledge function only as long as the will is silent. Only the disinterested intellect that looks at the world without desiring anything can serve as a faithful mirror or useful instrument of objective knowledge. Enhancement of intelligence involves "separating intellect from will." A complete separation occurs only in man, whose intellect, faced with greater demands and being incessantly exercised, produces a "free excess" capacity and thereby "becomes truly aware of the world, that is, grasps it with perfect objectivity and then creates, composes, thinks accordingly."

Though Schopenhauer emphasizes that the intellect is inherently "bent on truth," it is in effect almost constantly and badly deflected from this aim by the will. Because intellect derives from blind, unreasonable will, it naturally tends to "pollute knowledge." It can never deny being in the service of the will, and the impairment it thereby suffers becomes obvious when the will becomes in any way interested or engaged in an intellectual undertaking. The will, Schopenhauer says, is the "secret antagonist of the intellect."[15] Any noticeable excitement of the will disturbs the functioning of the intellect by directing its attention to things that are the object of desire, and by forcing it to choose from the multitude of impressions only those that appeal to the will while neglecting all the rest. The will, "when itself aroused, obstructs and paralyzes the intellect, diverts it from its own object to what at the moment happens to be the favorite object of the will, bribes it unawares." The result of intellectual activity is thereby falsified. Only at its highest level, when freed from this servitude, does the intellect become capable of objective knowledge. Still, owing to its origin, this capacity is secondary. In case of conflict, it may be presumed that the will forces the intellect back into its primary function, which consists not in the true knowledge of things, but in sustaining and enhancing the will's ex-

---

12. Ibid., 3:224. 13. Ibid., 2:209.
14. Ibid., 3:233. 15. *Nachlass,* 4:386.

istence. Thus, the intellect is forever interfered with, and our power of judgment is distorted by inclinations and interests that find expression in the prejudices of social classes, nations, and religions.

To put the intellect in a subordinate position and to regard it as a product and tool of the will, without any power to influence it, has important consequences for anthropology and for political and legal philosophy. When intellectual activity is directed to social questions, the effect is both concealing and revealing. Because of their known dependence on the will, knowledge and judgment are suspect of reflecting merely the interests of certain groups or classes. As Schopenhauer says, human judgment "is mostly corrupt and pronounced in favor of some party or class."[16] Interest turns judgments into prejudices, and objectivity bows to what is advantageous. At this point, Schopenhauer's theory harks back to Bacon's theory of idols.[17] Philosophy is assigned the task of revealing the subjective interest concealed in prejudices in order to neutralize their corruptive influence on objective understanding. A tendency to militant enlightenment inspires Schopenhauer's thought.

This exposition of the relation of intellect to will would be incomplete if we left out of account the general role Schopenhauer assigns to consciousness in the will's understanding of itself. He repeatedly makes the point that the world does not lie, "that the character of the world is perfectly honest."[18] Error and deception make their appearance only in consciousness. Only a conscious being is capable of deceiving itself as well as others, of forging its real motives by pretending to act according to what society qualifies as moral. "All that is original and therefore authentic in man acts, like the forces of nature, *unconsciously*," whereas to consciousness attaches a suspicion of disingenuousness. It is able to cover up the plain, direct operation of the will, be that good or evil. Knowingly or not, it creates a false appearance that makes it difficult for us to pass moral judgment.

It is in the nature of reason to replace concrete individual motives with abstract concepts. It is also capable of depicting our life as an unbroken chain of decisions and consequences, letting us anticipate the results of future resolutions and so to regulate our behavior. "Reason is the capacity for all-inclusion" and hence the cornerstone

16. *Werke*, 5:479.   17. Ibid., 3:244.   18. *Nachlass*, 4:18, 19, 24.

of human freedom. "It enables us to see our whole life, action, and thought as unified, to have an overview, and to act in accordance with maxims."[19] By weighing and comparing motives, we acquire a capacity for prudence and circumspection, which is "the root of all our theoretical and practical accomplishments, of our care for the future, and our methodical procedure in every enterprise, including co-operation toward a single aim."[20] But prudence has a seamy side, which consists in the dissembling of motives for the sake of creating a false appearance. In contrast to nature, "which never lies," consciousness is the sphere of deception. "Everything that is conscious has been improved upon, is intentional, and so passes into affectation or fraud."[21] Fraud or deceit, according to Schopenhauer, is necessary and morally justifiable in the interest of human collaboration, "for much that is evil and bestial in our nature needs to be covered over."[22]

It appears, therefore, that the intellect, in addition to being the servant of the will, is employed in the production of masks. Most human views and convictions are masks. Schopenhauer calls "our civilized world nothing but a great masquerade."[23] "As our body is cloaked in garments, our mind is wrapped in lies. Our talk and our doing, in fact our entire being, are mendacious. One can only sometimes guess at our true conviction behind the mask, like the real shape of the body underneath the garments."[24] And once more: "There is only one mendacious being in the world, and that is man."[25] Will by itself being whole and uncorrupted, it is in consciousness and with the aid of the intellect that the lie makes its appearance. To quote Schopenhauer: "Nature, reality, never lies; on the contrary, it is through it that truth is made true." The source of the lie is "always man's intent to extend the rule of his will over other individuals."[26]

The analysis of Schopenhauer's conception of the intellect needs to be carried one step further. As has been shown, the original use of the intellect as a tool and weapon of the will did not entirely prevent it from developing a capacity for objective knowledge, and it is owing to this development that Schopenhauer's world-will achieves self-consciousness. Only when the knower "cuts himself loose from

19. Ibid., 4:146–7, 22–3.   20. *Werke*, 1:101.   21. Ibid., 6:637.
22. Ibid., 5:487.   23. Ibid., 6:224.   24. Ibid., 5:447, fn.
25. Ibid., 6:617.   26. *Nachlass*, 4:162.

the service of the will" and is transformed into a subject pure and devoid of will, has the truth found its proper organ. It is now possible for the intellect to expose the will to life in its insatiable greed and brutality as well as to confess its own lies and prejudices committed in the service of the will. Through self-analysis and the renunciation of his will, the knowing subject is able to enlighten himself. More broadly speaking, it is in philosophy that the will strips off its veil and comprehends itself as the one and all. In philosophy the masquerade of the world is exposed because the intellect has here at last acquired the requisite intellectual honesty. On this level, it is possible also to prepare the foundation of a new morality. Like other distinguished European moralists, Schopenhauer insists on the abolishment of human self-deception and prejudice as the indispensable condition of ethics. "There are no venerable lies," he declares; "we want the truth and will proceed remorselessly with the vivisection of lies."[27]

Schopenhauer's metaphysic is, however, flawed by contradiction. The vivisection of lies and the unmasking of prejudices are presented as the work of the intelligence, which, in contrast to the world-will, he praises for being "guiltless" and "pure." In view of this exceptional attainment, the originally limited, servile function of the intellect and its derivation from the will must appear doubtful. In one passage Schopenhauer describes the intellect as a gift or "endowment" bestowed on man "by heaven—that is, by eternal, mysterious destiny and its necessity."[28] He seems to be referring to his idea that only through the philosophic self-knowledge of the will can deliverance from the will—the meaning and aim of cosmic evolution—be effected. The irrationalistic, voluntaristic monism with which he began appears to have been abandoned in favor of a dualism in which will and intelligence figure as the two equal attributes of the world substance. The contradictions that beset his analysis of the intellect have often been commented on. The intellect in its capacity for causal thinking is presented as a condition of the multiplicity of things, but it is also the product of the will to life, indispensable to it at a certain phase of its development.[29] It is not explained how the non-rational will can produce reason from within

27. Ibid., 4:252.   28. *Werke,* 5:491, fn.
29. For criticisms of Schopenhauer, see the following works: Otto Liebmann, *Kant und die Epigonen* (Stuttgart, 1865), pp. 157 ff.; Wilhelm Windelband, *Geschichte der neueren Philosophie,* 8th ed. (Leipzig, 1922), 2:376, gives an excellent

itself, or how reason "suddenly" breaks the fetters that chain it to the will. Finally, it is unclear how the will can be purpose-oriented since purpose is a concept pertaining to the intellect.

It is unnecessary to analyze these contradictions further. Instead, we summarize Schopenhauer's conception of the intellect as follows:

(1) Created by the will as its servant, the intellect must function as a tool, yet at the same time aim at objective knowledge.

(2) The intellect's ability to know the truth is continually, though not absolutely, prejudiced by the will to life. The latter prescribes the intellect's aims and influences its choice of means; and it generally determines that the world, including social ethic, religion, the legal and economic systems, be shaped according to its interest.

(3) Following Bacon's example, Schopenhauer designates as prejudices the sum total of all ideas biased by interest. The liberation from prejudices is accomplished by an uncompromising philosophy that establishes the truth on the "plane of reflection and candor."

---

discussion of Schopenhauer's dependence on post-Kantian philosophy; and Ernst Cassirer, *Das Erkenntnisproblem in der Philosophie und Wissenschaft der neuern Zeit,* 2nd ed. (Berlin, 1923), 3:430.

V

Nietzsche's Philosophy as the "Art of Mistrust"

Nietzsche's Influence and
Some Interpretations of His Work

NIETZSCHE'S philosophy and its influence have been ill-starred. For over half a century those who have tried to interpret his work have come to no agreement. The aspects from which it has been viewed and the practical purposes for which it has been claimed have varied. About its influence there is no unanimity even among professionals, apart from the trite observation that it has been profound and almost incalculable. And how few could resist adorning their own intentions with fragments and baubles taken from his writings?

Though a number of people think they are his legitimate intellectual descendants, their claims are highly dubious. In any case, such questions are to be decided when we know what the essence of his philosophy is. That requires not only a comprehensive knowledge of his work and how it evolved through different stages, but familiarity with the effects it had on different periods. The history of these effects is best suited to make us conscious of the possibilities for misinterpretation and misuse contained in the work itself. It can also sharpen our sense for the power of the written word and the responsibility of the thinker. Nietzsche's work is ambiguous and contradictory; it combines, in ways that are strangely captivating as well as repelling, so many conflicting elements—vision and delusion, sublime spirituality and cynical brutality, abysmal depth and exalted provocation, overwhelming insight and noncommittal aesthetic playfulness, superior serenity and cramped turgidity—as to give rise to a wild profusion of interpretations and initiate a veritable history of misunderstandings.[1] Nietzsche, who had extolled a perspectival philosophy, seemed almost to encourage the wealth of perspectives his interpreters applied to him, for he hid his true face behind many masks, right down to his collapse. It was possible to refute every thesis by a counter-thesis out of his own writings. Where, then, was the synthesis, and did a "whole" Nietzsche exist at all? A unifying interpretation clearly presents a problem because the unity of the work and of its author is in question.

Nietzsche and the political philosophy of the twentieth century is a topic worthy of reflection. Though he was not a first-rate political theorist, he did supply the early part of this century with some effective political slogans. In the view of one of his most faithful disciples, Oswald Spengler, he also paved the way for the "ultimate understanding" of historical life. In this opinion, Nietzsche's merit consists in having provided, by his "grand" critique of morals, a means of measuring the value of historical moralities by their success, rather than by some supposedly "true" morality. If the will to power justifies itself by its success, a universal theory of ethics supported by philosophical argument becomes superfluous. Then, too, politics and history are relieved of "doctrines" and "principles," "ideologies" and "reformist plans," all declared to be reflections of social sickness and decline. In Spengler's words, Nietzsche "has shown the most history-hungry people of the world what history really is. His legacy consists in the task of living history accordingly."[2]

With regard to twentieth-century totalitarianism, Nietzsche may be cited as an opponent or an advocate. Like Jacob Burckhardt, he foresaw and warned against the all-powerful modern state made necessary by the welfare of the masses. From this point of view, nineteenth-century socialism was nothing but the "fantastic younger

1. Gisela Deesz, *Die Entwicklung des Nietzsche-Bildes in Deutschland* (Würzburg, 1933). The author appears to have neglected the book of Lou Andreas-Salomé, for which see fn. 12 below.

2. This is the interpretation of Spengler, who calls himself Nietzsche's disciple, presented in a talk on "Nietzsche und sein Jahrhundert" (1924), contained in *Reden und Aufsätze* (Munich, 1937). The passages cited in the text are from pp. 122, 124.

brother of an almost extinct despotism" aimed at the destruction of the individual or his reduction to "an efficient member of the communal state." Socialism was said to "desire a Caesarist, absolute type of state" requiring the abject submission of its citizens. To the battle cry "as much state as possible," the aristocratic individualism of Nietzsche opposed the opposite of "as little state as possible."[3] Yet it is just as easy to show that certain of his concepts, symbols, and postulates—perhaps because they were misunderstood and torn out of context—helped substantially in the ideological preparation and actual building of the total state. For its apology and glorification Nietzschean ideas and phrases could be resorted to very nicely. The doctrine of the will to power, for example, which affirmed harshness and truculence as an excess of vitality, had a catastrophic effect unforeseen by Nietzsche. He was generally not one of those willing and able to estimate the consequences of their visions and ideas, though he did fear that "mischief" would be done with his work. He intended to permit only chosen and exceptional men to invoke his name.

The fact is, however, that Nietzsche left a whole arsenal of metaphors, insights, and intellectual weapons that invited extensive unscrupulous abuse for which he must himself be held responsible. He disdained to concern himself, in his visions, with the real conditions of political and economic order in the nations of the world. His rejection of democratic liberalism, socialism, and nationalism is not balanced by any constructive principles with which a new social order might be constructed. This defect is not remedied by his call for a "morality with the intent to breed a ruling caste";[4] for an elite may lead only if supported by certain conceptions of social order unless, of course, one regards the mere possession of power a sufficient justification for a new aristocracy. Nietzsche assumes that the shape of future social orders will be determined by the opposition between elite and mass. The gradual vulgarization of culture, made evident by the renunciation of individual responsibility and autonomy in favor of material security and entertainment provided by the absolute state, seemed to him inescapable, and he therefore

3. Friedrich Nietzsche, *Gesammelte Werke,* Musarion ed. (Munich, 1923–29), 7:334–5. Hereafter cited as *Werke.* "The democratization of Europe is also an involuntary arrangement for the breeding of tyrants, taking the word in every sense, including the intellectual," ibid., 15:197.

4. *Werke,* 19:315.

thought a world-wide ruling caste, legitimized by the creation of a new culture, was required. But the polarity between "herd-animal" and "lead-animal" yields no organizing principle.[5] Every society has a leading group; the question is for what kind of order such a group asks respect, and by what political means it secures consent to its policies and general leadership. On such matters Nietzsche never clearly expressed himself.[6] Though believing "global government" to be near at hand, he only lamented the "complete want of principles for it."[7] He prided himself on being the initiator of the "grand politics" with Europe and the world as its field, and for having declared war on "brutish nationalism" and the "paltry provincialism of petty states." But, preoccupied with the "lawgivers of the future" who would realize the aims he saw shining in the distant future, he neglected the concrete problems involved in forming a new state.

These deficiencies became apparent when a politically inspired in-

5. Friedrich Mess, *Nietzsche als Gesetzgeber* (Leipzig, 1930). The author attempts to give a comprehensive exposition of Nietzsche's philosophy of law and politics, and to prove that the German philosophy of law has not yet recognized what a great thinker it has in him. Such merits as the book has lie in the first part. The second part is, in the author's own words, an "audacity." And, indeed, he fails to clarify and give concreteness to Nietzsche's vague notions about law, government, and world order.

6. The same failure afflicts Walter Lemke, *Die Entwicklung des deutschen Staatsgedankens bei Friedrich Nietzsche* (Leipzig, 1941). As already stated in the text, to proclaim a new nobility or elite tells us nothing about what kind of political order is wanted. Lemke admits that Nietzsche did not "definitely" project a future German state; the same vagueness surrounds Nietzsche's ideas about the future political order of Europe and the world. Lemke does not get beyond such statements as that the "idea of breeding a strong master-race" is the "central fire of his later philosophy of the state," "the philosophic deed by which his metaphysical principle of the will to power receives its first political realization," p. 56. Equally uninformative is Kurt Kassler, *Nietzsche und das Recht* (Munich, 1941), who simply assets that Nietzsche's ideas about right are related to those of national socialism. p. 108. Jean-Eduard Spenlé, *Nietzsche et le Problème Européen* (Paris, 1943), too, has to admit that the philosopher's ideas about the "good European" and the legislation of the future are "fairly vague and unsettled." However, he believes that Nietzsche did not intend to offer any "political doctrine or European statute," but regarded as his central problem "the cultural and eduational values that portend and form the future," p. 245. This view is scarcely tenable. The cultural and educational values of the future are meant by Nietzsche to be attributable to a ruling caste. If the educational system is to be of any use, the aims it serves need to be clearly stated. But neither the aims nor the means receive that attention from Nietzsche.

7. *Werke*, 19:327.

terpretation of his work pulled Nietzsche right into the "grand politics" of the twentieth century. His secret divinations of a new eschatology about the "future lords of this world" and the "hierarchy of values" were now treated as precise prognostications of current political and intellectual movements. He acquired the dubious fame of having found his "true fulfillment" in this period: National-Socialist writers described him as the "best trail blazer of the new events."[8] In their judgment, fascism and national socialism were the rightful heirs of Nietzsche. To those mindful of his *entire* work, and not seduced by certain aphorisms and expressions, such as the "blond beast," this political exploitation was a grotesque abuse.[9] It

8. The appalling misuse of Nietzsche for Fascist and National-Socialist purposes is illustrated by two German writers of the 1930ies: Friedrich Giese, *Nietzsche: Die Erfüllung* (Tübingen, 1934), and Richard Oehler, *Friedrich Nietzsche und die deutsche Zukunft* (Leipzig, 1935). Neither conveys any insight; both are indicative of the decay of the critical mind at a time when ideological adjustment to the prevailing political powers was deemed advisable. Giese looks on the first third of this century as having brought Nietzsche to "fulfillment." Mussolini is the historical figure who will forever remind us of Nietzsche, and Fascism is the European political reflection of his doctrines. His philosophic heritage is said "to permeate the Third Reich," too. The breeding of a "daring, dominant race," we read, "was written in 1886, but lived in 1933 and subsequent years," p. 150. Compared with Giese, Oehler is concerned only with demonstrating Nietzsche's agreement with, and realization in, National Socialism. Special emphasis is given to Nietzsche's militaristic utterances. His ideas on education and breeding are said to have been faithfully embodied in Nazi cultural policies. Oehler displays astonishing vulgarity in discussing Nietzsche's complex position on the Jewish question. Since he was responsible for the two-volume index to the Musarion edition of Nietzsche's works, he could not help knowing what Nietzsche wrote about the Jews. Yet his absolute rejection of anti-Semitism and his pro-Jewish utterances are suppressed. Richard Maximilian Lonsbach has presented a Jewish view of this whole question in *Nietzsche und die Juden* (Stockholm, 1939). Exaggerating on the other side, the book is only partly satisfactory. Finally, we mention Alfred Baeumler's article, "Nietzsche und der Nationalsozialismus" (1934), reprinted in *Studien zur deutschen Geistesgeschichte,* 3rd ed. (Berlin, 1943). Baeumler sees the "deeper relation" between Nietzsche and Nazism in their radical rejection of bourgeois life and its morality, which Nietzsche replaced with the philosophy of the will to power, the quivalent of the philosophy of politics, p. 282.

9. See Edmond Vermeil, *Doctrinaires de la Révolution Allemande, 1918-1938* (Paris, 1938), who distinguishes carefully between the general European character of Nietzsche's work and "Pan-Germanism." Spengler, Moeller van den Bruck, and National Socialism are criticized for "distorting Nietzsche ruthlessly and taking from him everything that can lend support to their militant racism," p. 33.

should be mentioned, however, that to certain national socialists, Nietzsche's political views were suspect. His criticism of imperial Germany, its nationalism and materialism, seemed to them to imply hostility to the imperial ambitions of national socialism as well.[10] After all, he had raised the question of whether the military success in the war of 1870–71 was not a foreboding of the "extirpation of the German spirit in favor of the German 'realm.'"

From the political aspects of his writings, we pass now to the philosophic substance of his work and, more particularly, to his criticism of the Christian religion and morality and to his critique of reason. Nietzsche was convinced that the moral ideas of Western culture had lost their force and meaning, and that this bankruptcy announced the inevitable advent of nihilism. Though he himself embodied the "nay-saying spirit" and promoted the process of destruction, he also attempted to find a way out of mere negation. As he put it in a letter to his friend Erwin Rohde, he hoped to find the "exit and the hole through which one reaches the 'something.'"[11] To surmount nihilism and to arrive at a new "affirmation of life in spite

10. Nietzsche's hostility toward the German *Reich* is the central topic of Christoph Steding, *Das Reich und die Krankheiten der europäischen Kultur* (Hamburg, 1938). This National-Socialist author accuses Nietzsche of "deviation" from the central regulative power of Europe as ideologically represented in the imperialistic concept of the Third Reich. He begins his book with an attack on the autonomous "German"-Teutonic marginal states of Scandinavia, Denmark, Holland, and Switzerland, all of which are said to be guilty of "deviation" from, and hostility to, the *Reich*. Culture, objectivity, and neutrality are denounced as concepts typical of small states, and for having initiated the decay of the idea of a powerful *Reich* in Germany. This decay is then related to the "military defeat of 1918 and the subsequent rise of a specifically unmilitaristic, even antimilitaristic, un-Prussian, and unmanly type of man who . . . found his possibilities realized in the Weimar Constitution and the politics of Locarno," p. 56. Nietzsche is described as the exponent of this hostility to, and flight from, the idea of a greater German empire, having himself been infected by the Swiss mentality. Steding's book is typical of a political science that frames and trims its material according to predetermined political goals. It is not by accident that it gained the consent of Carl Schmitt, the man who propounded the politicizing of science and scholarship and for nearly twenty years "justified" the acts of whoever happened to be in power in Germany with, of course, strictly "scientific" arguments. Schmitt's comments on Steding are to be found in his book *Positionen und Begriffe im Kampf mit Weimar-Genf-Versailles, 1923–1939* (Hamburg, 1940), pp. 271 ff.

11. Letter to Erwin Rohde, 23 May 1887.

of its most severe and difficult problems" was the strong desire of his basically religious nature.[12] Nietzsche's work contains both criticism and prophecy, and one has the impression that his assault on Christianity increased in vehemence as he became aware of and intoxicated by his own mission. Whether he succeeded in creating a philosophic substitute for the lost Christian faith is doubtful. We

12. Concerning the religious aspect of Nietzsche's thought, the following works are instructive. Lou Andreas-Salomé, in *Friedrich Nietzsche in seinen Werken* (Dresden, 1894), anticipated important perspectives of present-day Nietzsche interpretations. The philosophic unity of his system is set forth in aphoristic fashion, and the psychology of religion is rightly regarded as providing the point of view for a proper understanding of it. Nietzsche is recognized for what he was, namely, the herald of a new message of salvation after the traditional forms of the Western religious sense were exhausted. In this role, he is said, however, to have been diverted into self-deification as into a substitute for the God that had been lost. See pp. 38, 40, 41. Important documents from Salomé's papers about this subject were first published by Erich F. Podach in *Friedrich Nietzsche und Lou Salomé: Ihre Begegnung, 1882* (Zurich, 1937). This woman was struck right away by Nietzsche's religious concern, and she is quoted as referring to his "religious nature," to his having been the "promulgator of a new religion" who wanted "to convert, not to instruct," pp. 142, 144, 146. Similar comments came from such men as Jacob Burckhardt, Karl Hillebrand, and Erwin Rohde. In a letter to Marie Baumgartner, Burckhardt already in 1877 mentioned the "religious tone of apostles characteristic of Nietzsche." This letter was first published by Edgar Salin in *Jacob Burckhardt und Nietzsche* (Basel, 1938), p. 242. For Hillebrand's judgment from the year 1883, see C.A. Bernoulli, *Franz Overbeck und Friedrich Nietzsche* (Jena, 1908), 2:487. Rohde wrote to Overbeck in 1886 that Nietzsche looked on himself, "openly and secretly," as the model of the hoped-for Messiah. See E.F. Podach, *Gestalten um Nietzsche* (Weimar, 1932), p. 56. Emphatic confirmation for Nietzsche's opinion of himself as a religious messenger is provided by the organization of all his posthumous writings from 1880 on that forms the basis of Friedrich Würzbach's book *Das Vermächtnis Friedrich Nietzsches* (Salzburg, Leipzig, 1940). In praising Nietzsche's legacy as the "New Testament of a new humanity," Würzbach confuses, however, the philosopher's subjective claim with his objective achievement. One may well recognize his criticism of Christianity as at least in part justified, and yet question whether his ideas about eternal recurrence and the superman will be able to satisfy the religious needs of Western men. Peter Gast's enthroning of *Thus Spake Zarathustra* as the "bible for exceptional men" has hardly been effective. A fair presentation of Nietzsche's struggle with the problem of religion is given by Walter Nigg, *Religiöse Denker: Kierkegaard, Dostoevski, Nietzsche, Van Gogh* (Bern, 1942). He calls Nietzsche the "religious revolutionary who embodies the metaphysical fate of modern man," p. 205. We must not omit, however, Overbeck's testimony about Nietzsche: "Seriously religious he was as little as I." He was a "reformer of culture (somewhat like Rousseau), but not of religion." Quoted from C.A. Bernoulli, 1:217, 218.

need not pursue this question since we are concerned primarily with his philosophic achievement.

Still, Nietzsche's epistemology and metaphysic are closely related to his criticism of religion. He argued that contemporary philosophy works with concepts that have their origin in untenable religious beliefs. This holds true especially for teleological concepts as applied to nature and history. Such categories as purpose, being, and unity are in his opinion "crooked ways to back-worlds and false divinities."[13] They have nothing to do with the real world, which realizes no purpose, has no being and no unity. Its essence is eternal flux, in which individual "quanta of will" struggle against each other. This insight replaces man's erroneous conception about the world, and when it becomes general intellectual property, mankind lapses into nihilism. "The cause of nihilism is the belief in reason; we have measured the value of the world with categories that apply to a purely fictive one."[14] Even though religious motives entered into Nietzsche's critique of reason, there can be no doubt that he sought to give it a philosophic and scientific foundation. Generally speaking, to understand Nietzsche well, it is important to bear in mind both the religious and rationalistic components of his thought. The new "truth," the affirmation of life he proclaims, is a message of salvation for which he attempts to provide rational and scientific confirmation.

The Biological and Sociological Critique of Reason

Nietzsche's criticism of the human capacity for knowledge continued unbroken from his earliest to his last writings. The first scattered indications are contained in the fragment *Critique of the Philosophy of Schopenhauer,* which presumably dates from 1867, and the notes on *The Teleology of Kant* (1868). They are then unified in notes prepared for an essay on The Philosopher (1872), and especially in the reflections *On Truth and Lying in the Non-moral Sense* (1873); and from there the line of this criticism continues down to his very last writings, such as *The Will to Power,* which develop

13. *Werke,* 18:16.   14. Ibid., p. 17.

the early suggestions more fully and consequentially. The point of departure for all this was Schopenhauer, whose "true" critique of reason aimed to separate reason from religious associations formed when the dogmas of the Christian faith penetrated Greek philosophy. "By undertaking to interpret the world out of itself," as Wilhelm Dilthey put it, Schopenhauer cast doubt on the supernatural origin of the instruments of knowledge. "None of the concepts of God retains any power over him."[15] Reason for him was no longer a part of human nature, with which the creator had endowed it. However, Schopenhauer still held that the structure of human reason as manifested in the formal conditions of thought was unchanging, and that the same was true of the structure of experience because it was based on stable properties of the intellect and sensual perception.

Nietzsche radicalizes Schopenhauer's critique of reason by reducing the entire instrumentality of knowledge to its biological foundations; and he also extends it to logic and the formal conditions of thought left untouched by his predecessor. Nietzsche dissolves the stable forms and laws of logic into manifestations of the will to power. It is true that Schopenhauer, too, described intellect and reason as products of the will, but he still held that man developed a "superfluity" of cognitive power that put a limit to domination by the will. Nietzsche, however, recognizes no such limit. To him, all forms of knowing reflect the will to power, which is not interested in universal truth, but rather in the control of things for the sake of life enhancement. Thus, the question of truth becomes a question of power.

Nietzsche first applies the critique of reason to nature and history, and in both cases he takes issue with the concept of purpose. Evidence of a universal teleology would be tantamount to evidence of a universal reason, but no such evidence is obtainable in nature or history. In nature the attempt founders on her obvious inefficiency, the fact that only by an immense waste of life can species be maintained and evolved. "Nature is ruled by chance, or the opposite of purposefulness."[16] Teleology and the idea of a higher reason must

15. Wilhelm Dilthey, "Die deutsche Philosophie in der Epoche Hegels," *Gesammelte Schriften*, 4:262.

16. *Werke*, 1:420. Nietzsche's ideas on teleology are contradictory and conceptually unclear.

therefore be rejected. Thus far, Nietzsche's critique is based on the identification of reason and purpose. From this, he advances to the insight that the interpretative mechanism employed in the explanation of natural phenomena is a product of human organization. "Teleology, like mechanism, is a way of perceiving,"[17] imposed by us on nature. Such imposition is inevitable, but it is also wrong.

One easily recognizes in these ideas the influence of F.A. Lange, of whose *History of Materialism* Nietzsche said that "it offered infinitely more than its title promised."[18] He took over from Lange the views that the sensual world is a product of our organization; that our visible bodily organs, like all other parts of the phenomenal world, are merely pictures of an object unknown to us; and that the transcendental ground of our organization remains as obscure to us as the things that act upon us.[19] Under Lange's influence, Nietzsche came to doubt that Schopenhauer had penetrated to a knowledge of the thing itself. He now regards the expression of the will to life as a metaphor all too clearly reflecting the anthropomorphic structure of our understanding of the world; and the belief that "thought reaches into the deepest chasms of being and is able to know, or even to correct it," he dismisses as "a profound delusion."[20]

But Nietzsche agrees with Schopenhauer's definition of the intellect as a tool employed in the service of life. It is, he says, a "resource bestowed upon the most unfortunate, delicate, and transient of creatures."[21] The intellect as servant of the will assumes two particular roles, the first of which is to seduce us into affirming life. The "frightful struggle" for existence in which all living creatures devour each other, and the "recognition of the absolute illogic of the world order" produce in man a pessimism "nature despises as something utterly unnatural."[22] Hence, the intellect is drafted to fight this pessimism threatening life at its root. "To support life, to seduce to life, is therefore the intent behind every act of knowing. It

17. Ibid., p. 416.

18. Elisabeth Förster-Nietzsche, *Das Leben Friedrich Nietzsches* (n.p., 1895), 1:270. As C. A. Bernoulli (see fn. 12, 1:142) rightly emphasizes, the importance Lange had for Nietzsche's philosophy and his knowledge of natural science cannot be overestimated.

19. Friedrich Albert Lange, *Geschichte des Materialismus und Kritik seiner Bedeutung in der Gegenwart,* 10th ed. (Leipzig, 1921), 2:402–3.

20. *Werke,* 3:102.   21. Ibid., 6:76.   22. Ibid., 3:278.

is this illogical element that begets all knowledge and defines its limits as well."[23] Similar to religion and art, the intellect is engaged in "world correction" in order to make life appear "to be worth living." The construction of a world worth living in is accomplished with the aid of "noble delusive images produced by an artistic culture." The intellect triumphs in denying the illogical, as though it were only appearance, and by erecting a true counter-world. Yet this counter-world of being and permanence is in fact illusionary, produced by the will in order to make us go on living. The intellect thus becomes the creator of those illusions that make life bearable. "Illusion," Nietzsche writes, "is the foundation of everything that is great and vital. The passion for truth leads to decay."[24]

The second role of the intellect is to dissemble and deceive. Living beings unequally equipped for the struggle of existence develop the ability to deceive as a "means by which weaker, less robust individuals maintain themselves. . . . In man, the art of deception reaches perfection. Here deception . . . the wearing of masks, the veil of convention, play-acting before others and oneself, in short, the continual fluttering about the *single* flame of vanity is so much the general rule that it is almost incomprehensible how an honest and pure desire for the truth should have arisen among men. They are steeped in illusions and dream images."[25] Deception takes various forms: self-deception, deception of others, and deception about the nature of the world. The very possibility for it arises because of the prevalent misconception about the intellect: people ignore the fact that it is an organ of the will, and that man does not exist in order to know.

In view of all these obstructions, the question is where in the world the desire for truth comes from.[26] Nietzsche believes that it is generated by the state. Because "man out of need and boredom wants to live socially and herdlike, he requires peace and strives to eliminate from his world at least the crudest *bellum omnium contra omnes*. The conclusion of such peace entails something that looks like the first step toward that enigmatic urge for truth. People come to an agreement of *what* the 'truth' from now on is to be; that is, a generally valid and binding nomenclature of things is invented, and

23. Ibid., p. 311.   24. Ibid., 6:74.
25. Ibid., p. 76.   26. Ibid., p. 77.

the legislating of the language contains also the basic laws of the truth."[27] Only then do men distinguish between truth and lies. "Man insists on the truth and adheres to it in moral dealings with other men, all common life rests on that."[28] Without such truth, "man would live a life of mystification. The founding of the state is a stimulus to veracity."[29] Being truthful or sincere in one's relations with others is a quality born of human need and a "means of social existence."

The truth current in society gains expression in a uniformly accepted designation of things through language. If language were an adequate reflection of reality, one could not well deny objectivity to what society calls truth. Unfortunately, language is metaphorical and anthropomorphic through and through. Besides, an analysis of how concepts are formed shows that every concept is made by "equating the nonequal."[30] "Concepts require us to overlook what is individual and real," and nature remains for us an "inaccessible and undefinable X."[31] What we call truth has no relation to reality; it is no more than "a sum of human relations" which never reveal the nature of a thing but only its consequences. Since the urge for truth is rooted in the attempt to avoid war, truth itself is bound to exhibit the general character of an urge, namely, its being regulated by pleasure and unpleasure. "There is no urge that does not anticipate pleasure from its satisfaction," hence the urge to truth, too, must be eudaemonistic. Men do not want the truth as such, only the use or gain it promises, namely, the possibility of a social existence.

Though men feel an obligation to the truth, they usually are in error about the reason for it. It is not the "alleged truth" that puts one under an obligation, but the "belief of possessing it." "It is necessary to believe in the truth; but since truths are proved by consequences and not by logical demonstration, the illusion of truth is sufficient." "Truth and effectiveness are identical; one bows to force here, too." This pragmatic train of thought announces Nietzsche's radical social interpretation of the concept of truth. He writes: "In the battle of 'truth' against 'truth,' men look to reflection for an ally. All genuine truth-seeking has come into existence through the struggle for some 'sacred conviction,' through the passion of the

27. Ibid., pp. 77–8.   28. Ibid., p. 29.
29. Ibid., p. 38.   30. Ibid., p. 80.   31. Ibid., p. 81.

fight itself, aside from which man takes no interest in the logical origin of the truth."[32] To be able to believe in truth presupposes two things: "an independent capacity for knowledge" and the conviction that with its help truths binding for all men can be established.[33] Nietzsche refers to the "complete uniformity of the instrumentality of perception" and thinks that the "overwhelming consensus about things" proves it. But he adds that this uniformity does not vouch for a knowledge of things as they are. All that we possess are relations that tally, but which, though they are conditioned by things, do not touch their nature. "None of these relations is the true, absolute relation, but each is tinged anthropomorphically."[34]

In addition to these critical comments on the theory of knowledge, Nietzsche's early fragments also contain the beginnings of his critique of the science of logic. The central problem is posed by a skepticism that undermines faith in the truth and thereby "destroys all the blessings of faith," that is, life-sustaining and life-promoting illusion. Skepticism overlooks, however, that it, too, contains an element of faith: "the faith in logic," a science built on the falsity of equating the nonequal. "The ultimate step, therefore, is to abandon the science of logic—that *credo quia absurdum est*—and to doubt reason itself, to deny it."[35] Yet nobody can live with such total doubt, "which demonstrates that faith in logic and faith in life generally are necessary."[36] Nietzsche concludes that the "truth" is a cloak and cover for quite different drives and urges. Implied, too, is a certain conception of man which, at this point, may only be indicated with the help of two exclamations. "Man equals thinker—that's where madness lies";[37] and, "To regard 'spirit,' the product of the brain, as something supernatural and even to deify it—what folly."[38]

To summarize, we have shown how Nietzsche's critique of reason broadened, already at its beginning, into a critique of traditional epistemology and logic. Guided by biological and sociological considerations, he maintains that knowledge and its functions must be explained in terms of the preservation and enhancement of life. He makes use of F.A. Lange's concept of human organization, but

32. Ibid., p. 17.   33. Ibid., p. 94.   34. Ibid., p. 58.
35. Ibid., p. 95.   36. Ibid., p. 95.   37. Ibid., 3:241.
38. Ibid., 6:36.

shifts it from physiology over into psychology. Categories and patterns of perception lose their a priori character, and are assumed to be purely sensual and instinctual, or they are consigned to the region of conventional fictions.[39] The mechanism of human perception, formerly held to be common to all men, Nietzsche individualizes. He transforms cognition into active and reactive behavior marked by uniquely psychic traits, so that individual "quanta of will" project individualized, incomparable world-pictures that need have nothing in common except the relation to an unknowable X.

The basic assumption of Nietzsche's philosophy is the eternal flux of things. Everything is in the process of becoming, it arises and passes away. "There are no eternal facts, just as there are no absolute truths." He concludes from this that henceforth philosophy will have to be modest, limited to the tasks of the epoch. Yet in a world of perpetual change no living being would be able to find its way; efficient, sensible behavior directed toward survival would be frustrated. Such behavior always relies on a minimal regularity in the course of events and on the reification of reality. Reification means that what is originally sheer process is being transformed into relatively stable properties that can be counted upon. Regularity, similarly, means that man creates and then lives by the illusion that under the "same" conditions the "same" events recur. Both these mental operations imply that the knower proceeds from the very start by falsifying reality. The view of reality that is favorable to survival alone prevails. The question is not what faith is truest, but which is the most useful. "Thought would be impossible," Nietzsche says, "unless it basically misconceived the nature of being: it has to insist on substance and sameness because knowledge of what is wholly in flux is impossible. For its own sake, thought has to fictionalize being."[40] The supposition of partial stability and "relative bodies" falsifies the facts, yet such "error is the presupposition of

---

39. On this question, see the excellent study of Erich Hocks, *Das Verhältnis der Erkenntnis zur Unendlichkeit der Welt bei Nietzsche: Eine Darstellung seiner Erkenntnislehre* (Leipzig, 1914). Erika Emmerich, in *Wahrheit und Wahrhaftigkeit in der Philosophie Nietzsches* (Halle, 1933), offers an interpretation that naively accepts the point of view of Martin Heidegger and Oskar Becker and overlooks the contempary philosophizing that left its mark on Nietzsche. Another important study is by Maria Bindschedler, *Nietzsche und die poetische Lüge* (Basel, 1954).

40. *Werke,* 11:149.

knowledge" and thought.[41] Language on its part encourages this error. It leads us to erect a "world of our own next to the other" so that we may establish a place sufficiently firm from which "to lift the other world out of its hinges and make ourselves its master."[42] The manifestation of the same error in logic has already been mentioned. There, reason is compelled to work with such "prejudices" as unity, identity, permanence, substance, thingness, and being.

Error has still another dimension, morality. Reason creates not only such concepts as have just been mentioned, it also introduces the ideas of meaning and purpose. Man interprets the world as if it realized some sort of aim. It is a matter of indifference whether this aim purports to be a moral world order, a general state of human happiness, or non-being. In any case, the effort to realize the aim is what gives life its meaning. All transitory things are made to justify themselves in the service of what is everlasting. Life's worth is measured by what it contributes to the attainment of some overarching goal, which in turn gathers all individual efforts into a harmonious whole. If, however, we should withdraw these concepts of purpose, unity, and being from the world, then it would "look worthless."[43] The reason why we oppose the world of change with another seemingly permanent one is found not only in our inveterate tendency to falsification, but in our need for some cosmic meaning, without which our own existence would be bare of meaning, too. In Nietzsche's words: "Unless some infinitely valuable whole is active in him, man loses faith in his own value: that is, he himself conceives that whole in order to be able to believe in his own value."[44] In short, the world that makes sense and has meaning owes its origin to man's will to justify his existence and make it bearable.

Nietzsche's critique of reason culminates in the doctrine of the will to power. With the introduction of this idea, Nietzsche turns away from the antimetaphysical bias of his earlier thought that was in evidence when he regarded himself as a follower of Schopenhauer. He then still objected that will was nothing more than a word, a "false reification," by which the unknowable was humanized but not grasped. Now, he no longer denies the validity of metaphysical questions; and to the oldest of them all—what is the innermost

---

41. Ibid., p. 147.   42. Ibid., 8:25.
43. Ibid., 18:16.   44. Ibid., p. 15.

nature of being—he answers that it is the will to power. It is also the profoundest, most terrible human desire. "Not physical need, not greed, but love of power is man's demon."[45] The philosopher's task, therefore, is to see in every expression of life a particular form of the will to power, and that includes human understanding with all the instrumentalities it has developed in the course of human history. The concept of knowledge thus acquires a "strictly anthropocentric and biological sense." Knowledge is both a tool and a product of the will to power. Cognition, being originally a creative and poetic capacity that falsified reality by transforming the multifarious and infinite into something uniform, finite, and "dependable," cannot really be expected to grasp reality. It is more like taking possession of something and assimilating it to ourselves. "The entire apparatus of human understanding is an apparatus for abstraction and simplification—not aimed at knowledge but at controlling things."[46] Man is said to be interested exclusively in self-preservation. "For a species to survive and grow in power, its conception of reality must contain that amount of calculability and stability which will enable it to construct a pattern of behavior." A species "takes hold" of reality "in order to gain mastery over it and to place it in its service."[47]

The doctrine of the will to power also provides an answer to the problem of truth. Earlier, Nietzsche raised the question as to why beings that were neither equipped for, nor interested in, knowledge should feel any urge to know the truth at all. Now, having broadened his critique of reason into a biological and sociological interpretation of man and the world, his answer is that the will to truth, as also the truth itself, are expressions of man's demon. The sense for truth has to "legitimize" itself as a means of survival, as a form of the will to power. Since the human intellect is "dependent on our valuations" and these in turn reflect our urges, both intellect and urges are "reducible to the will to power."[48]

The will to truth consists in fastening things down, lending them permanence, moving the false character of the world out of sight (which is, in fact, its "true" character—a continual process of becoming and a flux of self-active "will-quanta"), and of casting

45. Ibid., 19:161.   46. Ibid., p. 22.
47. Ibid., p. 12.   48. Ibid., 14:287.

it into the mold of being. It is clear, therefore, that the truth is not something that exists, that can be found or discovered, but that it is something which has to be made; it is a name for a process, or better still, for an unceasing will to vanquish the world: truth is a matter of endowing things with truth, a *processus in infinitum,* an active determining—not a becoming conscious of what is in itself fixed and determined. It is a word for the "will to power."[49]

What we call truth is the attempt to establish a limited number of useful, life-sustaining rules that make "the world manageable and predictable." Man "invented his reason" to be able to dwell in the world. The categories of reason are not a gauge of reality but a "shrewd way of misunderstanding it."[50] Philosophers have failed to recognize that logical categories and forms have no other use than to arrange the world, and thereby to falsify it, for our purposes. Nietzsche's definition of the truth is contained in the proposition: "The criterion of truth is the enhancement of the sense of power."[51]

Nietzsche's views of what constitutes truth are not free of contradictions. His criticism assumes the correctness of the common-sense concept of truth, according to which true propositions are those that possess universal validity; all men, in so far as they are reasonable and equipped with equal intellectual powers, must necessarily agree to them. This everyday notion of truth further supposes that true propositions are intended to be statements about reality, and that they should generally be verifiable. In short, it holds to the correspondence theory of truth without taking account of all the tacit philosophical assumptions contained in the idea of a correspondence between thought and being. Even if this theory were generally agreed to, it would leave open the question of the nature of things themselves. Nietzsche does not concern himself with these problems, but instead shifts the discussion to psychology. He asks how the "drive" to truth originates, and what sociological conditions give rise to an interest in the truth. As has been shown, Nietzsche thinks that society requires truth for its very existence because social work and communication would be impossible without some consensus as to what reality is. But even if it were the case that social need is the source of the will to truth, this has

49. Ibid., 19:53.   50. Ibid., p. 76.   51. Ibid., p. 43.

nothing to do with the epistemological question of the possibility or impossibility of knowledge. Just as the misuse of truth is no argument against truth itself, so its utility does not prove that its value is exhausted by the worth society puts on it.

The assertion that the truth does not reach beyond the psychological and sociological factors by which it is conditioned and determined is intended to undermine certain other and older conceptions of truth. Among these, the everyday notion of truth discussed above provoked Nietzsche less than the metaphysical search for an ultimately true and rational world. Kant's critique of pure reason appeared to him, when he came under the influence of Lange, to have demolished metaphysics for good, at least as a science with any claim to truth. Nietzsche therefore placed it alongside poetry and religion as a source of edification, calling it a "poetry of concepts."[52] From the outset this metaphysical agnosticism has the effect of devaluating the human capacity for knowledge; the alleged failure of metaphysics prejudices his analysis of epistemology. Metaphysics is suspected by Nietzsche of being motivated by "contempt and hatred of all that perishes and changes," and "by longing for a world of permanence."[53] Thus, again, human psychological need is exposed as the true source of metaphysical constructions. But Nietzsche also took issue with the notion of truth common in the empirical sciences. That knowledge should establish a connection with objects is termed a "nonsensical" idea because truth is not a relation between knowing and being. Ascriptions like true and false apply exclusively inside the web of human relations. They are devoid of trans-subjective significance and do not apply to anything outside human control, nor are they urged on us by reality. There are no logical criteria for statements about empirical reality, any more than for those about metaphysical reality. In both cases the only gauge of true or false is biological value.[54]

Nietzsche never carried out a systematic inquiry into the idea of truth. If he had, it could not have escaped him that the will to power, which is itself a metaphysical principle, would be put in question if he tried to maintain the premises of his own theory of

---

52. Letter to Paul Deussen, Easter 1868.   53. *Werke,* 19:77.

54. I here follow Raoul Richter, *Friedrich Nietzsche: Sein Leben und sein Werk,* 2nd ed. (Leipzig, 1909), p. 281.

truth.[55] Unless that principle is dismissed as a purely subjective opinion, these premises have to be revised. If "proof by force," that is, success and utility, is made the criterion of an idea, no intellectual discussion is possible anyway, because in that case an idea cannot be objectively refuted, it can only be overcome by a new force. We then are no longer in the realm of the mind, but in the political arena. For Nietzsche, to know is to gain power over and to transform something. But to equate knowing with falsifying, fictionalizing, or transforming presupposes that we possess some gauge for registering falsification. Unless the opposite, verification, is possible, there is no sense in talking about falsification. Transformation, similarly, presupposes something "given" that can be subjected to transformation. To speak of "misconceiving" being already implies some knowledge of being. Nietzsche thinks that cognition "falsifies the true facts," which implies the possibility of distinguishing between true and false. Yet his own position is that we know nothing at all about what the "true facts" are. What our consciousness accepts as given is already preformed. Nietzsche's premises do not permit the conclusion that the eternal flux of things is the ultimate truth.

There is another difficulty. The predictability of events and the solidification of the process of becoming into bodily form, by means of which man orients himself in the world, are inconceivable without there being some ground in reality for such predictability. The very idea of knowing one's way about in the world indicates that man experiments in a medium where some order, however minimal, prevails. If events were wholly unpredictable, so that men could form no expectations—a supposition suggested by the idea of "eternal change"—orientation would be impossible. The world that man creates and in which he lives and acts cannot be wholly fantastical, without any relation to the nature of things. For this man-made world which changes with time, place, and intellectual and psychic dispositions, interacts with the other world which Nietzsche,

55. Raoul Richter, *Der Skeptizismus in der Philosophie und seine Überwindung* (Leipzig, 1908), 2:470. The author rightly calls attention to the fact that Nietzsche "never thoroughly examined the concept of truth in a logical sense," and that his usual criterion of truth was the agreement of an idea with an intended or assumed reality.

because of its "eternal change," regards as unknowable; and in this interaction, both the nature of the world and man's perspectives equally assert themselves. At the least, the varying degrees of resistance that reality puts up against human activity create a constraint on purely subjective interpretations. Ideas are subject to a certain test because the world is constituted in a certain way. This also holds for Nietzsche's idea of biological usefulness: it is determined by conditions of inorganic and organic nature, in comparison with which human interpretations and perspectives are irrelevant.

One may agree with Nietzsche that cognition requires us to ignore what is individual, and that concept formation involves "equating the nonequal." Still, the "identification of the nonequal" is confined to certain limits set not by subjective arbitrariness, but grounded in reality. How this "grounding" occurs can only be demonstrated in each individual case. It is possible, of course, that owing to a temporary or final cognitive inability, such "grounding" remains impenetrable to man. Whether things are equal or unequal can only be determined when we have decided in what perspective they are to be viewed. Certain characteristics of life are shared by the simplest and the most highly differentiated organisms. Different things may appear equal in one perspective and unequal in another. But the comparability of things is always grounded in themselves, which means that equating the unequal, or concept formation, is not exclusively a matter of cognitive arbitrariness. Nietzsche generally tends to emphasize the subject's part in the process of cognition; and since the subject is already conceived as the center of the will to power, cognition assumes the character of active interference with the object. But the sphere in which cognition can automatically project the categories of reason onto the world is limited because cognition is not a matter of forming something that is inherently formless. On the contrary, man always confronts a world whose structure is autonomous.

By cognition Nietzsche never means the act of grasping what is before us, what offers resistance and proves to be something existing independently and in a relatively stable state. He does not, it is true, deny the basic situation in which cognition takes place, that is, the relation between the knowing subject and the object to be known. But in this relation, only the subject is of any weight while the object appears but vaguely as "that which acts upon us." The natural and social conditions under which the subject lives, and his physical and mental organization so predominate in the process of cognition that all that is left to the object is to let itself be formed and mastered by the subject. Although Nietzsche does not wish to deny the world its "perturbing and enigmatic character,"[56] he asserts that it can be grasped "only from within" and "not through its infinite protean nature."[57] Like Schopenhauer, Nietzsche relies for a description of the essence of things on personal experience, where that essence is apprehended as the will to power. This metaphysical definition of ultimate being does not tell us anything about how the problem of cognition is to be solved empirically, in the here and now. Since Nietzsche's definition of being remains general—it is simply effect-producing and power-exhibiting—such being cannot really become an object of cognition. When its effectiveness and power touch the subject's sphere of life, it becomes at once a matter for "interpretation." The real effects of things remain unknown because they are from the beginning interpreted and arranged so as to suit the subject's existential interests. Interpretation so predominates over the real effects that the latter seem not to exercise any constraint over it. Otherwise Nietzsche could not assert the "infinite explicability of the world."[58] Though the world as mediated by the senses is without doubt formed in accordance with the conditions of our own organization, one may suppose that the latter does not determine exclusively the variety of what is given in sense perception.

The deficiencies of Nietzsche's idea of cognition are particularly noticeable in respect to the knowledge of history. An understanding of people who lived in other times as well as an insight into contexts of meaning are scarcely intelligible in terms of domination. His idea of explication derived from philology seems at first sight more serviceable. But even here his general bias in favor of interpretation and against objective description of the facts is a disadvantage because subjective perspectives are thereby encouraged. His assertion that there are "no facts, only interpretations"[59] needs to be countered by the reminder that interpretation, too, has reference to brute facts. Of course, scientifically ascertained facts are found at the end, and not at the beginning, of an investigation. Nor is it

56. *Werke,* 19:88.   57. Ibid., 16:47.
58. Ibid., 19:88.   59. Ibid., p. 13.

necessary that a fact be the primary given thing; interpretation plays an important role in the way "a fact" comes into being.

All historical knowledge has to reckon with two changeable quantities. One is the historical object which, though of a certain identity, is always being transformed by being placed in new contexts of meaning. The other is the historian who, though heir of a certain historical tradition, also expresses in his work his unique individuality. Both form part of a historical tradition and encounter each other with varying degrees of open-mindedness and blindness. Obviously historical knowledge is difficult, but this does not mean it should be renounced, or the effort to at least approach the truth be abandoned. If, however, one recognizes nothing but interpretations, there can be no truth, but only "truths" that are valid for those who created them in the first place. Radical biological skepticism is self-defeating because it undermines the philosophical basis of its own argumentation.

Generally speaking, Nietzsche succeeds when it is a question of showing the influence of individual or collective types of interpretation on cognition. He is genuinely enlightening when he discloses how vital human interests and drives inform our knowledge of nature and enable us to predict and control; similarly, when he demonstrates the anthropomorphic nature of language. And when, as in the middle years of his work, he declares war on psychological, moral, and philosophical prejudices, he himself claims to carry forward the "banner of enlightenment."[60] Yet, to brand something as prejudice requires a criterion of judgment. The Enlightenment of the eighteenth century found such a criterion in universal and normative reason. Nietzsche first adhered to the ideal of a scientific philosophy, as is reflected in the works written between 1876 and 1881; he also followed the commandment of intellectual honesty which renounces moral self-deception. Later, when he tried to replace the Christian and Stoic morality with a new ethics, his criterion changed. He introduced a "new enlightenment" to "show commanding characters their way," and to demonstrate "why everything not permitted herd animals is permitted them."[61]

The prejudices of reason, morality, and religion constitute the ideology Nietzsche wants to crush with the hammer blows of a new

60. Ibid., 8:43.   61. Ibid., 18:357.

philosophy. The new enlightenment he promises is preceded by the "twilight of the idols" *(Götzendämmerung)*. This was the title of his penultimate work, whose French translation, *Crépuscule des Idoles*,[62] clearly confirms the connection between the nature of his undertaking and that of the eighteenth-century Enlightenment. However, Nietzsche goes beyond the latter in that he unmasks even the belief in absolute reason, and in the ethics based on it, as Christian and therefore life-denying. His enthusiastic fawning disciple Peter Gast confirmed, though unconsciously, the connection between the earlier Enlightenment and Nietzsche's program when he wrote his master: "What illuminations, what ecstasies of learning I owe to your world-mastering mind. . . . It is because of you that there exist again hopes, goals, and delineations of a new culture."

The examination of Nietzsche's criticism of the common-sense notion of truth has shown that his attempt to expose the biological and sociological conditioning of cognition confirms, but does not negate, the logical principles of truth.[63] Nietzsche himself presupposes their validity when he tries to demonstrate the origination of logic in the non-logical and when he contrasts the "misconception" of being with "true" being. The charge he raised against Schopenhauer, that his metaphysics of the will to life was nothing but a metaphor and a mistaken reification, falls back on Nietzsche himself. For the will to power is likewise only an imagery whose serviceability in the interpretation of inorganic nature is doubtful. It is more useful in psychology and sociology, especially when it is a matter of demonstrating how certain interests condition the formulation of political theories and the establishment of social systems. It cannot, however, help to answer the question whether systems of legal, political, and social philosophy aspire, despite their undeniable dependency on certain interests, to a supratemporal validity.

62. In a letter to Overbeck, Nietzsche writes that "Crépuscules des idoles" is being considered first for a translation. See *Friedrich Nietzsches Briefwechsel mit Franz Overbeck,* ed. Richard Oehler and C.A. Bernoulli (Leipzig, 1916), p. 453.
63. See Richter, *Der Skeptizismus,* 2:489. Also Karl Jaspers, *Nietzsche: Einführung in das Verständnis seines Philosophierens* (Berlin and Leipzig, 1936), pp. 161 ff.

Ideological Theory and the
Method of Reduction

According to Nietzsche's metaphysics, life and all its manifestations are to be understood as metamorphoses of the will to power. Included are the organic functions, the forms and contents of emotional and intellectual life, and the different types of social order. The philosopher's task consists in deriving all of these from the will to power and so to reduce them to it. To illustrate, psychology is viewed as a "morphology and developmental theory of the will to power,"[64] and ethics is "nothing but the sign language of our drives,"[65] which in turn are reducible to the will to power. Behind our conscious motives lies the "struggle of drives and conditions—the struggle for power."[66] This origin is, however, being concealed. All previous systems of morals, according to Nietzsche, aimed to deceive in this way, whereas his formulation of morality is free of this reproach because he identifies the powerful with the good, giving egoism back its "good conscience."[67] His criticism of morals, then, proceeds by uncovering the deception hidden in them, and this work comes to characterize a good part of philosophy itself. Nietzsche remarks that "one of his philosophies" would still like to be called the love of wisdom, but another is content with a "more modest name": "this philosophy . . . calls itself the art of mistrust."[68] It is by this means that "boastful words" and nobly unselfish gestures are unmasked as modes of human self-deception.[69]

Nietzsche's work contains a theory of ideology whose importance has thus far been little appreciated and which is here presented for the first time.[70] The opinion that his philosophy of culture and

64. *Werke,* 15:32. The study by Slata Genia Rudensky-Brin, *Kollektivistisches in der Philosophie Nietzsches* (Basel, 1948), is instructive concerning aspects of social philosophy in Nietzsche.

65. *Werke,* 16:192. 66. Ibid., p. 67.

67. Ibid., p. 152. 68. Ibid., p. 312.

69. See in this regard Hans Prinzhorn, *Nietzsche und das 20. Jahrhundert* (Heidelberg, 1928), who gives an excellent account of Nietzsche's psychology of unmasking and its significance for psychoanalysis. See also Ludwig Klages, *Die psychologischen Errungenschaften Nietzsches,* 2nd ed. (Leipzig, 1930).

70. Karl Mannheim's judgment is correct that Nietzsche along with Marx helped bring the modern theory of ideology and the sociology of knowledge into

education culminated in an aristocratic individualism caused his readers to overlook the fact that in his later writings, beginning in 1882, sociological points of view are introduced. The traditional morals that he subjects to criticism are treated more and more as the expression of certain social classes. At the same time, his "philosophy of the future" projects not only a model for individual ethical conduct, but also for the conduct of a social group. He begins to see that the social and moral theories he has viewed as manifestations of the will to power need to be related to the social position of those who create them. Every class subscribes to a morality appropriate to its interests and its particular will to power. The general principle of social order results from the polarity between domination and submission, command and obedience, leaders and followers. Society is divided into those who rule and the others who are ruled, and these two strata have different types of morality which Nietzsche calls the morality of masters and the morality of slaves. The sociological aspect of his criticism is concerned with examining ideas of moral conduct to discover whether they belong to an elite or to the masses.

Nietzsche rarely mentions the science of sociology, which arose in the nineteenth century. Its findings are not reflected in his work, but when he does refer to it, it is by way of criticism and a very special one at that. The fault of sociology is that "it knows from experience only the decadent form of society and inevitably adopts its decadent

---

being. See his article in *Handwörterbuch der Soziologie,* ed. Alfred Vierkandt (Stuttgart, 1931), p. 678. Helmuth Plessner, whose view of nineteenth-century intellectual history is the same as this author's, also touches on Nietzsche's importance in these respects in his good book *Das Schicksal deutschen Geistes im Ausgang seiner bürgerlichen Epoche* (Zürich, 1935).

The present author is the first to attempt a presentation of Nietzsche's contribution to the problem of ideology that takes into account his theory of knowledge and his metaphysics. The role of Schopenhauer in this context has also been insufficiently appreciated before.

Concerning Nietzsche's use of the term ideology, the following passages are illuminating: "For every strong, natural type of man, love and hatred, gratitude and vengeance, kindness and anger, affirmation and negation go hand in hand. One is kind at the price of knowing how also to be angry. Then whence that sickness and ideologically perverted nature that rejects this duality . . .? Man is being asked to lop off those instincts that allow him to be inimical. This unnaturalness corresponds to the dualism that divides characters into wholly good and wholly evil ones," *Werke,* 18:247. Hence, there "has been no more dangerous ideology and no grosser mischief in matters psychological than this will to the good," ibid., 248–9.

instincts as the criterion of sociological judgment."[71] This criticism becomes intelligible in connection with Nietzsche's posthumous fragments on the revaluation of values. It implies two things: first, that the societies of the nineteenth century are forms of a decaying will of life;[72] and, second, that sociology contains "variants of the Christian ideal of value" which must be combatted because they conceal the basic laws of social life.[73] Nietzsche's criticism of sociology is identical to his censure of types of ethics preceding his own—the neglect of a hierarchical order in societies by which the idea of dominion can alone be rightfully reinstated. The topic occupying the foreground of his last work is the "breeding of the legislators of the future," but he is in this connection thinking not of exceptional individuals, but of a ruling social group or caste. The vision of such a group helps explain Nietzsche's intention to replace conventional sociology with a "theory of patterns of dominion,"[74] for a hierarchical order is essential to society. What is called "modern society" is no society at all, but a sick conglomerate whose egalitarianism is the antithesis of rank, superiority, and subordination. Nietzsche is out to destroy the postulate of the moral equality and rationality of men proclaimed by the French Revolution. For equality is a chimera in whose belief only the underprivileged have an interest, and rationality is no more than a tool for acquiring as much as possible of the world. Thus, Nietzsche leads a counterrevolution against enlightened rationalism and the "absolute authority of the Goddess of reason."[75]

Nietzsche's ideological interpretation of everything historical materialism lumps together under the term superstructure rests on two assumptions. The first is that reason is an instrument of organic life and arises in response to its needs and interests. The second is that reason is made not for knowledge, but exclusively for the mastery of things. The problem of truth is thereby eliminated from the discussion of ethics, religion, and social philosophy, and the autonomy of the mind generally abolished. "What is commonly said to be a property of mind," Nietzsche writes, "seems to me organic in

---

71. *Werke,* 18:42.

72. See Hugo Fischer for a view of Nietzsche's philosophy as representing the "degenerative life" and "decaying bourgeois society" in *Nietzsche Apostata oder die Philosophie des Ärgernisses* (Erfurt, 1931).

73. *Werke,* 18:41.   74. Ibid., p. 330.   75. Ibid., 16:89.

nature. I regard the highest functions of the mind as no more than a sublime variety of organic functions (assimilation, selection, secretion, etc.)."[76] In addition to this biological reduction of intellectual activities, Nietzsche's theory of ideology leans on the political sociology just mentioned. Every society is divided into ruling and ruled classes whose members acquire different ideas of morality. The ruling class seeks to expand its power while the other, to make its lot bearable, attempts to erect moral inhibitions and legal restraints against it. The ruled class also attempts to share in the power and to supplant the ruling group. To summarize, having eliminated truth as an intellectual problem, Nietzsche's ideology retains only the "will to truth," and this appears in three forms: "conquest of, and struggle with, nature," "opposition to ruling authorities," and "criticism of what is harmful to us."[77]

It may be worth repeating at this point what has been established in the earlier chapters of this book, that the principle of ideological interpretations of cultural and intellectual life is to deny the autonomy of mind and the existence of universal truths. Intellectual life and its creations are reduced to social and economic conditions and to the complex of human drives. This reductionist procedure generally assumes that every intellectual product has a double sense, one obvious and self-proclaiming, the other hidden and requiring a special effort to bring it to light. Moreover, the first or self-evident sense is not regarded as the key to a true understanding of the cultural product in question. That is reserved to the second sense, which emerges only when the product is related to some other force whose "expression" it is alleged to be. Ideological reduction does not deny that every creation of the higher culture embodies some meaning describable in such terms as truth, beauty, or justice. But it assumes that this meaning does not exhaust the full significance of the object, which is disclosed only when it is shown to be the representative of certain vital forces. To effect this disclosure is the intent of the reductive procedure of ideology.

---

76. Ibid., p. 116. Concerning the sublimation of human urges, see Karl Jaspers, *Nietzsche: Einführung in das Verständnis,* pp. 115 ff. Unfortunately, Nietzsche never closely examined the process of sublimation for which he also used the term transfiguration. The sublimation of erotic love he regarded as a lie, due to the pressure of Christian values under which the "sexual drive was sublimated into love," *Werke,* 15:115.

77. *Werke,* 15:51.

How is one to describe the relation that exists between the product of the higher culture and the basic underlying vital forces? Nietzsche indicates an answer when he refers to morality as a "sign language of the emotions" and to the emotions as a "sign language of organic functions."[78] These organic functions, finally, may be "translated back" into the original master will from which they were split off. It would appear that these repeated references to language contain an analogy of the relation between intellectual activities and vital forces that we are trying to describe. The key concept here is expression. "Our thinking and valuing," Nietzsche writes, "is only an expression of desires at work behind them. The desires become increasingly specialized, but their unity lies in the will to power."[79] The concept corresponding to expression is reduction, for to reduce something is to present it as the expression of another thing. What presents itself as being beautiful, just, or true falls under the suspicion of being, in fact, a manifestation of the will to power, and to certify it as such becomes the task of the ideologist. Reductionism goes farther yet. The idea of justice, for instance, even though special interests may be shown to be promoting it for their own sake, might still claim universal validity if it could be proven an inalienable property of the human mind. In that case, the reductionist procedure might still demonstrate how the mind is misused by the will to power, its functions disturbed and inhibited, without, however, succeeding in abrogating the autonomy of mind itself. It is this last possibility of escape that Nietzsche wants to close. Consciousness, reason, and mind must be deprived of their claims to autonomous functioning by proving them to be metamorphoses of the will to power.

To revert for a moment to Nietzsche's critique of morality and religion. It asserts that man creates eternal verities and religious beliefs with which to oppose a transient world forever in the process of becoming. This dualism Nietzsche intends to replace with a monism that will enable him to derive all values and ideas from the sole reality of the will to power. The world human reason creates in order to make life meaningful and worth living is declared a fiction, as the contents of religion illustrate particularly well. God and the

78. Ibid., p. 190.
79. Ibid., p. 61. A similar passage is found in 18:279: "The history of morals reflects the will to power by which now the slaves and the oppressed, now the ill-begotten and mediocre attempt to assert values that favor them."

Beyond are "errors of the creative urge,"[80] and the whole idea of a truly permanent world is an "emergency measure."[81] Nietzsche regards such notions as compensations for the satisfactions life denies us. As the reductionist procedure is applied to religious consciousness, we see that its contents, too, are simply manifestations of the will to power, that is, illusions without a source of reality, yet suitable for making life bearable. The "world-correction" undertaken by reason and religion is still an expression of the will to power, but in this instance of a will too feeble and too sick to endure the ups and downs of becoming. The world created by those intellectual interests is therefore a symptom of decadence.

A fragment of Nietzsche's posthumous writings best summarizes his intentions by revealing the mechanism at work when a true and just world is manufactured by the human mind. Aside from war, which aims at physical annihilation, there is another form of struggle used by those who have no violent means at their disposal—the "war of the mind." It, too, is a struggle for power in which one's own value judgments are asserted while those of the opponent are ideologically devalued. In this intellectual war, in which the powerful, the healthy, and the strong are marshaled against the underprivileged, the lowly, and suppressed, the mind reveals its purely instrumental character. It displays denunciatory and disguising functions, not as accessories but as constituting its very nature. The war of minds is thereby relieved of the constraint truth previously exercised upon it, and moves into the political and economic arena where success becomes the sole criterion. All that the mind produces is now exclusively a means for asserting "value judgments" favorable to promoting one's own existence.

The game plan is as follows. Question: "How does one make war against feelings and valuations of a manly character?" Supposing physical violence is not available, and "only a war of cunning, defamation, lies, in short, a war of the 'mind' can be waged." Answer:

> First rule: claim absolute virtue for your ideal and deprecate the older ideal until it turns into the opposite of an ideal. This requires the art of defamation. Second rule: make your own type the general measure of worth, project it into and behind things,

80. *Werke*, 14:290.   81. Ibid., 19:66.

behind the fate of things—as God. Third rule: declare the foes of your ideal to be God's enemies; invent for yourself the right to grandiloquence, to power, to damn, and to bless! Fourth rule: attribute all suffering, everything that is threatening, terrible, and disastrous in existence to the opponents of your ideal so that suffering becomes punishment, even for one's followers, unless it may be a trial. . . . Fifth rule: go so far as to portray nature as the antagonist of your ideal and present your existence in it as a great test of endurance, a kind of martyrdom; train yourself to exhibit in mien and manner disdain for "everything natural." Sixth rule: project the triumph of the unnatural, of the ideal of castration, of all that is pure, good, sinless, blessed, into the future and announce it as the end, the grand finale, the great hope, and the "coming of the realm of God."[82]

As already observed, Nietzsche's reductionism is radical and aims to abolish belief in the autonomy of the mind. To this end, intellectual activities are made to appear as organic processes. The only remaining difference between the two is a degree of "refinement": intellectual functions are sublimations of organic functions, such as adaptation, nutrition, elimination, procreation, selection, and growth. The method of reduction terminates in the conversion of the philosophy of mind into biology.

Nietzsche's theory of ideology is a continuation of the psychology of unmasking as practiced by Mandeville and the French moralists of the seventeenth and eighteenth centuries. It also follows the sociological analysis of moral concepts introduced by Helvetius and Mandeville.[83] This aspect of Nietzsche's ideological theory has a

82. Ibid., 18:152–3.

83. Bernard de Mandeville is mentioned only once by Nietzsche (16:148). Whether he knew *The Fable of the Bees* and *Search in the Nature of Society,* I am unable to say. Albert Lévy, whose study *Stirner et Nietzsche* (Paris, 1904) lists the books Nietzsche borrowed from the library of the University of Basel between 1869 and 1879, found no record of Mandeville's works among them. Nor, according to Elisabeth Förster-Nietzsche, did Nietzsche's personal library contain any copy. See her contribution, "Nietzsches Bibliothek," to Arthur Berthold, ed., *Bücher und Wege zu Büchern* (Berlin and Stuttgart, 1900), pp. 429 ff. F.A. Lange's *History of Materialism* mentions Mandeville several times. The influence of the French moralists on Nietzsche has been investigated by Charles Andler, *Les Précurseurs de Nietzsche* (Paris, 1920), and Ernst Kroeckel, *Europas Selbstbesinnung durch Nietzsche: Ihre Vorbereitung bei den französischen Moralisten* (Munich, 1929).

permanent value, for there is no doubt that political, legal, and moral ideas are never isolated from the struggle for economic and state power. To recognize this, however, is not to say that those ideas and theories contain no knowledge whatsoever and merely serve to provide moral justification for the actions of interested parties. The historian Leopold von Ranke struck the right balance when he wrote: "In conflicts of power, certain theories emerge that often appear to be a justification of positions the parties concerned have taken or are about to take. It would be an injustice to the thinking mind to derive the theory solely from the fact, for it has also a movement of its own."[84]

The principal concern of Nietzsche's theory of ideology is to present political, legal, and moral philosophies as "expressions of the will to power." His argument assumes, first, that social analysis and historical experience show every society to consist of rulers and subjects; and, second, that the entire ideological superstructure is completely dependent on the legal and economic conditions of life. "Our valuations," he writes, "are related to what we believe to be the conditions of our existence;" and, he continues in a way reminiscent of Marx, "if the latter change, our valuations change, too."[85] The same holds true for religion. What a people reveres in its God are "the conditions that make it flourish, its own virtues; it projects its own pleasure in itself, its sense of power, onto a Being to whom one is grateful."[86] What he says about valuations and religion applies, of course, to the entire ideological superstructure. Morality, for instance, is a "system of values connected with an organism's conditions of life." Moral values are "inspired and regulated by our will to power"; they are indicators of "processes of physiological prosperity or degeneration."[87] "A belief generally reflects the pressure of circumstances, a subjection to the power of conditions under which an organism flourishes, grows, and gains in power."[88] "He who has the power to degrade others to a function of himself, rules; but the vanquished conquer others in turn and have continual battles on their hands. To sustain them is, to a degree, necessary for the life of the whole. The whole again pursues its advantage and confronts its enemy."[89]

84. Leopold von Ranke, *Zur Geschichte der Doktrin von den drei Staatsgewalten*, Sämtliche Werke, 24:237.

85. *Werke*, 16:177.   86. Ibid., 17:185.   87. Ibid., 16:249.
88. Ibid., 18:22.   89. Ibid., 11:218.

Men's concepts of law and morality are determined by their place in the social hierarchy. Looking back over the analyses that demonstrated the dependence of ideology on social position, it is obvious that for Nietzsche the superstructure contains only two types of attitude. Those who are in power attempt to justify it, while those seeking to acquire it attempt to disguise their drive: the ideology of the rulers confronts the ideology of the suppressed. Both, however, regard as moral and lawful "whatever upholds their caste" and maintains their type. But since the conditions of self-preservation as well as the aims of the two castes differ considerably, their morals also differ. The morality of the powerful consists primarily of "self-glorification and contempt for the powerless." Law, to them, is the "will to perpetuate the existing power relationship." The superior and the strong type "proclaims and imposes his *own* feeling as the law for others."[90] Generally speaking, "we try to find the philosophy that suits our possessions, that is, gilds them."[91] The ideology of the oppressed, in contrast, feeds on the will to change existing economic and political conditions; it is revolutionary and works with the ideas of freedom, justice, and equality. These ideas, according to Nietzsche, merely mask a will to power. He writes: "Christianity, revolution . . . equal rights . . . love of peace, justice, truth: all these great words have value only as battle cries. They do not refer to realities but are pompous words for quite different, even opposite, things."[92] The powerless employ such words as part of their strategy of power, of which Nietzsche marks out four steps. "On the first step, they demand 'justice' from those in power. On the second, they call for 'freedom,' that is, they want to 'cut loose' from them. On the third, the slogan is 'equal rights,' which means that so long as they have not gained the upper hand themselves, competitors must also be prevented from doing so."[93] Finally, on the fourth step, they are in sole possession of the power.[94]

The preceding analysis of Nietzsche's reductionism confirms the view that his work contains a comprehensive theory of ideology. It is a work largely critical in nature, and the result of his criticism is to discredit intellectual activities and the products of the higher culture

90. Ibid., 16:187.   91. Ibid., 11:217.
92. Ibid., 18:64.   93. Ibid., p. 66.
94. Though Nietzsche did not always follow this sequence of steps exactly, his view of the history of the struggle for power by the lowest social classes remained the same.

by showing them to be essentially ideological. The mind is thereby deprived of the possibility of attaining universal and timeless truths. Claims to this effect are dismissed as manifestations of the power of ruling groups or of those aspiring to it. The concept of knowledge is treated similarly. Instead of being object-directed, verifiable, and so capable of producing generally valid statements, knowledge is taken to mirror subjective mental states and social interests dictated by one's membership in a certain class. Nietzsche greatly advances this devaluation by expounding a theory of knowledge that likens cognition to a seizure of power.

The Analysis of Decadence and the Contradiction in the Anthropological Foundation

A critical discussion of Nietzsche's theory of ideology is inevitable and necessary. It should not proceed, however, from the point of view of the philosophy of mind. That approach would lead to the simple conclusion that the reduction of intellectual life to biological terms is self-contradictory precisely because mind is by its nature irreducible. More promising is another approach. We will inquire whether Nietzsche's philosophy, and especially his concept of the will to power, offers internal grounds for criticism. Several questions need to be asked. Did he really succeed in deriving mind, reason, and consciousness from the facts of physiology and biology? More important, is it not likely that what later emerges on the highest evolutionary level, in man, through "refinement" and "specialization"—and what we call mind—lies concealed in Nietzsche's concept of the will to power from the beginning? One has to ascertain whether Nietzsche is consistent in his reductionist procedure or whether he compromised the intended identification of intellectual and organic processes by loading the will to power with the very dualism he sought to abolish.

Before pursuing these questions, we wish to say that we are not going to treat Nietzsche's philosophy as the product of an individualized will to power, even though he himself invites this kind of subjective, psychological interpretation. He confessed to having brought forth his philosophy from his own will to health and life,[95]

95. "I produced my philosophy out of my will to health, to life," 21:178.

and regarded other philosophers as "roguish advocates of their prejudices, which they baptize 'truths.'" Every great philosophy, he thought, was the "self-confession of its author, a sort of involuntary and unnoticed memoir." These conjectures about philosophy and philosophers may well be correct, but this does not preclude the possibility of a philosophy being more than a reflection of such things as passions, interests, prejudices, sicknesses of body or mind, and national or racial qualities. Psychological interpretations of any philosophy do not really touch its truth content; they are merely interested in whether it adequately expresses a certain psychic condition. If, therefore, we were to accept Nietzsche's theory of truth, his work would, philosophically speaking, be discredited. To do him justice, it is necessary to uphold what he himself denies, namely, that our cognitive capabilities are able, within limits and under certain conditions, to penetrate to the objects themselves. After all, what Nietzsche's philosophy really intended was a knowledge of the world, not a private interpretation of it. He had what Karl Jaspers called a "boundless will to truth."[96] Having clarified the general question of how to approach Nietzsche, we now ask where in his work internal criticism may best begin.

Even a cursory acquaintance with Nietzsche's writings indicates that the central concern of his philosophy of culture is the diagnosis and therapy of decadence. The first and simplest meaning of decadence is decrease in the will to power. "Whenever the will to power declines in any way," he writes, "this is inevitably followed by a physiological decline, a *décadence.*"[97] Decline and decay are not matters for moral condemnation; they are to be accepted as necessary consequences of life that occur in every epoch and happen to every people.[98] Though Nietzsche describes all organic life in terms of growth and degeneration, and though he assumes the same will to power among plants and animals, it is odd that he should attribute *décadence* to man alone. One is therefore inclined to think that degeneracy on the highest level of organic nature is related to human characteristics alone. The manifestations of degeneracy, it should be noted, are not the cause of a diminished will, but its symptom. On the human level, decadence may take moral, intellectual, and social forms, but these can tell us nothing about its cause.

96. Karl Jaspers, *Nietzsche: Einführung in das Verständnis*, pp. 175 ff.
97. *Werke*, 17:186.   98. Ibid., 18:33.

If decadence "belongs" to life in general, then it is a natural process whose inevitability falls on man and all other organisms alike. But in fact, Nietzsche does not treat it as being inevitable in man. He believed with an almost religious fervor that his own philosophy contained both a ruthless diagnosis of the decay of the West and an infallible cure for it. It would appear, therefore, that the inevitability of the natural process has somehow been breached. This is confirmed by an examination of Nietzsche's anthropology, the result of which may here be anticipated and roughly outlined.

Nietzsche's views concerning the rise of "ascetic ideals" and the "bad conscience," which accompanies the development of human collaboration, mark a breakdown of his attempt to derive mind and its activities from the processes of organic nature. His determination to treat life, including the life of the mind, as a manifestation of the will to power becomes extremely strained when he tries to explain why men, once they exchange the state of war for the social state, develop modes of conduct that are the complete opposite of naturally determined behavior. Nietzsche is, of course, aware that such a change has taken place. He refers to those "half-animals happily adjusted to war and adventure" who upon their entry into society "no longer possess in this novel, unknown world their former guides, those regulative, unconsciously reliable drives; they fall back on thinking, inference, calculation, and on their 'consciousness,' which is their feeblest, most error-prone organ."[99] The characterization of man as "half-animal" suggests that he does take account of a specifically human constitution. This specificity appears in connection with man's social existence, at which point a "violent separation from his beastly past" occurs, which is "like a leap and fall into new conditions of existence," and which necessitates a "declaration of war on the old instincts on which his strength, pleasure, and fertility formerly rested." "Let us add at once, however," Nietzsche continues, "that the fact of an animal soul taking sides against itself created something so novel on earth, something so profound, unheard of, enigmatic, contradictory, and so *significant for the future* that the aspect of the world was thereby changed essentially."[100] In other words, man is capable of resisting his urges, including the will to power, and, in this sense, of turning against himself.

99. Ibid., 15:352.   100. Ibid., p. 353.

This forces Nietzsche into ambivalence. On the one hand, he is compelled to deplore the inhibitions society and moral scruples place upon the will to life. For the "oppressive narrowness and regularity of custom" produces the "bad conscience" on which Nietzsche blames the "worst and most sinister sickness of mankind." The state prevents man from discharging his instincts outward so that these become directed against himself. On the other hand, Nietzsche cannot deny that this organized war against the instincts brought with it a "hope" and a "great promise." He is compelled to affirm that by inhibiting the will to life, man arouses an "interest, a tension, a hope, almost a certainty, as though something in him is being announced and prepared, as though man were not a goal but only a way, an incident, a bridge, a great promise."[101] Still, man pays a high price for being among nature's "most unexpected and exciting lucky throws": he becomes sick because he denies himself.

Where Nietzsche founders is in the attempt to derive the denial of the will to power from this elemental force itself.[102] Refinement and sublimation of the organic processes, far as they may be carried, cannot explain how the self-denying principle can emerge out of the self-affirming principle. Since Nietzsche equates life with growth and increase of power, but designates as decadent or corrupt the organism that chooses what is disadvantageous to itself, it would seem that the "unnatural" must be original to human nature. It is the characteristic that distinguishes man from the animal and makes it possible for ascetic ideals and an ascetic way of life to arise within a sphere that is supposed to be ruled exclusively by the unqualified affirmation of life. Man is capable, at least in part, of breaking out of the chain of natural determination because his reactions to events in the outside world or to internal urges are less immediate and direct. Reflection and prudence may interpose themselves. Since a need may be satisfied in different ways, reflection takes into account the relation between end and means. This presupposes a conceptual apparatus and language, both of which come about when the mind

101. Ibid., p. 354.

102. The reasons why the principle of denial cannot be derived from the will to life are discussed by Paul Deussen in *Allgemeine Geschichte der Philosophie*, 2nd ed. (Leipzig, 1920), II, 3:572 ff.

fixes attention on common elements, and not, as Nietzsche believes, by intentionally overlooking individual traits. Conceptual thought and language, aided by the experience of regularity in nature and in human behavior, make life sufficiently predictable to plan the gratification of future needs. Nobody would deny that these intellectual instrumentalities serve to sustain life. But is this all they do, and is their obvious usefulness the cause of their development? To be equipped with a conscious mind is obviously of advantage in the struggle for existence, but this does not prejudice the question as to the origin of mind. Adaptation, as Charles Darwin understood it, does not produce man's intellectual equipment, nor is it at all certain that mind can be explained as the result of the evolutionary development of animal behavior.[103] Nietzsche inclines to the view that man has intellectual capability because it is useful and indispensable in the struggle for existence. But this view would represent a regression to the traditional religious teleology he consistently opposed.

All the characterizations of man Nietzsche employs, that he is a "half-animal," a "sick animal," "less determined than any animal," and an "experimenter with himself," lead to the conclusion that the metaphysical will by itself is insufficient to determine the nature of human nature. Man's capability to resist the natural compels Nietzsche to resort to the concept of mind after all. "Mind," he writes, "is the sort of life that cuts into life."[104] But what exactly he

103. Nietzsche's argumentation was under the influence of Charles Darwin's work *The Origin of Species* (1859), although Nietzsche also voiced vigorous opposition to Darwin. See 19:111. Scientific criticism of Darwin has come to the conclusion that the survival of the fittest through adaptation and the struggle for existence cannot explain the origin of new inherited characteristics. See Richard Hesse, *Abstammungslehre und Darwinismus*, 7th ed. (Berlin, 1936), p. 74

104. *Werke*, 13:133. A fragment from the Dionysos-Dithyrambs (20:24) runs as follows:

> This greatest hindrance,
> the thought of thoughts,
> who erected that?
> Life itself created
> its own hindrance:
> now it leaps across its own thought.
> . . .
> From this idea
> I draw the whole future.

means by mind is not easy to say. Various and contradictory influences he came under prevented him from clarifying his meaning. Mind, as we have seen, was for him a "tool in the service of the higher life." Disassociated from any myth of creation or divine spirit, man is regarded as only the strongest of animals "because he is the most cunning: intellectuality is a consequence of this."[105] Yet, the cunning Nietzsche speaks of is a human attribute, not the kind animals exhibit in the hunt for prey, for it implies intentional deception to induce others to certain actions. Besides cunning, mind also includes such qualities as "caution, disguise, patience, self-control, in short, everything of the nature of mimicry."[106] Self-control permits man to delay the action of his drives, to renounce them, or to satisfy them by such means as civilization approves. Self-control need not imply hostility to life, but in any event it transforms human life so that it is not exclusively controlled by the elemental will to power. If one surveys these and similar descriptions of intellectuality in Nietzsche, one characteristic stands out as the hallmark: "intellectuality" is "unnatural."[107] Leaving aside the accusatory tone in which this word is usually uttered, as well as the sense of degeneracy associated with it, mind signifies the ability to become detached from, and to objectify, life.

We return to the phenomenon of decadence, which was the point of departure for our internal criticism of Nietzsche's philosophy. If decay really were a "necessary consequence of life" for "every epoch and for every people," it would be inappropriate to speak of it in valuational terms. Also, the refutation of religion and modern philosophies as manifestations of human decadence would be useless. For as surely as life declines, so it must revive, because according to Nietzsche these are "natural" processes, not a result of man's doing. By the same token, it would be futile to expect a new ascent from a new knowledge of the world and man, or to try to restore the "innocence of becoming" through fresh philosophic insight. Yet, Nietzsche obviously takes intellectual activity seriously. His criticism of many values of Western civilization and his unmasking of the Christian religion are inspired by the conviction that values and attitudes noxious to life can be exposed by knowledge and enlightenment.

105. *Werke.* 17:182.   106. Ibid., p. 117.   107. Ibid., p. 55.

Similar contradictory views come to light when we examine Nietzsche's account of the origin of decadence among men. It coincides, he says, with the founding of states and societies, which suppress the natural expression of the will to power, beget the "bad conscience," and place high value on renunciation, sacrifice, and like moral acts and dispositions, all of which run counter to the will to live. How was it possible that man could be compelled to adopt so unnatural a behavior? Nietzsche's answer is that man is a relatively imperfect organism, "less thoroughly determined than any other animal," and dependent on reflective consciousness for his survival. This means that Nietzsche, much against his own will, acknowledges that what is unnatural or contrary to nature has its root in the condition of man himself. Nietzsche's biological and metaphysical monism fails because mind proves to be irreducible to a form of the will to power.

Nietzsche's view of the acceptance of Christianity by the Germanic peoples illustrates especially well how problematic is his concept of decadence. Christianity, he says, has made an "ideal of contradicting the sustaining instincts of the strong life."[108] Why, then, did not the "strong races of northern Europe reject the Christian God . . . this hybrid produce of zero, concept, and contradiction, which sanctions all decadent instincts, the cowardices and weariness of the soul?"[109] All he is able to answer is that the refusal to do so does no honor to the "taste" and "religious talents" of these peoples. This amounts to a confession of helplessness. In the light of his own analysis of the phenomenon of decadence, the question remains unanswerable.

Finally, Nietzsche considered the possibility that the life process itself is a continual decadence, with man as the "greatest aberration of nature" occupying its lowest level. Teleologists and Darwinists held the opposite view: they agreed that higher forms of life arise necessarily. "But," Nietzsche observed, "this is all a hypothesis constructed on the basis of certain value judgments, and the most recent at that. The reverse is equally demonstrable, that everything down to man is decay. Man, and especially the wisest of men, would accordingly be the greatest aberration of nature and, as the being suffering the most, a contradiction in terms: nature sinks as low as

---

108. Ibid., p. 173.   109. Ibid., p. 188.

this."[110] Nietzsche did not defend this view, but merely mentioned it as a possibility. His metaphysics of the will to power, at any rate, permits the assumption that any judgment as to whether life generally is on the rise or decline is made according to human criteria. Since, however, these criteria, along with their respective hierarchies of values, must also be a symptom of a developing or degenerating life, the idea moves in a circle.[111]

The Limitations of Nietzsche's Theory of Ideology, and His Political Philosophy

The preceding critical discussion has shown the unattainability of Nietzsche's aim to reduce the activities and products of the mind to the will to power. His own philosophy presupposes intellectual processes independent of that will. The attempt to explain man's rational equipment by his need for it fails because a need does not necessarily generate the means for its gratification. Moreover, Nietzsche never succeeds in explaining how language and conceptual thought are to be understood as "transfigured" organic processes. He merely asserts them to be such. These defects are bound to affect one's general judgment of Nietzsche's theory of ideology. It would, of course, be foolish to deny that ideology serves to justify and disguise special interests and power, and that it mirrors changes in power constellations. The question, however, is whether the relation between base and superstructure, between power constellation and ideology, is such that the latter simply translates into a readable "sign language" what the underlying facts express. Is the correspondence between the two inevitably such that the sum total of intellectual creations represents nothing more than the material conditions and power relations under which organisms flourish? If the answer is in the affirmative, as it is for Nietzsche, and if one defines knowledge, as he does, to be the mastery of things at the behest of the will to power, then any question as to the truth of

110. This posthumous fragment is to be found in Elisabeth Förster-Nietzsche, *Das Leben Friedrich Nietzsches,* II/2:437.

111. See Raoul Richter's paper "Nietzsches Stellung zur Entwicklungslehre und Rassetheorie," in *Essays* (Leipzig, 1913), p. 139, which also touches on the problem of decadence.

intellectual creations becomes nugatory. For in that case those in power will decree whether a proposition is true or false: truth and falsehood become functions of the will to live. Nietzsche's equating the good with what augments man's power proves disastrous because it gives license to any arbitrariness and violence.

Some critics of Nietzsche have been content to classify his theory of knowledge as a biological skepticism and to confine their criticism to his epistemology. That would leave out the question about the social and political effects of his philosophy. But to do so is to minimize its practical intent. By Nietzsche's own confession, the "refrain of my practical philosophy" is the question as to "who is to be the master of the world."[112] Another type of interpretation and criticism has been preoccupied with Nietzsche as the critic and reformer of culture, and with Nietzsche the psychologist and educator. So far as these interpretations took account of his censure of liberal, democratic, and socialist ideas, they helped to establish a certain kind of educational elitism in which those who feared the cultural leveling of the coming mass society took refuge. But until the early years of this century, Nietzsche's political philosophy and his excursions into sociology provoked little comment.[113] It was only then that French and Italian writers discovered in his philosophy political ideas that could be exploited in the struggle of conflicting ideologies and social interests.[114] The revolutionary syndicalism of Georges Sorel and the imperialistic nationalism of Enrico Corradini found one of their roots in Nietzsche's doctrine of the will to power: Sorel offered an "apology of violence," and

112. *Werke,* 14:185.
113. The fact that Nietzsche played only a minor role in political philosophy and in the examination of political ideologies in Germany is clear from Paul Barth, *Die Philosophie der Geschichte als Soziologie,* 2nd ed. (Leipzig, 1915). Barth terms Nietzsche's ethic "sociological Darwinism" and rebukes it for its sociological onesidedness. Man's socialization, he maintains, is not subject to the struggle for existence, but a consciously contrived means against it, pp. 291, 269. Karl Heinz Pfeffer, *Die deutsche Schule der Soziologie* (Leipzig, 1939), contains an insignificant chapter on Nietzsche's theory of society.
114. Nietzsche's significance for French political thought is discussed in two books: Geneviève Bianquis, *Nietzsche en France* (Paris, 1929), pp. 79–103, and Julius Wilhelm, *Friedrich Nietzsche und der französische Geist* (Hamburg, 1940), pp. 62 ff. Both works are useful, but incomplete.

Corradini inaugurated the "cult of war morality."[115] French royalism, led by Georges Valois, celebrated Nietzsche as the pacesetter of a new aristocracy opposed to the egalitarianism of the French Revolution. Valois referred to him as *le grand homme de l'anarchie*,[116] whose criticism of Western culture revealed the noxious consequences of the Protestant Reformation and the French Revolution and demonstrated the need for a new social order. Nietzsche, wrote Valois, "gave us a whiplash that compelled us to take an honest look at the actual reality"; he was the liberator who pulled us out of the "democratic and humanitarian muck."[117] It is worth noting that Nietzsche was used in an attempt to restore a nationalistic, Catholic social order. Oswald Spengler was the first, in Germany, to draw on Nietzsche's political ideas for his own purposes.[118] His interpretation, as fiercely onesided as his writings

115. Nietzsche's influence on Corradini, one of the intellectual forebears of fascism, is great. Corradini testifies to it himself in *Discorsi Politici, 1902–1923* (Florence, 1923), pp. 172 ff, 67 ff. A preliminary attempt to give at least a rough idea of Nietzsche's effect on political thought since the beginning of the twentieth century is made in several articles by Hans Barth, reprinted in his book *Fluten und Dämme* (Zurich, 1943). Since the history of Nietzsche's long-lasting influence on European political thought since 1900 is not a part of the present book, these brief references must here suffice. An objective presentation, one not inspired by a gushing Nietzsche enthusiasm, is urgently needed.

116. Georges Valois, *D'un Siècle à l'Autre: Chronique d'une Génération, 1885–1920* (Paris, 1921), p. 132.

117. Georges Valois, *L'Homme qui Vient: Philosophie de l'Autorité*. Ed. definitive (Paris, 1923), pp. 32 ff. The 1st ed. appeared in 1906.

118. See the quotations in the early pages of this chapter. What Spengler took from Nietzsche's work can be seen in the final version of *Der Untergang des Abendlandes*, published in 1922. The epoch of "Caesarism" in which the development of the cultural souls reaches its final phase is characterized by the growth of technology and military might for which success is the sole criterion. The later writings of Spengler, especially *Der Mensch und die Technik* (Munich, 1931), reflect the same misunderstanding of Nietzsche as an apologist of success. Alfred Baeumler's essay, *Nietzsche der Philosoph und Politiker* (Leipzig, 1930), is highly tendencious and politically biased. Nietzsche is presented as pioneering an imperialist, nordic German *Reich*. Baeumler, too, fails to extract from Nietzsche's vague suggestions a clear picture of a practicable world order, and what he offers is a political mysticism that contributes nothing to an objective discussion of the problems involved. Worth mentioning is the fact that Franz Mehring described Nietzsche already in 1891 as the "social philosopher of capitalism." See his *Gesammelte Schriften und Aufsätze*, ed. Eduard Fuchs (Berlin, n.d.), 6:177.

generally are, left standing little more of Nietzsche's work than the ruthless glorification of success. True morality is the morality that succeeds, and power, truth, morality, and success are lumped together as basically identical. Spengler applied the method of ideological reduction to Nietzsche himself, with the result that nothing remained of the promise of a new salvation through a life-affirming ethic.

Our critical discussion of Nietzsche has come full circle. As has been shown, he thought that his salvational philosophy, by which the decadence of the West would be overcome, was solidly "confirmed and sustained by truth and science." His theory of knowledge, however, affords no grounds on which to base such a universal claim. It was pointed out that the objective criteria to which his critique of knowledge and reason deny validity must, in fact, be presupposed if his claim to the truth of his own philosophy is to be taken seriously. But to do so compels one to recognize as untenable large parts of his epistemology and his monistic metaphysic of the will to power. If truth generally consists in what the will to power decrees as such, then Nietzsche's "new enlightenment" is subject to the same limitation. To call it truth would have to be considered an intentional deception, an attempt merely to borrow the halo of universal truth for a doctrine of quite contrary persuasion. Moreover, to claim for one's philosophy the confirmation of science would be idle if science, deprived of objectivity, ranks only as another way of so arranging and fictionalizing the world that man may the better obtain mastery over it. To sum up the result of our internal criticism: the truth intended by Nietzsche's philosophy is the strongest argument against his theory of knowledge and the doctrine of ideology derived from it. [119]

119. For basic philosophic criticisms of Nietzsche, see Alois Riehl, *Friedrich Nietzsche: Der Künstler und Denker,* 6th ed. (Stuttgart, 1920), esp. pp. 128 ff.; and Johannes Volkelt, *Gewissheit und Wahrheit: Untersuchung der Geltungsfragen als Grundlegung der Erkenntnistheorie* (Munich, 1918), pp. 288 ff., 291 ff.

VI

A View of The Present

WE HAVE attempted to present the work of Marx and Nietzsche under the aspect of the doctrine of ideology, quite aware that this treatment could not do justice to their whole thought. It was, however, a reasonable assumption that this special aspect, under which both men developed a marked and powerful influence, would grant access to problems of central importance. It was possible, at least, to lay bare the philosophical anthropology underlying certain conceptions of history and economic life, and also to anticipate those ideas which nowadays dominate a large part of the discussion and controversy in the sociology of culture and knowledge. When one compares what Marx and Nietzsche said about the problem of ideology with the analogous intellectual endeavors of our time, it is clear that the important elements and assumptions constituting the whole ideological consciousness were almost completely developed by them. This relieves us of any extensive presentation of the present situation.

The theory that there exists an ideological or false consciousness and that ideology is the intellectual superstructure overlying the mechanism of human drives and economic life presupposes a certain view of the development, function, and structure of consciousness. In this respect, there were basic and obvious differences between Marx and Nietzsche. Marx, a Hegelian and descendant of the En-

179

lightenment, remained a representative of Western rationalism who expected history to realize the realm of reason. Nietzsche, inspired by Schopenhauer and his opposition to the constitutive elements of Western thought, endeavored to revise radically all the ideas and values by which man had previously conceived and interpreted himself and the world. Whereas Marx's anthropology was heir to the Western notion of humanity and to the declaration of human rights by the French Revolution, Nietzsche reduced all intellectual forms and contents to functions of the will to power. It is true that Marx, too, functionalized ideas. But his attempt was limited to the ideas of ruling social classes. Moreover, it was influenced, at least in the early writings containing the philosophical foundation of his work, by ethical norms derived from Western humanist ideals. To his own detriment, Marx later eliminated all ethical elements from his theory of history; and in presenting history as an automatic process, he regressed, intellectually, to Hegel's untenable notion of an inevitable historical teleology. Strangely enough, Marx's theory of history, because it employed such concepts as finality, necessity, and predictability, claimed to have discovered the natural law of history and thereby to be in agreement with the nineteenth-century ideal of natural science. Nietzsche broke with such interpretations. Still, his criticism of culture, too, operated with anticipations of what is to come, with the image of a culture yet to be created. He, too, was future-oriented; and if it were possible to give a more concrete content to his vision of the "great politics" and "world government," it would become apparent that he also replaced current conceptions of justice and truth with new ones. From these basic differences between the two writers followed different positions regarding the problem of ideology. To Marx, ideologies proved the lack of rationality in social conditions. Because the world does not make sense, man produces ideological surrogates, such as religion which promises eternal happiness in another world, and philosophy which construes existing conditions as being rational. To Nietzsche, all intellectual traditions were ideological in nature. His biological and sociological critique of reason transformed intellectual activities and contents into sublimations and metamorphoses of the will to power.

In the twentieth century, a new element in ideological thought appeared in Germany through the linkage with historicism. Historicism refers to the method which seeks to understand man, his culture, and society in their historical uniqueness. This method, with its concepts of development and individuality, was elaborated when history, owing to efforts of men like Vico and Herder and to the impact of Romanticism, had attracted special interest and became an object of inquiry different from the nature with which scientists were occupied. Historicism as a method must, however, be distinguished from the philosophical historicism which arose as a consequence of it. The more intensive and objective historical inquiry became, the more compelling the conclusion that the existence of an inexhaustible variety of philosophic systems argued against the application of universally valid criteria of judgment. The conception of man as the historic being par excellence began to invalidate ideas that assumed human reason to be essentially unchanging. Truth became relativized: every epoch, every unified social group, every nation or culture was said to have its own truth.

This relativization was reflected in Spengler's morphology of cultures, according to which historical inquiry no longer distinguished between true and false, but only between shallow and deep.[1] Hand in hand with this substitution of depth for truth went a change in the concept of knowledge. Knowledge no longer sought to establish what objective importance things and events may possess, but instead looked on these as the expression of a collective soul.[2] The historicizing of thought signified, according to Spengler, "insight into the historical relativity of its results, which are themselves the expression of a discrete, single form of existence."[3] This meant that the contents of knowledge were no longer related to an object, but that they were examined as to whether they adequately expressed the individuality and intentions of a collective soul. This view rested on the fiction of some spiritual essence or substratum lying back of

1. Oswald Spengler, *Der Untergang des Abendlandes,* 33rd ed. (Munich, 1922), 1:131.

2. Ibid., p. 390.

3. Ibid., pp. 31, 56, 469. An excellent criticism of the degeneration of the idea of knowledge from objective understanding to "expression" is given by Johannes Thyssen, *Der Philosophische Relativismus* (Bonn, 1941). Theodor Litt, *Philosophie und Zeitgeist,* 2nd ed. (Leipzig, 1935), offers a trenchant criticism of the view which regards intellectual life as the expression of a "racial soul" or a folk spirit. See pp. 24 ff., 56 ff.

our knowledge. The distinction between expression and substratum was made to enable the historian to qualify the expression as authentic or inauthentic. This overlooked the fact that the substratum was objectified in the creations of culture and present in them alone. The so-called substratum was nothing but a result of abstractions and interpretations which was then related to the cultural creations from which it was extracted in the first place. Thus, the intended comparison between the expression and an underlying something that manifests itself proved to be illusory.

It is also obvious that the substratum in this model of historical interpretation can be one of a number of entities. For Spengler it consisted of cultural souls; in the social philosophies of the Romantics, it was national folk spirits. But it may also take the form of the class situation, as in Marx, when economic and social conditions are hypostatized. In each case, the intellectual world is given the character of a superstructure in which some kind of substratum finds expression.

It seemed inevitable that the historicist mode of understanding man and his societies would result in an "anarchy of convictions." The German historian and philosopher Wilhelm Dilthey described this painful situation repeatedly. "This infinite, incomprehensible universe is multifariously reflected in religious seers, poets, and philosophers. All are under the power of place and hour. Every world view is historically conditioned, hence limited, relative. A terrible anarchy of thought seems to emerge from this."[4] The relativity of truth, which is the last word of historicism, gave rise to a tragic frame of mind. Those who suffered from it declined from intellectual honesty to evade the consequences of the relativity of truth and moral principles which historical science seemed to exact. Yet, so as not to be lost in a sea of facts, some, like Ernst Troeltsch, for example, attempted a synthesis of European culture as if to surmount history by historical means.

It is odd that the fully developed historicism of the latter half of the nineteenth century led to a mood of resignation which did not in

---

4. Wilhelm Dilthey, *Gesammelte Schriften*, 8:222. Dilthey's position in modern intellectual history is well characterized by O.F. Bollnow, *Dilthey: Eine Einführung in seine Philosophie* (Leipzig and Berlin, 1936), pp. 3–21.

the least afflict its early phase. Historicism in its late phase was felt to be a threat because it declared all claims to universal truth and moral principles to be invalid. The sense of insecurity and crisis did not result, however, from the knowledge that man is an historical being and that his various philosophies are likewise historically conditioned. It stemmed from the feeling of being part of a historical movement that had no aim. The fact that different legal systems, religions, and philosophies exist was ancient knowledge, not a discovery of a highly developed historical consciousness. It may be assumed for example that the theological and philosophical differences that existed during the Christian Middle Ages weighed upon the people of that time not less heavily than did the diversity of post-Cartesian philosophy on modern men. Why, then, did these suffer more from this diversity, as they evidently did in the period of historicism? The answer seems to be that formerly philosophical disagreements did not carry the force of compelling decisions and ultimate insight. They appeared, in a religious perspective, as emanations of God who revealed Himself in a variety of shapes and names; and to secular minds, they seemed legitimate as necessary steps toward the attainment of an inclusive realm of reason. As long as man and nature were thought of as God's creations, there remained a kinship between the laws of nature and the laws governing man's social existence; and as long as all being was related either to a transcendental unity or fitted into a permanent rational structure, whose ultimate source was also divine reason, the discrepancy between rival conceptions of truth was bearable and relatively unimportant. As to the general impact of historicism, the discovery of the rich variety of historical individuality first brought with it a greatly heightened sense of life, of which Herder supplies an impressive example. Nothing was farther from those pioneers of historical understanding than despair and lament over philosophical or religious anarchy.

In the later nineteenth, and in the early twentieth, century, however, the Christian view of the world, which was generally still unimpaired when historicism began, disintegrated. When Dilthey wrote that "thought cannot penetrate to what lies back of life,"[5] he

5. Wilhelm Dilthey, *Gesammelte Schriften,* 5:5.

meant that man's relation to some transcendental unity was lost; he could have no experience of whoever might be the ultimate source of life. Dilthey admired Schopenhauer among the post-Kantian philosophers because he did not attempt to transcend the world by some sort of mysticism, but interpreted it as it was. With Dilthey's philosophy of life and its exclusively this-worldly orientation, history lost the possibility of realizing a divine plan or human reason. The chasm that separates him from the founders of the German historical school may be illustrated by a comparison with Ranke, for whom every epoch was equally immediate to God, "before whom there is no time and who overlooks historical mankind in its entirety, finding it all to be of equal value."[6]

Modern historicism renounced the idea of cosmic reason. One of the symptoms of this change is that at the turn of the century Schopenhauer's influence began to override that of Hegel. Dilthey recorded it in his student diary in a phrase explicitly directed against Hegel: "This rational construction of the world proved an illusion both in nature and history."[7] As a mature scholar, he elaborated on this same idea in his essay on "Experience and Thought," where he presented the history of modern rationalism in outline. Again, the agreement with Schopenhauer is remarkable. Dilthey concluded that reason is not the "principle of the construction of the world," but an "episodic secular fact." The analysis of both nature and human nature can do without any relation to a "higher nature." He stated:

> These two developments imply a third: the religious connection between creature and creator has ceased to be for us a compelling fact. This means that it has become impossible to dismiss the view according to which the sovereign intellect of Descartes is but a passing singular product of nature on the surface of this earth or perhaps other celestial bodies. Many of our philosophers combat this view. Yet none of them takes reason as the background of the whole world for granted.[8]

6. Leopold von Ranke, *Über die Epochen der neuren Geschichte,* ed. Alfred Dove, 1888, IX/2. First lecture: "Weltgeschichte."

7. Clara Misch-Dilthey, ed., *Der Junge Dilthey: Ein Lebensbild in Briefen und Tagebüchern 1852–1870* (Leipzig and Berlin, 1933), p. 82.

8. W. Dilthey, *Gesammelte Schriften,* 5:88.

Dilthey's philosophy of life developed further what Schopenhauer's "true" critique of reason had intended: Dilthey presented a critique of historical reason, at the center of which stands a concept of life that is radically this-worldly, finite, historical, and antinomical. Common to both philosophers was the destruction of reason as a cosmic principle; as a part of man's equipment, reason is treated as something ephemeral which developed as an instrument of life.

When projected against the historical intellectual background of the preceding chapters, the theory of ideology in the twentieth century is seen to rest on the following four assumptions:

1. The dominant themes in the concept of man are an irrational will and his drives. Intellect and reason are epiphenomena which develop from the organism's need for orientation and which function essentially as tools in the struggle for existence. Man's intellectual equipment is a form of adaptation to this struggle.

2. The primacy of will over reason implies that practical behavior, designated as economic in the broadest sense of the word, is assigned great weight. The predominance of the will helps confirm the view that human economic activity, along with its institutional forms, relates to intellectual life as the material base to the superstructure. This view is dangerous in so far as it tends to separate cognitive from practical behavior, and to create the impression that the economic maintenance of life proceeds without the aid of the intellect. But economic activity, as Marx rightly observed, always requires both mental and physical labor. The reproduction of life requires an understanding of objective relations and the laws of nature.

3. Since intellectual activity first developed in close connection with the maintenance and secular orientation of life, it is assumed that even the seemingly "pure" activities of the mind remain under the control of concrete practical interests.

4. The relation between the forms of objective and subjective mind and the economic, social foundation is characterized by the dependency of the first upon the second. The questionable and captious metaphor "expression" is employed to explain the nature of this dependency.

The impulse to the modern discussion of the problem of ideology came from Karl Mannheim's work *Ideology and Utopia*.[9] It represented a confluence of the relevant ideas of Marx and Nietzsche, Dilthey and Spengler, and culminated in the contention that all thought is inevitably determined by the cultural and economic

9. Vilfredo Pareto, especially his *Trattato di Sociologia generale* (1916), could serve equally as well as Mannheim for a discussion of a representative theory of ideology in the twentieth century. The basic ideas of such a theory were already presented in the first two chapters of an earlier book, *Manuale di Economia politica* (1906). Pareto, of course, approached the problem with different assumptions from Mannheim: the scientific ideal of his time, which he transferred uncritically to social phenomena, misled him into construing sociology according to the "pattern of heavenly mechanics." Pareto regarded all intellectual creations, including religion, ethics, political and social theory, as "derivations" of human drives and economic conditions. Unless engaged in causal investigations according to the model of mechanics, the mind was cognitively unproductive. Pareto dismissed the intellectual world as a chaotic mixture of rationalizations used to disguise the struggle for social power. Like Nietzsche, he sought to unmask all intellectual contents as manifestations of irrational drives. Because he viewed social life as a struggle for the maximum possession of goods, Pareto's theory of history and elites assigns a central place to power.

Opinions about Pareto's work still fluctuate widely. While some deny his sociology scientific qualification, others regard it as the foundation of the whole discipline. He himself has been taken for a politician who disguises his counsel in the form of dispassionate scientific statements. His work *Les Systèmes socialistes* (Paris, 1902-3), certainly lends support to this view. Pareto there attacks both bourgeois humanitarianism and socialism, and bewails the decay of the sense of power and leadership among the bourgeois elites of the European nations. For these reasons, he has been regarded as a predecessor of fascism. It should be remembered, however, that even after fascist Italy began to make use of his ideas, Pareto did not entirely surrender the liberal part of his intellectual heritage.

For criticisms of Pareto, see the following works: Benedetto Croce, "Economia filosofica ed Economia naturalistica," *Materialismo storico ed Economic Marxistica*, 4th ed. (Bari, 1921), pp. 259 ff. Heinz Ziegler, "Ideologienlehre," *Archiv für Sozialwissenschaft und Sozialpolitik* (Tübingen, 1927), 57:661 ff. Pitirim Sorokin, *Soziologische Theorien im 19. und 20. Jahrhundert* (Munich, 1931), pp. 12 ff. Leopold von Wiese, "Pareto als Soziologe," *Zeitschrift für Nationalökonomie* (Vienna, 1936), 7:433 ff. Arnold Gehlen, "Pareto und seine 'neue Wissenschaft,'" *Blätter für deutsche Philosophie* (Berlin, 1941), 15:1 ff. Raymond Aron, "La Sociologie de Pareto," *Zeitschrift für Sozialforschung* (Paris, 1937), 6:489 ff. C.H. Bousquet, *Vilfredo Pareto: Sa vie et son oeuvre* (Paris, 1928). Lawrence J. Henderson, *Pareto's General Sociology: A Physiologist's Interpretation* (Cambridge, Mass., 1935). Franz Borkenau, *Pareto* (London, 1936).

Some might perhaps wish that Georges Sorel's work, too, were made part of this discussion. Certain of his writings, such as *La Ruine du Monde antique*, 3rd ed. (Paris, 1933), *D'Aristote à Marx* (Paris, 1935), and *Les Illusions du Progrès*, 4th ed.

position of the thinking subject.[10] Mannheim's theory of ideology planned to dissolve the forms and contents of thought into functions of the existing social and historical conditions. Every social group or stratum possessed a definite ideological superstructure corresponding to its material base. The "process of the complete destruction of

---

(Paris, 1927), do contain ideological investigations concerning the relations between the material conditions of a class and its intellectual production. Yet, Sorel's central concept is that of myth, as developed especially in *Réflexions sur la Violence* (1908), and it does not fit the Marxian meaning of ideology. Though a vehicle of history and especially of revolutionary uprising, Sorel's myth makes no claim to truth but is a plain political slogan with which to whip up political energy. Sorel was also too much the rationalist to believe that class conditions so deform human understanding as to obviate the distinction between true knowledge and intellectual partisanship. His main concern was the restoration of European morality from a process of decay. The means to this end was a revolution that would help revive the soldierly virtues of discipline, courage, and sacrifice. Because of his interest in the power of revolutionary myth, Sorel dismissed the scientific part of Marx's work as untenable. See his *La Décomposition du Marxisme*, 3rd ed. (Paris, n.d.), pp. 48 ff.

The literature about Sorel includes the following: *Gaétan Pirou, Georges Sorel* (Paris, 1927). Michael Freund, *Georges Sorel: Der revolutionäre Konservativismus* (Frankfurt a. M., 1932). Four works by Edouard Berth: *Les Méfaits des Intellectuels*, 2nd ed. (Paris, 1926); *Guerre des Etats ou Guerre des Classes* (Paris, 1924); *La Fin d'une Culture* (Paris, 1927); *Du "Kapital" aux "Réflexions sur la Violence"* (Paris, 1932). Jean Wanner, *Georges Sorel et la Décadence: Essai sur l'idée de décadence dans la pensée de Georges Sorel* (Lausanne, 1943). Hans Barth, *Masse und Mythos. Die ideologische Krise an der Wende zum 20. Jahrhundert und die Theorie der Gewalt: Georges Sorel* (Hamburg, 1959).

10. It is strange that the discussion of ideology in Germany did not begin earlier in connection with Max Scheler's work *Die Wissensformen und die Gesellschaft* (Leipzig, 1926). Scheler made use of Freud's psychology and Marx's theory about base and superstructure in contructing his own dualism concerning human drives and the mind without, however, sacrificing the autonomy of the latter. Though he adopted some of Marx's views and in some passages even his wording, Scheler could have offered a more profitable treatment of the problem of ideology than Marx because, in his book *Die Stellung des Menschen im Kosmos* (Darmstadt, 1928), he gave a precise definition of mind. Crucial to Scheler's thought is the concept of sublimation which he, like psychoanalyst writers, postulates and employs, but without explaining it satisfactorily. On this, see Kurt Lenk, *Von der Ohnmacht des Geistes: Darstellung der Spätphilosophie Max Schelers* (Tübingen, 1959).

Psychoanalysis regards the capacity for sublimation as an inherent disposition of the ego. See, for example, Siegfried Bernfeld, "Bemerkungen über 'Sublimierung,'" *Imago* (Wien, 1922), 8:334. According to Freud, sublimation occurs when a "drive is projected onto another goal that is remote from sexual satisfaction." See his paper "Zur Einführung des Narzissmus," *Theoretische Schriften 1911–1925* (Vienna, 1931), p. 48. Psychoanalysis assumes the "plasticity of sexual drives," by which their

all spiritual elements"[11] which began with Schopenhauer, continued with Marx, and reached its climax in Nietzsche, entered the general intellectual consciousness through Mannheim's work. To describe the influence of the various external conditions on thought, Mannheim employed the term *Ideologiehaftigkeit:* thought was ideology-bound, or ideologically confined, tied to the prevailing mode of being, and, more particularly, to a definite locus in society. To expound the ideological liability of thought presupposes a certain reinterpretation of the process of human understanding: the primary question is not whether knowledge is objective and object-related, but what are the conditions under which it is formed. Slanting the question this way brings to light the dependence of historical and social knowledge on a multitude of nontheoretical conditions which, however, indisputably exert an influence on theorizing and its results. The task then is to draw up a catalogue of these con-

---

energy is easily shifted from one object to another, and so removes the "natural" determination of the drives. See Heinz Hartmann, *Die Grundlagen der Psychoanalyse* (Leipzig, 1927), p. 150. Scheler argued similarly. It is the mind, he wrote, "which introduces the repression of drives because the will, guided by ideas and values, denies to the contrary impulses of the id the images it needs in order to act; at the same time, images measuring up to those ideas and values are dangled like bait before the drives that lie in wait, so that the impulses may be coordinated in the execution of projects of the will set by the mind." *Die Stellung des Menschen im Kosmos,* pp. 72–3. What Scheler failed to explain is why a drive should put its energy at the disposal of the mind at all. Is not the assumption inescapable that drives are originally directed toward the mind and values?

We wish to mention in this connection the work of Alfred Seidel, *Bewusstsein als Verhängnis,* posthumously ed. Hans Prinzhorn (Bonn, 1927). Seidel shifted the problem of ideology to psychology, where he sought a solution through the concept of an originally harmonious humanity. Though he failed, he was not necessarily on the wrong path. But his tragic fate shows how radical ideologizing can attack the very roots of a person's intellectual and emotional existence.

11. Karl Mannheim, *Ideologie und Utopie* (Bonn, 1929), p. 242. The extensive discussion of this book is recorded in the bibliography attached to the English edition: *Ideology and Utopia: An Introduction to the Sociology of Knowledge* (London, 1936), pp. 281–304. Those who followed this discussion must have felt the need to examine the historical antecedents of the problem of ideology in Marx and Nietzsche, for the interpretation in terms of "vulgar Marxism" proved inadequate and at times misleading. In this respect, see Hans-Joachim Lieber, *Wissen und Gesellschaft: Die Probleme der Wissenssoziologie* (Tübingen, 1952). Theodor Geiger, *Ideologie und Wahrheit: Eine soziologische Kritik des Denkens* (Stuttgart and Vienna, 1953). Werner Stark, *The Sociology of Knowledge: An Essay in Aid of a deeper Understanding of the History of Ideas* (London, 1958).

ditions in order to secure the objectivity of understanding against possible sources of error. In this sense, the theory of ideology appears as a continuation of Bacon's theory of idols. But the concept of ideology in the Marxian sense as developed in the twentieth century contains more than this. To characterize knowledge as ideology-bound implies a relation between the result of thought and the social situation of the thinking subject that is "necessary" and hence irresistible. According to Mannheim, the act of knowing is a "method of penetrating the life of a vital being of a certain kind in a living space of a certain order. All these three factors, the structure of the penetration, the constitution of the vital being, and the character of his living space, particularly the place and position of the thinking subject within it, condition the result of thought as well the 'ideal of truth' he may construe from it."[12] This would be an acceptable definition, were it not for the unclear meaning of the verb "condition" and the suspicion that important philosophical prejudgments lie concealed therein. Let us attempt, therefore, to clarify what is meant by saying that an organism is conditioned.

The fact that an organism perceives wave motions of different frequencies as light or sound, and perceives matter of a certain consistency as solid, fluid, or gaseous obviously depends on the organism's physical constitution; and some wave lengths it does not perceive at all. Generally speaking, the organism's constitution conditions the scope and form of the environment's effect on it. This sort of conditioning, however, seems not to be in question here and so may be left aside. In the case of man, one may assume that his individualized system of drives conditions the manner in which he responds to the actions of his fellows and pursues his own plans in the social and natural world. Conditioning now comes to mean reacting and behaving similarly to similar events and circumstances. Since, however, experience and insight also influence our actions and reactions, conditioning loses the character of inevitability and constancy, for caution and expectation make the individual react differently to similar environmental conditions. Already, the basis for being conditioned has been changed.

Mannheim further contended that an individual's ideas were conditioned by his social place and position, and that thought generally

---

12. Karl Mannheim, "Wissenssoziologie," in *Handwörterbuch der Soziologie,* p. 672.

was tied to a certain mode of being. Let us examine the meaning of conditioning also in this respect. To begin with, man is born into a certain environment, in which gradually and at first unresistingly he adopts through language and the behavior of his parents a picture of the world that transmits to him a felt experience of life. In his domestic ambience, the child acquires a conglomerate of values and views concerning all things of everyday life. His early passivity is later supplemented by personal spontaneity, and the tradition in which he grew up becomes transformed. School enlarges his horizon, and with the start of an occupation, technical and economic interests claim his attention. His belonging to a people and his entrance into a moral and political order enlarge his earlier, largely emotional, ties into the conscious acceptance of duties and rights by which his social existence is constituted. A cluster of views develops by which he learns to understand and interpret events; his judgment and behavior begin to be determined by certain criteria of value.

It is easy to see that in this context the concept of conditioning becomes increasingly vague. Personal insight and initiative, force and efficiency, conditions at home, and the general cultural situation are all capable of almost unlimited variability. In what sense, then, are we to understand the term "conditioning" in this context; and what is it that "conditions" individual thought? Most likely, it is the expectation by which the individual is guided.[13] Expectation is the framework in which an individual's life unfolds and in which interest, experience, knowledge, and emotional ties to traditional ideas and modes of behavior are combined. To say that thought is conditioned comes to mean that it is led in a certain direction by the thinking subject's will and interest. The subject moves within a frame of expectations which palpably affects the way in which he understands, interprets, and evaluates events. This frame represents a conceptual apparatus in which individual perspectives become objectified, and to which individual wishes and life aims impart their own direction. This was also Mannheim's opinion since he spoke of modes of thought "provided by struggling life itself," and directed

13. We chose the term "expectation" to stress the subjective form in which interests become objectified.

attention to those points in the sociology of political thought "at which otherwise latent impulses of the will break through."[14]

The contention that thought is tied to a certain mode of being and dependent on certain social conditions would hardly be philosophically momentous if it merely resulted in the recommendation to take into account in the understanding of intellectual achievements the social conditions under which they were produced. But more is in fact asserted. The conditioning of thought is held to be compelling so that the physiology of human drives and the power of economic conditions by themselves constitute what we think and how we act. But if intellectual conditioning were of so inevitable a character, the dependency of the intellectual superstructure on the base would prove impossible to ascertain. The most that we could know would be that in other historical periods people thought differently. We would even be unable to discover that thought rises in the form of a superstructure above underlying determinants. The differentiations into base and superstructure, social station and ideology, being and consciousness, would merge into an indissoluble unity which would afford no opportunity for comparison. One could as well assert that the base depended on the superstructure, or, as Hegel did, that the form of spirit, in the current phase of its evolution, imprinted itself equally on both.

In order to assert the dependency of an ideology on the material substratum, there must be an immediate apprehension of the difference between false (ideological) and true consciousness.[15] Insight into the determining function of the base is possible only if one can doubt the legitimacy of one's own position. To maintain that certain intellectual results "only" reflect the prevailing social conditions presupposes at least a minimum of comparability. It is in this

14. Karl Mannheim, "Das konservative Denken," *Archiv für Sozialwissenschaft und Sozialpolitik* (1927), 57:70.

15. See Ernst Grünwald, *Das Problem der Soziologie des Wissens* (Vienna and Leipzig, 1934), p. 223, for a useful critical history of the sociology of knowledge. The same goes for Alexander von Schelting, *Max Webers Wissenschaftslehre* (Tübingen, 1934). See also Florian Znaniecki, *The Social Role of the Man of Knowledge* (New York, 1940); Jacques J. Maquet, *Sociologie de la Connaissance: Etude critique des Systèmes de Karl Mannheim et Pitirim A. Sorokin* (Louvain, 1949); Robert K. Merton, *Social Theory and Social Structure* (Glencoe, Ill., 1949).

self-questioning stance of the mind that the idea of truth announces itself. The claim of a philosophic or scientific statement to be true remains unconditional even though the results of human knowledge always remain subject to revision. A political or economic theory may be shown to be incongruent with the interests of a social group, but such a demonstration tells us nothing about its truth. Conversely, the fact that concrete interests have a hand in the solution of certain problems is insufficient to term the solution ideological; nor do philosophic and scientific theories become ideological by being used in justification of political demands. Also, a self-declared ideology may well contain verifiable knowledge. Every political ideology intends to be more than an expression of interest, and this is the best argument against the ideological confinement of thought. If social philosophies and theories were to characterize themselves as ideologies—which has never happened—they would thereby pull the ground from under themselves. To charge consciousness with being ideological requires a prior distinction between "true" and "false" consciousness; and to make this distinction, it is sufficient that a concrete consciousness reckon with the possibility of being affected and restricted by the prevailing social conditions. The mere suspicion of finding oneself in such a situation signals caution in the acceptance of one's own findings. Thus, the insight that one's own knowledge is conditioned is arrived at on the ground that the idea of truth itself is unconditional.

To summarize and conclude our criticism of the theory of ideology, we have observed that the major ideologists set themselves two tasks, one scientific and the other political. The first was to be solved through the method of reduction as developed by Nietzsche, the second through the unmasking of intellectual systems and views as the machinations of special interests. The political aim was always to devaluate the opponent's position by showing it to lack any claim to universal recognition, while making one's own position appear to be true and morally justified, hence unassailable. It is obvious, however, that if the theory of ideology were applied consistently, no intellectual position could escape the conditioning force of its own interests and would have to allow this dependency to be exposed. If the nature of intellectual achievements is ideological, in that their appearance conceals their "real" meaning which is to manifest the will to power or a set of social conditions, the practical consequence will be that critical intellectual discussion is replaced by political decision.[16] In the chapters dealing with Nietzsche and Marx, we have shown that the reduction of intellectual content to social power is self-defeating. The ideas of truth and justice are not invalidated merely because under different conditions men hold

16. For an excellent diagnosis of the nihilistic consequences of "sociologism," see E.R. Curtius, *Deutscher Geist in Gefahr* (Stuttgart and Berlin, 1932), pp. 75 ff.

According to the legal theory of Carl Schmitt, a state of emergency is declared to exist by those who happen to be in power for no other reason than to remain in power. It is no accident that Schmitt supports himself mostly with arguments from Hobbes, who in his *Leviathan* referred religious controversies to the state for decision. To resolve problems this way is, of course, to silence critical intellectual discussion. Schmitt was a consistent apologist of total state power, which he worshiped. For his writings, see *Der Begriff des Politischen*, 2nd ed. (Munich and Leipzig, 1932); *Politische Theologie*, 2nd ed. (Munich and Leipzig, 1934); *Über die drei Arten des rechtswissenschaftlichen Denkens* (Hamburg, 1934); *Der Leviathan in der Staatslehre des Thomas Hobbes* (Hamburg, 1938); *Positionen und Begriffe im Kampf mit Weimar-Genf-Versailles 1923–1939* (Hamburg, 1940).

It is interesting to compare Schmitt's philosophy of law with that of Hans Kelsen. In the foreword to his book *Reine Rechtslehre: Einleitung in die rechtswissenschaftliche Problematik* (Leipzig and Vienna, 1934), Kelsen writes that his aim is to establish a "theory of law purged of all political ideology and all elements of natural science." He and his followers pride themselves on their legal positivism because it is applicable to all legal systems past and present, and provides the basis for a true understanding of law. See, for example, the paper by Aladár Métall, "Die politische Befangenheit der reinen Rechtslehre," *Revue Internationale de la Théorie du Droit*, X:3, 1936. Métall argues that opposition to the theory of pure law from the most diverse political quarters confirms the rightness and universality of the theory. Kelsen identifies power and law. Law is for him a "merely constraining apparatus without political or ethical value," a specific instrument of social life, and indifferent to its own content. "Any content," he writes, "can be law. There is no human behavior that, owing to its content, could be excluded from becoming the content of a legal norm. The validity of a legal norm is not put in question by the fact that its content does not correspond to postulated material values." *Reine Rechtslehre*, p. 32. The "identity of the state and law," which Kelsen asserts, implies that law, as a compulsive instrument, may be such as to destroy human existence, and still be law. "From the point of view of a consistent positivistic theory, law, like the state, is nothing more than a compulsory order of human behavior, whose morality and justice are irrelevant matters," p. 127. The gain achieved by liberating legal theory from political ideology is, however, dubious. By eliminating the philosophical problem of the relation of law to justice, legal positivism achieves a great simplification; but, of course, the problem has not been made to disappear, it has only been shifted from one discipline to another so that now social philosophers worry about it. Besides, the price paid for the liberation of law from politics is that law gets treated as a purely empirical matter.

different things to be true and just. Though all intellectual systems, including law and social theory, lay claim to these ideas, they may in practice well fall short of them. Yet this does not mean that the ideas themselves are reducible to other forms or modes of being, such as economic activity, folk spirit, culture soul, race, or social power. On the contrary, the ideas are inherent in human nature. The disastrous effect of ideological thinking in its radical form is not only to cast doubt on the quality and structure of the mind that constitute man's distinguishing characteristic, but also to undermine the foundation of his social life. Human association is dependent on agreement, and the essence of agreement, be it concerned with common behavior, rational action, or scientific investigation, is the idea of truth. If this idea is denounced as ideological, we are left, in Nietzsche's language, with individual quanta of will which, according to the measure of their power, arbitrarily determine what truth and justice are to be. Against this monstrous misconception, we set the insight of the German eighteenth-century philosopher Christian Wolf: "Truth and justice are the pillars of the common life: remove them and it crumbles."[17]

17. Christian Wolff, *Grundsätze des Natur- und Völkerrechts,* 2nd ed. (Halle, 1769).

Index